'On 5 January 2001 many persons came to the orphanage with different disabilities. I was scared because they seemed and acted like animals. For children with trauma, it is hard to know what they like or dislike, because their feelings change every time. So, for them you have to take time to learn many things about them, like knowing how they act when are happy, when they are sad, what they like and how to support them in every act they do, because they will then feel that you are a good person and try to show you who they really are.

'The time came when the government closed the orphanage, and the residents had to be treated like everyone else. To help the residents re-integrate into society, training was given to the people who will take care of them. Now these children have changed their aggressive behaviour, and they can spend a whole day with others. This was successful because of the support worker who worked hard to get to know them and understand their feelings. There are many things which are changing because they have been given dignity and independence. In order for the children to gain independence you have to spend quality time with them and build a good relationship with them by knowing their language, the words they use and so on, and knowing their moods.'

Amina Rugema, *genocide victim and NGO caregiver, Rwanda*

HOPE FOR CHILDREN OF TRAUMA

Hope for Children of Trauma: An International Perspective synthesizes all the existing evidence, policy and practice from around the world for children and youth who have experienced different forms of complex trauma – such as abuse, neglect and war violence – and also presents a real advance in the literature, by covering new material from the author's extensive visits and collaborations in low and middle-income countries in Asia, Africa and Latin America.

The book covers a historical and research overview of developments in trauma and child mental health, global policy and evidence on the impact of trauma on child mental health. In particular, this book communicates real experiences through narratives and supporting photographic material from children in slum areas, orphanages or on the streets, and explores the application of therapeutic approaches by frontline practitioners, therapeutic interventions, service development and training programmes.

Integrating testimonies, observations, therapeutic interventions and research findings, *Hope for Children of Trauma* shows how these problems can be addressed, and will be thought-provoking reading for child and adolescent mental health practitioners, NGOs and policy-makers.

Panos Vostanis is Professor of Child Mental Health at the University of Leicester and Visiting Professor at University College London.

HOPE FOR CHILDREN OF TRAUMA

An International Perspective

Panos Vostanis

LONDON AND NEW YORK

First published 2018
by Routledge
2 Park Square, Milton Park, Abingdon, Oxon OX14 4RN

and by Routledge
711 Third Avenue, New York, NY 10017

Routledge is an imprint of the Taylor & Francis Group, an informa business

© 2018 Panos Vostanis

The right of Panos Vostanis to be identified as author of this work
has been asserted by him in accordance with sections 77 and 78 of
the Copyright, Designs and Patents Act 1988.

All rights reserved. No part of this book may be reprinted or
reproduced or utilised in any form or by any electronic, mechanical,
or other means, now known or hereafter invented, including
photocopying and recording, or in any information storage or
retrieval system, without permission in writing from the publishers.

Trademark notice: Product or corporate names may be trademarks or
registered trademarks, and are used only for identification and
explanation without intent to infringe.

British Library Cataloguing in Publication Data
A catalogue record for this book is available from the British Library

Library of Congress Cataloging in Publication Data
A catalog record for this book has been requested

ISBN: 978-1-138-20564-2 (hbk)
ISBN: 978-1-138-20565-9 (pbk)
ISBN: 978-1-315-45077-3 (ebk)

Typeset in Bembo
by Keystroke, Neville Lodge, Tettenhall, Wolverhampton

To all vulnerable children, young people and their carers who are fighting against the odds all over the world

CONTENTS

Preface		*xi*
1	Ever-changing approaches to child trauma	1
2	Impact of trauma on child mental health	9
3	Child vulnerability in a global context	22
4	Looking for answers: from Birmingham shelters to Mumbai slums	31
5	An international perspective: the road to WACIT	40
6	Children's safety should permeate policy, attitudes and environments	56
7	Nurturing attitudes and approaches	66
8	Building resilience at school and in the community	75
9	Application of therapeutic approaches	87
10	Therapeutic interventions	102

x Contents

11 Always a service model, whatever the constraints   114

12 Training in a service context   126

Epilogue   *137*
Book references by chapter   *138*
Index   *159*

PREFACE

The stage was a workshop in Uganda, as part of the World Awareness for Children in Trauma (WACIT) programme. This innovative service consisted of a child protection team and a group of community volunteers who acted as advocates for children in the most adverse circumstances, raising awareness, while actively connecting with the team and other agencies. I had already visited some of the slum areas where the volunteers lived. Then I facilitated the first child mental health awareness workshop for the team, with particular focus on the impact of trauma on children, with the objective of adding a psychosocial 'layer' to their remit, as they were firmly established by now in their core child protection functions. This was followed by a workshop for the community volunteers, with broadly the same goal, but adapted to their roles and needs. This was really exciting, but also a trip into the unknown. We decided that I should slightly sit back and co-facilitate this second workshop with a team member, so that she would form the sustainable link in the future.

Then came a creative, albeit stressful twist in the tale. The co-facilitator was keen to capture participants' expectations and worries in open discussion, rather than through traditional but less threatening pre-training questionnaires. A few community volunteers contributed with their largely anticipated anxieties on the relevance of the training to them, whether they would understand it and how it would be conducted. Then this lady at the back stood up, and just said one word in English:

'Colour ...'

My co-facilitator shuffled uncomfortably. She immediately shifted to Luganda language and seemed to negotiate the wording with the community volunteer. Eventually, she went back to the flipchart, wrote the word 'language' instead of 'colour', and was keen to change the subject. She appeared to dilute what the community volunteer had said. I thought that I should respond to the agreed narrative, so I stood up and reassured them that few people in England understood my accent anyway, and that I would try to slow down! They laughed and the co-facilitator moved on.

But I could not move on. She had clearly said 'colour', not 'language'. What I really heard, was: 'You are White and so different to me. Can you relate to me? Can I trust you?' Having visited where she lived, she could not have been more right. The training worried me less, having cut my teeth in the region with community leads in Kenya and genocide survivors in Rwanda. This one seemed to run smoothly too, and some of the community volunteers were amazing with their intuitive observations:

The eldest volunteer during the child development session: What makes you worry in your role? How do you know?
Trainee: When a baby frowns.

But that early comment was still playing up in my mind. After we said our goodbyes and took our photos at the end of the workshop (see Photo 12.3 in Chapter 12), I waited in the shade for everyone to leave. That same lady approached me on her own. She smiled, asked me my name and where I came from. Then she shook my hand and thanked me for coming. How does that leave one feeling?

'There are very few – in fact, pretty rare – moments in life when you connect with another human being under the most unusual and unexpected circumstances. Don't let that moment pass. Just savour it for now. Then let it permeate not just your work outlook but, critically, your whole life stance ...'

1

EVER-CHANGING APPROACHES TO CHILD TRAUMA

Evolving concepts and attitudes towards children, trauma and mental health

Complex trauma and its correlates

Whilst 'trauma' as a concept goes back to ancient times, and even its psychological origins have at least one century of heritage originating from Sigmund Freud, its integration into practice and research is relatively recent, transcending the last two decades. Although a shift in viewing ex-soldiers as experiencing mental torment can be located to post Second World War times, its embedment into practice has taken considerably longer, certainly for children.

A number of factors appear to have played a part in moving from 'whether' to 'how', and then to 'what can we do?' Early clinical observations and psycho-therapy case studies were followed by epidemiological evidence on the nature and extent of trauma, and its loosely connected impact on children. Challenges were rather circular, in that conceptual doubts on how children could process experiences and how these could be captured, constrained the direct evidence that eventually focused more on the underpinning mechanisms and their complexities. When I looked at children's data from our first study in Gaza on their recollections of direct (experiencing or witnessing war violence) and indirect exposure to trauma (through parents, friends and neighbours, or through the media), I was astounded by their ability to process and articulate both their experiences and their resulting impact. And yet, this was barely 20 years ago. Although such evidence is hardly innovative in our days, youth reports still largely rely on adolescents, with some uncertainty on how to approach younger children with their cognitive and other developmental characteristics, hence research based on adult views and interpretations.

2 Ever-changing approaches to child trauma

Somehow a number of seemingly contradictory factors appear to have been involved in this gradual, and often frustratingly slow, process; namely societal attitudes about both children and vulnerability, and methodological limitations in extracting evidence. There are still many societies that claim that 'there is no abuse in our communities', despite the contrary evidence of fairly universal patterns where studies were methodologically comparable. So, how does one enquire about events that reflect fear? And how does one then change fear, if policy and attitudes do not capture the underpinning evidence?

Undercurrents on children's rights and gender issues seemingly run in parallel with advances in practice and research, before one catalyst turns the tide by raising public and media interest, thus leading to policy-making. But, what are such catalysts? These almost always seem to constitute individual or collective incidents that cross the threshold or public and political conscience. The fatal cases of Victoria Climbie in 2000 and Baby P in 2007 were hardly uncommon in England, yet they changed inter-agency communication, and resulted, at least in the short term, in an increase in the number of children being accommodated in care. So did the fatal gang rape of 23–year-old student Jyoti in India; or the case in Saudi Arabia of 5-year-old Lama, who was raped and killed by her father who was eventually prosecuted for murder, thus breaking a precedent of silence and collusion, largely because of the National Family Safety Programme beginning to take effect.

Views on the nature of trauma keep changing too. The simplistic distinction between dependent (e.g. abuse) and independent (e.g. accidents) life events was challenged by the realization that, even externally initiated accidents are more likely to happen in vulnerable situations such as families living in disadvantage, with parents being less available to supervise their children, and so on. Traumas are both inter-related and cumulative, in other words, 'trauma breeds trauma'. For this reason, other terms and pathways have been thrown into the equation, like primary and secondary effects; impairment; predisposing, precipitating and maintaining risks; and vulnerabilities. The more we search, the more we find, particularly over longer periods of study.

The 'past' and the 'present' are much more closely connected than originally thought, and this will be a key feature behind proposed interventions throughout this text. Children who experience war conflict are displaced from their host environment, before moving to the asylum-seeking or refugee phase. Communities that suffer seemingly independent human disasters can be disrupted or even uprooted. I witnessed this in Indonesia, where an ongoing volcanic disruption led to whole communities' displacement, parents constantly travelling afar to find work, consequent weakening of child protection systems, in turn leading to an increase in child abuse. A superficial glance at these systems would have probably missed these links, hence opportunities to intervene.

The more popular current terms of 'complex' or 'multiple' traumas are meant to demarcate from single traumatic occurrences, in otherwise stable situations, which tend to have a benign course and positive resolution. Some non-mental health organizations perceive uncomfortable connotations in the term 'trauma', mainly in pathologizing human emotional responses, for which reason terms such as 'distress' or 'stressors' are preferred instead. There can also be some identification of the term 'trauma' with its mental health expressions (mainly, but not solely, post-traumatic stress disorder) and the need for 'specialist' interventions. We will revisit the theoretical, practical and service implications, as concepts are likely to continue to fall in and out of favour, but the underlying drivers are certain to persist. When it comes to cultural contextualization, the question is not 'whether' (as everybody hurts), but rather 'how', i.e. on the mechanisms that affect children, and how these effects are expressed.

The never-ending mental health dilemmas

Few fields still cause as much debate as mental health constructs, ranging from well-being to problems and disorders. The roots of stigma and negative attitudes are still prominent. These apply to a variable degree in all societies, possibly more so in many low-income countries, although this does not equate with intolerance in other forms of psychosocial life. The implications for people with mental illness are too raw to ignore, but in some ways it is occasionally worth asking 'Does it really matter what we call it?' Instead we could focus more on how to engage young people, as such debates on mental health language sometimes reflect professional rather than societal cultures. Evidence on child mental health concepts across cultures is intriguing and relatively new, and has largely been based on qualitative and ethnographic rather than more traditional diagnostic methods. Nevertheless, when similar methodologies have been applied and children have engaged in the research process, differences were not as striking as originally assumed.

> When you talk t' them, they think that mental health means that, yer, a nutter (.) and they'll say "I'm not psycho."
>
> *Young homeless person in UK shelter*

> Mental health is a new concept in Africa. And many people are ignorant on the issue, on the issue of mental health.
>
> *Psychologist in Kenyan slum area*

> I don't want anyone say, [A] is crazy. And I was very crazy actually, because I try twice kill myself, I try hung myself; I cut myself, I really was crazy.
>
> *Asylum-seeking young person in UK*

These quotes are obviously selective from our research group studies on conceptualization of child mental health problems in different contexts. Nevertheless, they do reflect evolving public and professional attitudes, which cannot as yet shake off underlying stigma. It is also worth noting the interplay between mental health and vulnerability in all societies, i.e. being homeless or a refugee carries additional

4 Ever-changing approaches to child trauma

stigma, which is multiplied when mental health comes along ('Ah, of course . . . what did you expect?').

Little big people?

We then need to throw the whole concept of childhood into the equation. What constitutes a child-centred society, which can hence influence interventions and services? This is not just a scientific debate, but should be historically placed in socioeconomic context, and analysed from a sociological, philosophical and legal perspective, with these perspectives sometimes being conflicting or contradictory. For example, the notion or subtle acceptance that children are 'future adults', hence we need to prevent adult ill-health, was a decent starting point two decades ago to convince adult-driven policy and governments to identify and protect funding for children's services; this now seems, however, rather dated from a human rights angle. Defining children's needs through an adult lens – be it from parents, care-givers or professionals – brings its own biases. Although a corroborative approach is useful in incorporating multiple views, it can misleadingly avoid capturing children's narratives.

The 1989 United Nations Convention on the Rights of the Child has certainly gone a long way in at least being endorsed by 192 countries. But how much has it changed attitudes, legislation and practice? A pragmatic answer is that it has, albeit slowly and not in isolation from a multitude of other factors. More than 200 million children still work in labour worldwide, half of them in hazardous conditions. Can we make allowances for some communities fighting for survival? If so, where do we draw the line?

The wide range of the minimum age of criminal responsibility, i.e. the youngest an individual can be to be considered liable – thus charged – for a crime (although they can still appear in court and be given alternative punishment) reflects the global ambivalence towards children. This marker ranges as widely from 7 (in some US states) to 18 years (e.g. in Brazil), with an average of 14 years across the world. Interestingly, if one considered the 'child-centredness' of a society as a whole, they might not necessarily guess this country's age of criminal responsibility, i.e. these two are not always associated. The UK has advanced young user involvement in its service provision (although predominantly for adolescents rather than for younger children), yet still adopts one of the lowest ages of criminal responsibility at 10 years. In contrast, many African countries have a more liberal higher age of 14 years, but this can be rendered meaningless in other fields of life, from widespread child labour to children serving in armies; whether out of economic necessity, response to conflict or societal views. We will revisit similar dilemmas and discrepancies in interpreting what constitutes adequate parenting across different cultures and societies.

Status and sources of evidence

In an ideal world, we would be guided by pure and unequivocal evidence in our thinking and service planning. Yet, there are several challenges in this field of research. By definition, we are dealing with the most complex groups of children and youth, in that they attract multiple risk factors which act as confounders in understanding the mechanisms of impact of trauma and, what is more, in understanding what works and how. Children are not placed in care overnight, but rather after prolonged periods of abuse or neglect, often with intermittent returns to their family of birth; thus making it difficult to establish linear pathways and predictors of need for a particular group. Being homeless brings its own misfortunes and secondary impairments such as drug and alcohol use, sexual exploitation or offending; these in turn blur the relationship and prognosis between, for example, homelessness and mental ill health.

Such difficulties are pronounced in real world research, where it is extraordinarily tenuous to allocate children to one or another intervention by chance, whilst accounting for all other factors in their lives. Ethics play their part, as well as children's and adults' choices throughout the process. Consequently, although it is relatively difficult to establish the effectiveness of a psychological intervention on adolescents with depression living in relative stability, challenges are multi-fold with homeless youth or care leavers.

These constraints have somehow been balanced by the evolution and, in many cases, integration of methodologies. In other words, rather than merely relying on randomized controlled trials, there has been increased evidence viewed from different angles; and emerging from a range of qualitative research, needs analysis, service data, case studies or mixed methods designs. Children's narratives now matter as much in research as in the justification and improvement of existing services. New technologies allow access to populations much further afield than previously imagined.

It is hence interesting to note how complementary sources have influenced practice to variable degrees. Different methodological studies can be complemented by 'grey' literature from policy, practice or service reports, as long as this synthesis, and particularly its interpretation, is transparent. Epidemiological research with 'hard to reach' groups is, inevitably, well . . . hard! Yet, there have been several excellent studies, crucially some with comparable designs that allow us to draw relatively firm conclusions. One can quote population research in western countries, as well as Brazil, Pakistan or India, that point to similar prevalence rates of mental health problems accounting for similar socioeconomic factors; but also similar mechanisms of risk and protective factors.

As already stated, the interactions between these variables are pronounced among vulnerable groups; yet we do now have sound and fairly consistent evidence on how trauma affects children from research with victims of abuse, children in care, homeless, offenders, refugees, and victims of war conflict. One challenge is to distinguish between emerging themes and specific characteristics. In contrast, 'top-down' influences of evidence are less pronounced in relation to interventions, and remain

6 Ever-changing approaches to child trauma

limited in terms of service development. A number of studies give us sufficient confidence to roll out particular interventions, usually of individual nature. Equally, others evolve 'bottom up' before being evaluated, by practitioners being trained in generic child and family modalities, before adapting and applying them (knowingly or not) to vulnerable groups.

The expansion of posts and services for children in care (or looked after by local authorities) over the last decade in the UK constitutes such an example. Somehow, evidence on looked after children's needs filtered down through targeted policy to designated funding, before the evidence on how to use these new resources became available. The new posts and flurry of activity created their own dynamic, based on which research of initially small-scale and new methods emerged. One hopes that this can be continuously synthesized and fed back into the system. Creativity and innovation are not mutually exclusive with relatively dry but rigorous evaluation. Modern professional, health and welfare organizations are rapidly coming to realize the benefits of such synergy. Despite the consciously narrative style of this text, I will be highlighting the support from evidence, as well as existing gaps and limitations, throughout the book.

The whole is larger than the sum of its parts: why service modelling matters

Where child mental health is lagging behind other fields is in the realm of service models. Most of its provision still relies on evidence or good practice in parallel domains of diagnosis, assessment and intervention. These have been taken forward by professional bodies, and have been adapted to wider health, welfare and educational systems. This process has also highlighted a few gaps – or cracks. Why we behave in a particular way in a particular contextual setting should not happen by default, intuition or habit. Instead, decisions should rely on a service framework and arising evidence on implementation that links together key service components.

Such service ingredients start much earlier than when a child crosses the service doorstep, or indeed before a practitioner crosses the child's doorstep, wherever this might be. Help-seeking, care (or referral) pathways, operational criteria, staff competencies, links with other agencies, training and consultation are as important in the modern service world as the more traditional core diagnostic and treatment aspects. At least if one aspires to a seamless, comprehensive and sustainable needs-less service, rather than just providing 'good' interventions in what we are most used to and feel comfortable with. This should encompass the whole spectrum of help, from crisis-response to prevention, or indeed the other way round.

Here comes another fallacy, i.e. that these principles and aspirations only apply to specialist settings, namely what we tend to refer to as child and adolescent mental health services (CAMHS). If we accept the principle that everyone in contact with children has a mental health role of some kind, the service definition is certainly broader too. There has to be a theory, model and supporting evidence behind an educational psychology and counselling service, as much as for a humanitarian or developmental non-governmental organization (NGO) without the 'core' remit of treating mental health problems. This is where attitudes, needs and staff innovation have often moved ahead of policy and top-down service development.

Let us challenge a few other myths too. This is not just about scale and wealth of resources either. It would be an exaggeration to state that 'small is beautiful' or that 'money doesn't buy happiness', as high-income countries undoubtedly have a disproportionate amount of resources. Yet, there is evidence that the strongest predictor of public (and, of course, children's) well-being among a number of indicators is the extent of income inequality within a society rather than the absolute income, which is an encouraging message for Nordic countries and Japan, but less so for the US or the UK. Then there is a difference between the ongoing and sustained growth of child mental health services, and pouring funding into dysfunctional areas without seeking to understand the reasons for a chronic underperformance. If there was a linear association between the amount of resources and high quality service models, one would expect to find those in the better-funded countries and areas. Unfortunately, this is not the case, as the absence of evidenced service models transgresses income and reinforces further service inequalities. This is the reason that Australia, New Zealand and, recently, the UK have attempted to address such inequities with better evidenced payment systems. The drive is undoubtedly economic rather than philosophical, nevertheless, my colleagues and I did find a huge service variation across child mental health practice (intervention for the same problem) across English child mental health services, often within the same region or locality.

Consequently, there is disparity of service provision, which particularly affects certain groups of children. Factors such as lack of advocacy and support, social exclusion, poverty and mobility make such a type of service less accessible to vulnerable groups. Unfortunately, children and youth living in care, shelters, on the streets or in juvenile settings are strikingly less likely to be seen in mainstream services compared to the general population with lesser levels of need. There is strong evidence, for example, that homeless or refugee youth will only manage to access services in crisis, usually when they are very ill. In doing so, they have bypassed the usual service filters and pathways that rely on having supportive – or even vocal – parents, being in school or registered in primary health care.

The next myth to challenge is that service modelling is only required in high-income countries, because 'they have a lot of ingredients to mix'. I would argue exactly the opposite, in that the smaller the resource pot, the more important it is to use it wisely and efficiently. There will always be dilemmas and priorities resulting in 'something has to give', but avoiding them will not improve children's care. Instead it can make it worse by wasting limited staff time to ad hoc interventions, thus entering a vicious cycle of low staff morale and failure to convince authorities of the value of the service. In contrast, a targeted, justified and evidenced approach, albeit with a long-term and developmental strategy that understands the wider strengths and limitations of a society, is more likely to succeed and keep growing. Leadership is crucial, but not sufficient without an underpinning framework and vision.

8 Ever-changing approaches to child trauma

Finally, an argument that I have heard from some NGOs, including large international organizations, is that 'we don't do mental health'. Maybe language and past experience in linking with mental health services play a part in these perceptions. Nevertheless, it is difficult to argue against a common goal across all agencies of building children's resilience within their own remit. Deciding where to draw the line of this remit is a tough call, particularly when being overwhelmed by extreme need. However, avoiding an open discussion on the core duties as well as on the evolving role of a volunteer, practitioner or agency will at best miss opportunities to develop new skills, thus help vulnerable children. For example, an NGO geared towards working with adults could reasonably develop competencies and interventions for the 'parent' part of their target group, without diverting considerably from its mission. This will still require awareness and training in relation to children, as well as liaison with more child-focused agencies. This will eventually improve the service they offer, equip their staff and volunteers with new competencies, position the organization to compete for new funding streams and meet family needs without losing the distinct expertise of the existing service.

Placing a service in a particular sociocultural context is as important as relating to its wider public and welfare systems. Such a system may be skewed towards specialist services or be more integrated with primary care; have equally developed health, social care and education services; be overtly reliant on non-statutory agencies; sub-contract academic centres to provide a variable degree of services; or consist of mixed provision by the independent (for profit or not) sector and the state.

If this is not confusing enough, adding a child trauma perspective whilst seeking service consistency appears an impossible task. Why? Because the connection and integration of services becomes even more important for children with complex needs; developing a different approach can be testing where generic services are relatively underdeveloped; and vulnerable groups are usually low down the policy and funding priority list. Nevertheless, this is why we need to be able to 'see the wood for the trees', and thus make sense of patterns across seemingly different worlds. If we can agree on certain principles, seek evidence, then translate and apply these principles and evidence to different contexts, perhaps we can introduce some structure and rationale among the chaos. Isn't this, after all, what we try to achieve in making sense of children's fragmented experiences and inner worlds?

2

IMPACT OF TRAUMA ON CHILD MENTAL HEALTH

The complex relationship between vulnerability and trauma

Placing children or youth populations into groupings has both advantages and drawbacks. It highlights particular needs in terms of complexity, longevity and severity; the lasting interaction between the child and their environment; the mirroring of children's needs by agencies from social care, education, health and other sectors; the different methods of acquiring evidence; the direct or indirect exclusion from or limited access to mainstream services; and the pragmatics of redressing these inequities through designated policy, funding and resources.

There are dangers in doing so, as well. These groups overlap, as a child in care may be in contact with the juvenile system or become homeless at some point. There is a limit on how many groups one can define, and consequently fund, in a linear and cumulative way. Earlier debates on culture-specific services have demonstrated the risks of the well-meaning creation of protected resources inadvertently resulting in service silos. The rapid changes in our multi-cultural societies show that we can no longer afford to define service needs in terms of even two or three predominant cultural groups.

Overall, though, adopting a 'vulnerability' or 'trauma' framework (or whatever concepts predominate in future years), indicates a different way of viewing certain groups of children, both collectively and individually. From the moment we do so, policy, service modelling, interventions, research, training and practice will never be the same again. Then we will start considering the options and limitations of implementing these principles but, unless the thinking changes and the reasons become apparent to caregivers, practitioners and other stakeholders, it is not possible to change, among other things, policy, environments, media and public perceptions.

> For me, myself I think it's very I have a . . . new perspective, I have a . . . different point of view so I can . . . more easy to face the children with

> trauma when they have problems so it's more . . . easy to handle them and
> for others it is very useful because everybody who . . . attend the workshop
> have worked with children so it will help them to . . . the next feature.
> *Orphanage social worker, Indonesia, after trauma-focused training*

In spite of the somewhat artificial boundaries, notwithstanding within and across-country variation, children in public care (foster, residential, kinship, living in orphanages and care leavers), adopted, young offenders, drug and alcohol users, refugees (migrants, internally displaced, asylum-seeking, living with parents or unaccompanied minors) and homeless (single youth or younger children with their parents, usually victims of domestic violence) are the groups more likely to be viewed as having complex (rather than 'special' or 'specialist' needs). Their increased mental health problems are also strongly associated with learning difficulties or disabilities, other developmental delays and acute or chronic physical illness. Their identified traumatic experiences, usually abuse and neglect, but also exposure to violence (community or family) and war trauma are not only often inter-related but, crucially, they can lead to secondary trauma and impairment such as being placed in care and whatever else this might involve. Although traumatic experiences per se, such as abuse and neglect, transgress social strata, they tend to cluster with other adversities and socioeconomic deprivation. Some communities are collectively affected by human (war or political conflict, ethnic violence) or nature-induced disasters (e.g. earthquakes). What becomes increasingly evident and matters for interventions and services is exactly this complex, cumulative relationship between past trauma and current adversities (or secondary trauma), thus how to simultaneously tackle both.

Nature and extent of mental health problems

Children exposed to multiple risks are more likely to have more and, to some extent, qualitatively different types of mental health problems. Higher rates are consistent across studies with vulnerable groups such as homeless, refugee, in care or in contact with the courts. The characteristics of the samples and measures vary, mainly because studies using questionnaires tend to over-report prevalence rates compared to those using interviews. There are also cross-cultural differences in the use and interpretation of measures. Therefore, it is difficult to generate exact rates or patterns, but an average 4:1 ratio to the general population is a close estimate, i.e. one would expect as many as 40 per cent of children belonging to any of these groups to present with mental health problems of sufficient severity to justify assessment and possibly intervention; this in contrast with 10–12 per cent in the general population, or 20 per cent among children living in deprived areas, hence where some risk factors are present, but children live in relative stability. Therefore, there is a relatively linear association between risk and poor mental health. This applies to most types of mental health problems, although the reasons may be different. When methodologies are reasonably comparable, findings are strikingly similar in different parts of the world.

Epidemiological research, for example in Brazil and Pakistan, came up with similar conclusions with those from high-income countries, at least when one took into account the underlying risk factors, predominantly socioeconomic deprivation. The same applies to studies with collectively affected populations such as after natural disasters, or war conflict. Furthermore, these trends have been replicated in eastern European orphanages and residential settings in other countries, as well as with street children and incarcerated youth.

Notwithstanding debates on mental health concepts, their cultural validation or their threshold, emotional problems such as post-traumatic stress disorder (PTSD), depression and anxiety are the most obviously precipitated by exposure to trauma. Effects could be direct such as from abuse or neglect; or indirect, for example by witnessing domestic or community violence. Interestingly, pathways to different problems have been found to vary, with PTSD (as the term implies) being a direct outcome of trauma, whereas depression and anxiety are mediated more by 'here and now' adversities like living in a refugee camp, social exclusion, unemployment or parenting difficulties. This is an important finding that has influenced our approach to interventions and services that should ideally tackle child's adverse experiences and circumstances both past and present.

Behavioural problems (assuming that we classify them within ill mental health, a stance that many will not agree with) are clearly more related to adversity such as inconsistent or negative caregiving and community influences. These are not easy distinctions to make as, for example, neighbourhood violence will result in both trauma exposure and learned behaviours. However, the key qualitative difference, which is just beginning to permeate practice and which has been central to our training programmes in recent years, is the distinction between trauma-related and socially learned aggression. The former has a different genesis in the child, primarily reproducing their experience through fear and acceptance, in addition to the learned elements of their response. Such a conceptualization arises from attachment theory, and has influenced attachment-focused interventions that focus on the caregiver-child relationship in providing new nurturing experiences. This does not mean that no behavioural strategies should be implemented – far from it – but rather that caregivers and staff need to constantly operate at both levels.

We know relatively little about the causes of neurodevelopmental conditions such as autism (often viewed as a broader spectrum), attention deficit hyperactivity disorder (ADHD) and learning difficulties or disabilities. Although these clearly have a biological explanation, they are also over-represented among all vulnerable groups, possibly because children are exposed to a variety of risks, from as early as pregnancy. They are more likely to co-occur with emotional or behavioural problems than in the general population, and are difficult to distinguish in practice. It can take some time, with skilled observations and monitoring following a child's placement for adoption, before one can conclude with some certainty whether their difficulties in class can, for example, be attributed to impaired concentration span and overactivity – thus hinting at ADHD – or to an environmentally explained hypervigilance commonly seen in neglected children. Of course, there is also the

12 Impact of trauma on child mental health

possibility that both could be present. The distinction becomes even harder the older the child and the less stable their environment. In the previous scenario, an adoptive placement breakdown would compound presenting difficulties during adolescence.

Mental illnesses like schizophrenia or other forms of psychosis are also biologically determined and usually start in late adolescence or early adult life; but they have a much worse prognosis for those unfortunate young people who are either in a vulnerable situation, or become vulnerable – end up homeless or in prison – as a result of their inability to live independently. A psychotic presentation could mask a drug-induced psychotic episode, which will usually subside and have a better prognosis as long as the substance use is managed.

Finally, carers are bound to ask: 'Will the problems go away?', 'Can they lead a *normal* life?', 'Will they get into trouble in later life?' Although there are neither 'all-or-nothing' answers or accurate predictions, there are strong indicators that can either reduce or increase risk, thus break the cycle, at each stage of a child's or young person's life. These are often referred to as vulnerability or risk and protective or resilience factors.

Changing approaches to vulnerability and resilience

The debate on the relative effects of *nature* and *nurture* has evolved in accepting a more complex and dynamic relationship between multiple factors than originally thought. Early research was useful in identifying the merit of individual factors that placed children at risk or protected them from stressors and other adversities. However, more sophisticated designs gradually highlighted the interaction not just across factors, but also within them, thus challenging what were previously thought of as linear causal processes.

One example stems from a simple observation that, out of three children exposed to the same events within a family, only one may go on to develop mental health problems. The hypothesis and later establishment that inherent characteristics play a part from as early as birth was an important contribution, but subsequent research identified more complex patterns. In the majority of common emotional problems, both predisposition and experiences have an impact. We now know that a baby with a 'difficult' temperament can influence their caregiver's early responses, their bonding and ultimately their relationship; thus placing this baby at a relative disadvantage to their siblings. The change in knowledge though suggests that this is not a static characteristic, but rather that this dynamic relationship takes on a life of its own in predicting what will happen next. In other words, this sub-system in parenting or family life is more than a sum of its two parts. In a relatively stable environment, the effects on the child's later mental well-being can be marginal. In another context though, such as the mother being a victim of domestic violence or living in a refugee camp, if we fast forward two or three years, we may find this toddler in a foster home or orphanage, while their siblings still live at home. A whole new trajectory in front of them already . . . And yet, understanding these subtle mechanisms means that we can intervene early and make a difference.

Another example of interaction between risk factors concerns the changing concept of *life events*. Initially there was a relatively clear-cut distinction between 'dependent' events such as family conflict, which was known to be both cause and effect of other stressors; and 'independent' events like a road traffic or other type of accident. This distinction has become more blurred with the realization that only a few events truly happen by chance, with the majority having an increased probability in vulnerable environments. Extreme poverty, overcrowding and parental stress or depression mean impaired parenting capacity and supervision; thus a bigger chance of a young child wandering off into all sorts of hazards or exploitation. I recall a disabled teenage mum and her three-year-old son charged with energy in a Sao Paulo favela in Brazil. She was pregnant, had reduced mobility on account of some disability and looked utterly exhausted (Photo 2.1). As far as the environment was concerned, he had the options of narrow alleys in the burning sun, all sorts of protruding sharp metals used for cheap constructions, naked electric wires to illegally 'borrow' electricity from the surrounding neighbourhood and stagnant water – right in the middle of the Zika mosquito crisis. The mother was trying her best, but what chance would one give the boy *not* to have a serious, if not fatal, accident? The local NGO volunteers attributed two other mums' obvious apathy and exhaustion to domestic violence. They stared blankly past the volunteers on their door step, seemingly drained of all emotions. As we followed the clues to engage as many families as possible in the favela in basic tuition, the parents' trail often went cold, and we only found young children at 'home'. What was so scary was again their acceptance of their fate in their looks, staring right through us: 'Mum has gone to work' (Photo 2.2).

PHOTO 2.1 What are the chances of safety and optimal growth in a Brazilian favela?

PHOTO 2.2 Alone in a Brazilian favela

The increasing influence of socioecological and resilience theories

As the body of evidence on the relationship between various risk or protective factors and mental health problems has increased, the complexities of the mechanisms involved have become more prominent. This is perhaps a less neat and more confusing framework than originally believed, but it is also encouraging because each part of the chain offers opportunities to intervene. Overall, there have been several shifts in our knowledge.

As already discussed, most factors are inter-linked. Even some biological factors that predispose, for example, to developmental delay could themselves be affected by environmental factors such as drug use during pregnancy. Resilience is no longer merely assumed to be an absence of risk factors, but rather a more assertive, thus attainable, attribute with which to fight and prosper in the face of adversity. More importantly, and poignantly for children living in extreme conditions, Bronfenbrenner's ecological theory (1979) has hugely influenced how services and researchers conceptualize resilience. If it was initially perceived as a survival tool that a child is somehow born with, this is now viewed as a more dynamic and multi-level concept cutting across the child, family and peers (microsystem), interactions with the community (mesosystem) such as school and extended family (exosystem) and wider society (e.g. culture and beliefs – macrosystem).

Interestingly, this shift from an individual to a multi-level resilience concept has been the outcome of both research findings and service gaps. In many countries or settings such as refugee camps, individual interventions and specialist skills are sparse or absent, hence agencies had to look for other strengthening approaches beyond the child. The broadening of the previously narrow mental health spectrum has brought to the forefront enhanced input from teachers and frontline workers,

Impact of trauma on child mental health **15**

through mental health promotion, preventive and responsive interventions. Even if evidence is not as yet conclusive in this complex field, services and practice are increasingly underpinned by such a multi-level framework.

The implications are substantial, as this model gives us several options for intervention. These options are not merely philosophical, as they can provide practitioners with possible goals and achievable outcomes, rather than them becoming overwhelmed by the extent of unmet needs, limited time, the 'one-trick-pony' approach (i.e. pursuing one line of intervention in isolation from addressing inter-linked risk factors in the child's environment) and low morale in the absence of change. Introducing simplicity to a child's complex world sounds contradictory. Yet, this has often been the only approach to fragile systems that produce fragile young souls. A number of young people in residential care immediately come to mind. These people were exposed to several risks, and responded by acting aggressively to repeated attempts to engage in some form of trauma-focused individual therapy. Containing the immediate risks, bringing calmness to their environment, setting realistic short-term goals and employing behavioural strategies are not mutually explicit with further attempts to engage a young person therapeutically. It is just that, sometimes, this young person may not be ready or feel sufficiently safe to reach the therapeutic point we want them to.

Inter-linked vulnerability and resilience factors through an ecological lens

This is not an exhaustive or detailed list, but rather the intention is to put across the dynamic relationships between different factors, demonstrate their specificity to traumatized children and inform subsequent discussion of interventions.

There is a growing body of evidence on their contribution of *individual factors*. What is often lacking is knowledge about their exact nature and part in the chain of events, because as already stated, these individual factors may be implicated as both cause and effect, or act as confounders. Some of the literature remains inconclusive, for example, on the impact of age and gender, possibly because of multiple factors associated with them in the first instance. Adolescents and males may be more exposed to war conflict through active participation in protests and adopting a more adult-like role in certain societies. This can be balanced by their enhanced cognitive capacity and peer support, and resultant coping strategies. Age holds a different weight altogether among vulnerable children. In a developmental context, chronological age and real age of functioning are not necessarily the same. Child development is thus viewed along several dimensions, namely cognitive, emotional, social, physical, communication (receptive and expressive), moral and personal skills. These will vary across all children. However, a child who has suffered abuse and neglect, and has been placed in care, has a higher chance of functioning at a younger age in one or more of these domains. This is an important distinction, for which reason, I like to start training with an exercise to sharpen observational skills. Caregivers then have to relate to a child at different levels for different developmental tasks – not a negligible challenge.

16 Impact of trauma on child mental health

Learning difficulties bring their own vulnerabilities and also require adapted responses, whilst variants of intelligence, particularly the 'emotional' type, help to better equip children in their social surroundings. The mix matters again, with girls more prone to social understanding, although sometimes over sensitivity can turn against them in peer relationships. Emotional and other types of intelligence and learning are strong predictors of educational attainment, which is addressed below, although some classifications refer to it as an individual attribute. This in turn increases confidence and self-esteem, and thus adds another protective layer; vice versa, lack of such a layer can negate other attributes. For instance, children who suffer abuse find it hard to accept praise, indeed they quickly drop out of precious educational and social opportunities at the slightest hint that they are 'not liked' or are 'not good enough'.

The same could be claimed for coping strategies that children develop intuitively, by observing peers and adults, or through direct exposure within the family, care environment and school, as well through therapeutic input. There are several coping theories and resulting coping styles, with the model proposed by Lazarus and Folkman (1984) being the most widely adopted for research and interventions alike. Their focus on the importance of cognitive appraisal (primary, secondary and reappraisal) has been influential in shaping interventions. The two broad emotion-focused (such as dealing with negative emotions through mindfulness meditation or praying) and problem-solving styles (practical ways of dealing with a problem without being affected by emotions) have been widely studied in particular individual and environmental circumstances. Development, gender and culture are strong influences, the latter in the protective shape of religion and spirituality, which are discussed below within the macrosystem level.

Our knowledge about the role of biological, genetic (both real and feared, for example, for adoptive parents), biochemical and hormonal factors is constantly improving and thus enabling us to disentangle them from independent environmental effects, understanding how they might be inter-linked and, crucially, their underpinning mechanisms. These improvements are aided by new techniques such as neuroimaging and genetic testing, although the heterogeneity of both traumatic experiences and mental health conditions (such as autism) remains a constraint on the generalization of findings. Some biochemical changes, such as the decreased sensitivity of serotonin receptors in depression, may reflect a non-specific mediating path of abnormalities that go back to early neurodevelopmental stages, even if medication based on these findings has been found to have effect on symptoms such as low mood, irritability and loss of energy. Recent years have witnessed a better understanding of the early effects of abuse and neglect on the child's developing brain, particularly during the first two years of life. Studies with infants and young children raised in institutions showed the negative effects of lack of stimulation and social interactions on the experience-expectant brain plasticity, mainly by affecting the hypothalamic-pituitary-adrenal axis of the brain; although this is not an irreversible process and can be buffered by secure attachment and other protective factors. A degree of genetic predisposition exists in most types of mental health problems,

Impact of trauma on child mental health **17**

mainly in the more severe types of mental illness, although in absolute terms the risk remains low.

Family factors are the most widely studied, although these are not independent of other vulnerabilities. Parental and child ill mental health are strongly correlated. Controlling for a small potential genetic effect, the key mechanism is by impairing parenting capacity, whether through lack of discipline and consistency leading to behavioural problems, or through the longer-lasting impact of emotional rejection. This can be expressed through harsh parenting, the definition of which varies across cultures or, crucially, through lack or limited bonding and the resulting attachment difficulties. Parental drug or alcohol use are other common correlates, often more prominent with domestic and other types of violence. As the probability of helping children to escape from abuse and neglect are minimal without breaking those adult cycles, child protection and anti-domestic violence interventions are increasingly being integrated into family safety programmes.

All these factors are associated with socioeconomic adversities such as over-crowding and unemployment. The links with individual and collective trauma are striking. Few populations have suffered as many hostilities in recent or distant memory as the inhabitants of the Gaza Strip. The socioeconomic indicators are pretty bad too. About 10,000 people share each square kilometre, moreover Gaza city also boasts the highest global unemployment rate – 44 per cent according to the World Bank. No wonder that, over the years, our studies found different path-ways linking war trauma to PTSD, and poverty to depression. In Brazil, 22 per cent of the population in Rio de Janeiro live in 1,000 favelas, with the numbers on the increase. One in four Aboriginal women aged 25–34 are likely to report domestic violence (i.e. the true incidence is likely to be much higher), with a strong associa-tion to unemployment and disability. Both these populations have high rates of drug and alcohol use, male crime and imprisonment.

'Education is more than learning' is a principle widely debated between and within governments around the world. *Schools* often offer the only opportunity when all other protection systems have ceased. Some of its benefits are more obvious than others, yet the evidence is unequivocal. Attainment is not just about obtaining grades, but rather steps and realistic goals in maximizing a child's potential, whatever the extent of their vulnerability, lack of opportunities, disability or impairment; or, sadly, for some children, all of the above. These goals may be related to educational skills, sports, creativity, practical competencies or peer relations. As with previous resilience factors, these are both inter-linked and can snowball, thus breaking cycles of rejection and unfulfillment.

Adaptive coping strategies learned in school can balance negative influences in other environments. Children can make these distinctions and 'hold both baskets' from a young age. A pre-school teacher in a disadvantaged Sydney area impressed on me how some 3–5-year-olds would start swearing as soon as their parents arrived to collect them, after a whole day of abiding by structure and rules. A little boy confirmed this by reminding me of the time-limit on playing a computer game: 'It is the rule.' Achievement of any kind breeds confidence, and confidence breeds hunger for more achievement and harder tasks.

This process can be relatively easy within a nurtured and supportive peer environment, as it can be destroyed by social exclusion. Making and sustaining friendships does not come naturally to children with insecure, disinhibited or disorganized attachment styles. However, when they do eventually kick in they can be a great catalyst for learning and belonging. I stood behind an unaccompanied refugee boy in an Athens shelter while he drew his five fingers on a piece of paper. He then stopped and pondered for ages. The activity involved listing his five top qualities, one written within the shape of each finger. When I asked why he had left it blank, he honestly replied that 'he could not think anything good about him'. He seemed friendly enough with the boy sitting next to him, so I prompted, 'What would your friend say about you?', and got the response, 'Well, maybe that I'm kind.' Then he got going, as if peer confirmation was sufficient to free a sense of self-belief (Photo 2.3).

When academic attainment and social growth are accompanied by emotional learning, the school can make all the difference in instilling emotional regulation

PHOTO 2.3 Positive attributes were initially hard to define for a refugee boy, but eventually there were plenty

skills and weaving through difficult experiences. There are several theories to build on, although less so for traumatized children, ranging from individual emotional or mental health literacy to a whole-school approach. Observing primary school children take turns, be inquisitive and welcoming in an Indonesian orphanage school was consistent with my earlier impression of a nurturing style across the caregivers at the home.

Community influences inevitably reflect socioeconomic changes. The protective layer of social networks can partially compensate for the lack of organized systems in low-income countries, through the natural resources of extended families and neighbours; for example, stepping in to provide kinship care in the absence of systematic fostering provision. This does not mean that communities should be left to their own devices to fill a state vacuum, but rather that the policy-makers and organizations involved should make a conscious decision on how to maximize community strengths without neglecting the planned fostering and adoption. On the other hand, working with homeless families – usually victims of domestic violence – in English cities over the years, or looking at the feeding station for homeless youth in Chicago, made me realize that some natural supports cannot be easily replaced by services. In the lands of plenty, people are often left to fend for themselves. Still, there are ways of developing boundaried and safe havens in those situations. The worst combination may be in societies in transition, where urbanization and economic growth do not always match: is it psychosocially preferable to live in a poor Indian village than be poor in the slums of a growing Indian metropolis? The interaction with other fields and evidence is also important, and the implications are just beginning to be understood beyond common-sense initiatives. The strong finding that children can form multiple attachments means that sports, leisure and other community activities offer unique entry points to these havens. A sports coach at a slum school or a youth offending institution often fills a child's vacuum as a role model or substitute parent. Again, such impact should be cultivated and nurtured, rather than be left to chance; for example, by providing training and support for those role models, as one would for established professional groups.

The outer *societal* layer is not to be sniffed at either, even if changes are slow and sometimes beyond our control. Attitudes towards disability, mental illness, women, sexuality and child rearing (predominantly physical punishment) fluctuate through all sorts of contradictions; and inevitably impact on how children, trauma and mental health problems are viewed and addressed – or not. Cultural beliefs are of huge importance too, although one should remember that these are rarely homogenous or stereotypical, but are themselves subject to continuous generational and socioeconomic influences. When my colleagues and I interviewed third-generation young people of Indian origin in quite stable and affluent English communities, their views on mental health issues were much closer to those of their indigenous White peers than to those of their parents.

Culture cannot be easily disentangled from religion, religiosity or spirituality, all of which have been shown to exert a protective role. I smiled to myself during the first year of the World Awareness for Children in Trauma programme when it struck me that I had been near or inside more mosques than churches during a period of visits in predominantly Muslim countries. This came at a time when Islam was distorted in its association with terrorism by western media and with revenge by socially inept terror organizations. In contrast, disadvantaged communities seemed to draw strength from religion, whether during and after Friday prayers in Iran or Sunday mass in Rwanda. When such resilience is accompanied by messages of wider tolerance and inclusion, its potential is very powerful. It is worth visiting Coventry Cathedral to experience human connections that transport you to post-conflict regions with different religions. A Ramakrishna Mission Swami Vivekananda temple in Mumbai stunned me with its frescoes from different faiths, so did the Mount Mary Catholic Church in the same city, where local Hindus came to pray. This was so accepted that the note on the entrance encouraged them to do so whilst keeping their shoes on – so engagingly funny!

Conceptualizing resilience systems and their interactions

Viewing a child within different and interacting systems provides a dynamic perspective and opportunities for interventions, even if one is constrained by one's role to only address one, e.g. working individually or with the family (Figure 2.1). Nevertheless, awareness of the other levels and the constraints that these may impose (for example, the unpalatable likelihood that the family situation will not change) can help one focus and set realistic goals. We will revisit this model extensively, both within the interventions and training chapters.

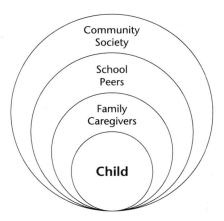

FIGURE 2.1 Resilience systems and the vulnerable child

REFLECTIVE EXERCISE

Claire is 15 years old and lives in a children's home. She has had three foster placements in the last five years which broke down because she ran away and took drugs. During this period, Claire has remained in contact with her birth mum, but this is a volatile relationship. Sometimes they get on great, only for a minor argument to escalate which results in them not seeing each other for weeks. Claire's behaviour then gets worse, as she stops going to school, stays out all night and cuts her arms. Her mum smokes cannabis and has been in and out of hospital with depression.

Claire had a good relationship with her foster carers when she was settled, but this would not last for long. She is an intelligent girl, who can be very creative but also fluctuating in her emotions. She went into care at the age of 10, after she disclosed to a teacher that she had been sexually abused by her mother's partner. Her mother did not believe her. It particularly hurts Claire that her two younger brothers (now aged 8 and 11 years) are still at home and that she can't see them when she falls out with her mum.

When at school, Claire is intelligent and does well 'when she puts her mind into it'. She particularly enjoys drama, 'the only time she can chill out and be herself'. She has some friends but tends to dominate them and lose them. Claire does not like herself. She has tried to lose weight, only to revert to comfort-eating. Throughout her years in foster care, her social worker tried hard to get her seen by child mental health services. Claire tends to attend after self-harming, only to drop out when she is introduced to a therapist for more long-term input. 'What's the point? Nobody can help me . . .'

Questions

1 How would you formulate Claire's mental health needs?
2 How would you define the relevant vulnerability (risk) and resilience (protective) factors on each dimension (young person, family, school and community)?

3

CHILD VULNERABILITY IN A GLOBAL CONTEXT

How much can we alter a child's life trajectory?

Where a child is born, across the world, within a country, region or community, will determine to a large extent their immediate, medium and long-term chances in life. These vary from survival, to having their basic needs met, living in a caring environment and having decent life opportunities. Of the nine million under-fives who die annually, the majority were born in Sub-Saharan Africa and South Asia, where an estimated 175 out of 1,000 children will not make it past their fifth birthday, a staggering contrast with 6 in high-income countries. When one considers countries officially defined as 'fragile' and 'conflict-affected', these account for 20 per cent of the low-income countries' population, whilst one third of their inhabitants live in extreme poverty; 50 per cent of their children do not attend primary school and, crucially, a sobering 50 per cent are likely to die before their fifth birthday. The major causes of pneumonia, diarrhoeal diseases and malaria are unnecessary too, as they are so easy to treat. These are not due just to poor or no access to basic health care, but also to sanitation, nutrition and a whole range of linked factors that form the focus of the global Sustainable Development Goals.

Worldwide, 400 million children live in extreme poverty and 100 million of those live on the streets. The current global refugee crisis predominantly affects children and young people under the age of 18, with 16 million internally displaced and 8 million refugee children; 600,000 children seeking asylum; and 25,000 unaccompanied minors across 80 countries. About 140 million children are orphaned, whilst in the least-developed countries 22 per cent of children are involved in labour and only one third attend secondary education. Evidence shows that nothing is set in stone, i.e. that mishaps are reversible, but also that risk factors play heavily and accumulate, thus form a chain of events that provide both opportunities to reverse the script and routes into criminality and abuse. It is obvious that there is no panacea or simple solution, as societies and systems reflect human and economic complexities. For this reason, placing such human experience into a service systems context is essential.

What do we define as *systems*? If our main focus is on child mental health or well-being in its broad sense, then all sectors in contact with children and youth matter. The 'big three' players of welfare, education and health vary globally, whilst their role may shift even within the same country, as governments, policies and structures constantly change. For example, the mantra that 'education is only for learning' can quickly turn into 'education is more than learning' after a swing in the votes. Similar ideologies impact on juvenile institutions. Child mental health is well down the list of most health policies, whilst even the more fundamental conceptualization of children's rights and protection can be absent, superficial, emerging or not yet finding its way through society and its services. These issues trespass socioeconomic strata, but if we follow the predominant classification of the world into high, middle and low-income countries, we will begin to establish some patterns that we can translate into both universal and specific solutions for children most in need.

High-income countries: policy, evidence and emerging models, but 'not everything that shines is gold'

Economic models can be difficult to understand and translate into health indicators, but a key public health finding is that it is not the absolute size of a country's gross domestic product (GDP) that predicts better health outcomes, but rather its interaction with the extent of socioeconomic inequalities. In that respect, Nordic countries appear to be at an advantage over technically wealthier nations. But what can we learn from each in relation to health and welfare systems for the most vulnerable?

Innovation, new technologies, intervention programmes and their more robust effectiveness largely originate from the US. The 'know how' is second to none, so is the ability to share and communicate competencies and treatment fidelity. Ambitious multimodal programmes like Multi Systemic Therapy (MST) and Treatment Foster Care (TFC) could not have been born anywhere else. Where they often struggle though is the next phase of 'real world' implementation. The fragmentation of policies and service structures between states is one reason. Proportionately high reliance on the private sector and health insurance has both direct and indirect effects. The former denotes second-class citizen care for poor youth, who also have a number of hurdles to jump to access decent education, employment and housing. 'Philanthropy' steps in on an ad hoc basis to salvage the luckier ones off the streets. Nevertheless, there are many inter-agency and preventive models that withstand the political trend such as Home Start and the 2,000 school health centres across the country. The specialist sector is influenced by the same contradiction of providing high-quality care if in tangent with health insurance guidelines. This is not without some benefits in targeting care more efficiently, but on the whole it comes at the expense of psychosocial and inter-agency approaches because of their higher cost – indirectly, this is where poor children and families lose out for a second time.

The UK has probably advanced the second implementation phase of translating technology and innovation into mainstream applications, because of its strong public

24 Child vulnerability in a global context

sector – or at least what used to be strong, as this is currently being clipped away around the edges. Primary health care is key to access, although there is strong evidence that even this is not enough for vulnerable youth with high mobility and disengagement, like care leavers, homeless and young offenders. This is where bridging policies in the early 2000s, like Every Child Matters, addressed the interface between health, welfare and education. Although policy implementation was disadvantaged by the lack of decent evidence, this policy led to a growth of posts, services and initiatives that often lacked consistency and evidence-base, but were innovative and crossed over traditional structures to enhance social inclusion.

Agencies were given financial incentives to work together, although these were often short-term, and core priorities made it hard for them to mainstream and sustain. Recently there has been a change in government policy that has led to substantial cost savings in local councils, which have primarily affected those at the bottom of the social ladder and in real need of inter-agency input. Privatization in social care and the growing independence of schools are likely to exacerbate this gap and mitigate consistency in years to come. Nevertheless, the lesson from the previous decade of service growth for vulnerable groups in the UK was that 'bottom-up' service development can only take you so far without evidence and a sustainability strategy. On a positive note, inter-agency principles, joint commissioning and key services like the youth offending inter-agency teams have largely survived, and may find their way through different processes and providers such as NGOs or social enterprises.

The rising costs of health care, particularly people living longer (a paradox from the earlier comment on low-income countries appalling mortality rates) and the high costs of new drugs such as in cancer treatment have stretched even the strongest public health systems. Australia now operates a hybrid model of citizens choosing between the public Medicare, contributing to costs in public settings, or full private care. The Netherlands adopt an interesting combination of state-provided insurance for long-term nursing and care, and client-paid basic insurance for medical care. The distinction between short-term and long-term care and the demarcation of mental health in its own right are useful safeguards for more vulnerable groups that require more than short-term interventions.

This leaves Nordic countries as the most stable in terms of welfare and health care provision. Although their systems differ slightly, they are largely strong in their primary care and preventive elements. These tend to favour children, in particular those with multiple needs and who cannot access routine care pathways. However, despite the well-developed health and social care interface in relation to elderly people, for example, service models of inter-agency working for vulnerable children and youth remain sparse. In other words, when core services encompass diverse and complex needs, they enhance engagement and access; but this remains relatively clinically and cost-ineffective without designated and integrated models for children in care, offenders or refugee children, who place increasing pressures on resources when they reach crisis point. In the case of similar systems, the reasons appear to be more related to lack of joint planning at national and local level than to ideology.

In high-income countries, children's public care tends to gravitate towards fostering and adoption, with a range of statutory and independent (both non-profit and profit-making) schemes, and a parallel reduction of residential care. The latter largely accommodates teenagers with multiple foster placement breakdowns because of challenging behaviours and/or late entry into the system. Kinship care by members of the extended family is usually the first consideration when accommodating children, although this provision is often not well defined and resourced. For example, foster carers may have access to training and support systems such as their own social worker, whereas a relative looking after an equally needy child may be assumed to be coping well, simply because of their blood link. Similar differences exist in adoption, with some countries such as the UK placing children from within their own care system, whilst others, like Nordic countries, demonstrate both national and inter-country adoption trends.

Political and economic responses appear to constantly influence agencies for asylum-seekers, refugees and economic migrants, including unaccompanied minors. Here a central legislative change, for example in the EU, can have a direct impact on which groups of asylum-seeking families will follow a clear path rather than rely on destiny. Examples of the former include accessing family support services, possibly with financial top-up and needs-led adjustments, accommodating unaccompanied children within the national care system or developing designated units. Detention centres are prominent in many western countries with strong welfare systems, such as Canada, and constantly raise concerns about their prison-like ethos and indiscriminating inclusion of adults, youth and children with different needs, not accounting for vulnerability and mixing legal (waiting for assessment of status and application), judicial (at risk of running away) and welfare reasons (nowhere else to go for protection) in their admission criteria.

Finally, education in high-income countries also varies and undergoes constant changes that are often politically and target-driven. However, in parallel there is a continuous endorsement of mental health literacy, and of social and emotional well-being as being central to a child's development. Recent years have seen an increase in programmes that are integrated into the school curriculum. Such programmes vary from being experimental to being driven by local or central government. Their integration into a whole-school ethos is more resistant to external influences, thus more sustainable, but also is increasingly viewed as particularly important in areas of multiple disadvantage, where the school may be the focal point for other agencies.

The constant flux of middle-income countries

What a strange term! This could be interpreted as 'both and', or as 'neither here nor there'. These are basically either countries on a temporary downslope, usually on the southern and eastern edges of a fragile European Union, thrown into an economic crisis; or on upward economic projections, which have been halted in recent years, like India, Brazil or Turkey. And, of course, China, which is difficult to either

26 Child vulnerability in a global context

read or predict, depending on the indices chosen. Their cultural, ethnic and geo-political diversity and heterogeneity are major hurdles in generating lessons and solutions. They do, however, share some denominators in relation to needs and supports for vulnerable populations. Middle-income countries are not in this group by coincidence. They are in constant flux, sometimes in turmoil, as shown by the recent political instability in Brazil in the face of economic downturn and the emergency state in Turkey following the attempted coup. There are other reasons too, predominantly the ambiguous role of the state, huge inequalities and rapid urbanization that deprives them of traditional compensatory support systems that still exist in rural areas.

Two decades of growth in southern Europe (Spain, Portugal, Greece, and the south of Italy) were not necessarily followed by structural changes and investment. Their health and welfare systems are variable in their quality, but largely geared towards acute care, diseases and hospitalization. Mental health services have improved, but remain largely influenced by professional bodies rather than by the state; and with ad hoc relations with the private sector. Social care is embedded in principles of child protection but not in universal application. For example, courts in Greece may devolve legal responsibility to an NGO to take up the overall care of a child who suffered abuse and neglect. This has some benefits for children within the system, for example receiving all levels of care – including therapeutic interventions – by the SOS Children's Villages; but there is a strong chance element, with many more children being missed out because of lack of alternatives. Both the economic and the refugee crisis have exposed this systemic fragility through the rise of youth homelessness, mental health morbidity, such as through incidents of deliberate self-harm, and the numbers of unaccompanied minors, particularly in inner cities.

Countries like India, Brazil and Turkey were until recently classified as 'developing'. Extreme social inequalities are blatantly obvious where Indian slums and Brazilian favelas pop up next to business centres and modern malls; whilst cultural and geographical differences place Istanbul and Anatolian villages worlds apart in Turkey. These contradictions can be a source of energy and development, but also of confusion and conflict over attitudes and policy that directly affect children and families. Different and rapidly changing values are reflected in emerging constructs and views on mental health, children, women and parenting. Destroyed communities can be left bereft of values and hope in the slums and favelas, placing more trust in local drug lords than the state or the police. The protective cover of rural and closely knit communities can sometimes turn into a wall of silence that 'abuse does not exist'. Consequently, middle-income countries are, well, somewhere in the middle . . . in terms of children's position in society, safeguarding, family structures and traditional vs new values. One, therefore, has to accept that working at both, and constantly changing, levels is a necessity.

So, where does this leave interventions and services? Largely, these are not state-driven or consistent, at least for the most vulnerable groups, and are usually professionally led in the case of specialist interventions, whilst NGOs increasingly fill the gaps. The paucity of mental health and therapeutic services means that they often concentrate on the severe end of the problems spectrum, and aim at achieving symptomatic improvement rather than broader psychosocial outcomes.

If one adds the societal stigma of mental illness and social issues like domestic violence, disadvantaged and multi-need families and youth are not likely to have much of a chance. This is where international, national or local NGOs are beginning to redress the balance from different perspectives, i.e. primarily targeting refugee children or particular schools in deprived areas. One can find innovation and adaptation of approaches such as visiting an NGO providing theraplay and eye-movement desensitization and reprocessing (EMDR) therapy for refugee children in Istanbul. Even the term NGO can be inconsistent though, as some organizations are funded by their government, with all the pros and cons that this might imply in terms of sustainability and autonomy. The main difficulty lies in establishing a clear picture (mapping), or even definition, of key agency objectives and capacity, thus maximizing their potential and directing them in a strategic way. Nevertheless, anecdotal evidence and service reports indicate that therapeutic initiatives cross-fertilize western therapeutic frameworks with local characteristics, and increasingly inform policy, albeit somehow opportunistically.

Care systems largely rely on residential care, from infant age (orphanages), in large numbers (units of 50–100 children) and limited community alternatives. As child protection policy and children's rights principles find their way through public, media and political conscience, there is an increasing will for reform and development of more formal kinship and foster care. Social stigma is more inhibiting for the expansion of adoption, with surrogate families being seen as an intermediate solution in some societies. Juvenile institutions are predominantly adult-like and have a limited welfare ethos, at least on a large scale. The same applies to provisions for refugees, which largely rely on external funding as in Greece and Lebanon, with variable and constantly evolving phased support (from short to long term) from local or international NGOs. These provisions range from admission centres, refugee camps, care homes to supported community living. The better developed models involve clear leadership and co-ordination between these organizations, sponsors and the host government; thus there is clarity on roles and more efficient use of resources to meet multiple needs. Unfortunately, this tends to be more the case in relatively settled (medium to long-term) populations. In the fluid circumstances of newly arrived and transitional families, solutions are rather ad hoc, with the nature and quality of care mostly relying on the remit, economic sustainability and networking capacity of NGOs. For example, their priority may be to get children off the streets and reunite them with their families where possible, as indeed with the general population. On a positive note, there is an overall shift towards more child-centred attitudes that influence professional standards, service ethos and, albeit less consistently, policy and legislation. Even where this is the case, releasing or designating state resources for vulnerable populations remains an exception, they tend instead to be aimed at improving the quality of mainstream children's services, this being a more realistic goal.

Low-income, developing or Third World countries?

The names reflect the western world's ambivalence – a mixture of acknowledgement, guilt, aspiration for growth, charitable mode and inference of partner status on an equal or unequal footing, depending on who you ask. In many ways, these countries reflect the characteristics of vulnerable groups within any given society, i.e. higher levels of multiple needs, lower growth, few support options and limited escape routes. With one difference, in that they claim the largest populations too. If one considers the most vulnerable individuals within low-income countries, these forces accumulate risk and trauma at a collective level, but with limited resilience-building systems.

The most notable absentees are child protection systems, at least as yet in making sufficient impact in reducing child labour, sexual and other forms of exploitation that are the direct result of living on the streets, or in conflict-driven states. Children's rights and international policies are beginning to filter through with more tangible outputs, but the pace is slow and still ad hoc. The extent of children being abducted and forced to serve as child soldiers or sex slaves is evidence of harsh realities in large parts of the world. In some African states, child sacrifice has neither been eradicated not criminalized by law. True, I saw street sweepers in Nairobi wearing fluorescent jackets with anti-abuse campaign slogans. Over the 12 months between my two visits to Jakarta, there were small but encouraging signs of getting children off the streets, although it is too early to assess outcomes in the absence of preventive and sustainable community alternatives.

Residential care settings predominate and can still play an interim role, although one hopes with a long-term strategy in mind of re-uniting and keeping children with their families where possible, as well as developing kinship and foster care for the rest. The scale and timescale of the closure of post-genocide orphanages in Rwanda in recent years shows that this is possible with the close co-operation of governments and international NGOs. Introducing viable community care options in the long run is, of course, much harder, as positive outcomes require more than a simplistic maths equation that living in any residential setting (thus potentially making allowances for punitive and abusive regimes) is better than living on the streets; or that living with any family is better than living in any care home (thus potentially falling into the trap of returning children to abusive situations or introducing new risks). What is so far missing is the parallel re-balance and growth of systems that are scarcely available. This possibly reflects other factors in the developmental stage of low-income countries.

A similar dynamic applies to the relationship between state, international, national and local NGOs. Marrying international principles with sociocultural needs, developing sustainable local capacity and training trainers are some examples of strategic co-existence with an eye to the future. The same applies to enabling national and local NGOs to become active and increasingly autonomous collaborators, by both bringing and developing expertise within already established and tested parameters. Naturally, strategy and constantly changing, or decreasing, funding priorities are contradictory. Over-relying on the state poses both benefits and risks, in terms of independence, economic transparency in the face of corruption and alliance with forces that may not be around for long. In contrast, the more central and local governments embed children's policies in their administration and service planning, the less ambiguous and more sustainable such relationships will become.

Challenges are equivocal across different sectors. Health care resource constraints inevitably focus on acute illness, and this also applies to mental health as a whole. The transition from institutional to community care for adults is at different stages of transition, largely with over-reliance on in-patient (with over-use of restraining methods) and pharmacological treatment (again, whether as an appropriate but single option, or by default in the absence of psychological interventions). Young people fall into this service pattern, with the additional concern of being admitted on adult psychiatric wards. Dilemmas and contradictions in embracing child mental health care range from parents opting for traditional healing, remaining fearful of the stigma of mental illness and disability, and the over-diagnosis and treatment of psychotic conditions for even pre-adolescent children. These barriers are further exacerbated as the poorest have to fund or contribute to their health care, the inaccessibility of appropriate new medication and its high and often prohibitive costs. Yet, there is a promising parallel development in counselling and psychotherapy modalities, usually in independent practice that can be afforded by socioeconomically self-selected families. Exposure to new ideas and approaches also means that NGOs working with vulnerable children and families increasingly provide their own 'psychological' arm, albeit with lack of integration with statutory services.

Although education is a constant around the world, in many low-income countries poor families are faced with the paradoxical injustice of having to pay school fees. Teenagers, in particular, often drop out of school and drift into illegal labour, drug use and crime. This can be the turning point in many of their young lives. Nevertheless, there are some encouraging trends in countries such as Kenya and Uganda which provide free primary school education, with the hope of extending it to secondary education in years to come. In the meanwhile, teachers often feel powerless seeing able pupils drifting away from education. This sometimes encourages them to innovate, as at a school that I visited in the Karachi slums that is run on social enterprise principles. The fees of better-off families subsidize children living in extreme poverty. Going against the social norms of not wanting their children to mix with those that are disadvantaged, the continuing academic excellence of the slum school is an incentive for them to enrol their children – perhaps an exceptional and romantic rarity, proof of what is possible with passion combined with a business nous, nevertheless.

Other untapped, albeit promising resources include educational psychologists, welfare officers and special needs teachers. However, exploiting their potential requires re-direction, clarity of roles, co-ordination, training and ongoing support. Many, for example, are restricted to psychometric testing rather than providing additional therapeutic roles (which, given the opportunity, they absolutely love and embrace – see following chapters). Education is thus increasingly central to charities operating in conflict and deprived areas, as it provides opportunities for mental

30 Child vulnerability in a global context

health literacy and integration with other functions such as trauma-focused interventions. This is more of a challenge for smaller NGOs, usually of national or local scale that have to conform to more circumscribed remits. Their commissioning by international bodies can be the catalyst for extending strategically to a more therapeutic ethos. Such collaboration brings the additional advantages of staff and volunteers having access to standards, training and supervision.

Both the bottom-up need to maximize resources and a more conceptual top-down drive from international organizations for a skilled though not necessarily specialist workforce, has led to the more purposeful development of key-working and family support posts that can more effectively encompass children's multiple needs. Their roles, requirements and position within their operating system are so far not consistent. The vacuum of specialist partners for consultation and training, in the absence of inter-disciplinary child mental health services (with the exception of professional 'pockets'), is often filled by academic centres that can contribute to training, course accreditation, evaluation and some clinical input. Triangulation between local service and academic providers and international institutions can be a way of kick-starting new initiatives, although eyes should always be set to the future and sustainability from within.

4

LOOKING FOR ANSWERS

From Birmingham shelters to Mumbai slums

Where have the last 20 years gone, in a blink of an eye? It only seems like yesterday when I rang the bell of a homeless family shelter in Birmingham for the first time. The reason for the visit was simple. Why were we not seeing any of these families, predominantly victims of domestic violence, in child mental health services? This was the start of the journey to understand and demonstrate why some groups of the population do not cross our service doorsteps through no fault of their own.

Exactly 20 years later, I walked into the heat of Mumbai to visit urban and rural slums, and ask the same question, only on a different scale. Were we ready to address children's mental health or psychosocial needs in the absence of specialist services and in sociocultural contexts that do not necessarily coincide with our beliefs and models? Have those 20 years been wasted, if we have been standing still, asking the same questions? Was it an inevitable evolution of merely 'wait and hope'? Have there been catalysts that we can learn from to bring knowledge, skills and ultimately hope to much larger numbers of collectively deprived children? Progress has actually been immense in several fields, which enables us to pose challenging questions. Let us consider them separately, then in their totality, before drawing definitive conclusions.

Societal, cultural and economic changes

The position of children and youth in many societies has clearly changed for the better, increasingly viewing them as individuals in their own right rather than as 'future adults' or anonymous numbers. Key international principles on children's rights have been translated into legislation, policy and campaigns, at various stages and with various outcomes so far. The essence of child protection has permeated welfare, health care and education, before making inroads into the public and the media. Child rearing is closely linked to cultural beliefs, nevertheless there is

32 Looking for answers

consistent opposition to the use of physical punishment – with plenty of evidence of its adverse effects and none to perpetuate folklore views such as 'it has done me no harm'. There are similar (but often painstakingly slow) parallels in societies, and services constantly redrawing their lines in fighting domestic violence, bullying and racial and gender harassment; but also frequent contradictions and setbacks. For example, some countries introduce legislation against domestic violence, but this is often negated in real life by covertly reinforcing it by selectively interpreting 'traditional' or religious values. The expansion of liberal and child-centred views can similarly be negated by giving mixed messages to youth that it is legal, thus acceptable, to use guns by not outlawing their use; or adopting a low age for criminal responsibility.

Progress in understanding and accepting mental illness and overcoming its stigma has been more linear, although equally slow. This is not independent of changes in attitudes to disability and inclusion. In many low-income countries, the shift is just beginning to show some centrally driven trends. Fear of mental illness and the absence of community alternatives to hospitalization are common remnants. In high-income countries, inclusive principles are being engrained in public conscience, but are devalued by the harsh reality of people with mental illness drifting down the ladder and homeless young people being seen as outcasts who have to fend for themselves. Ultimately, fear, stigma and exclusion tend to underpin a number of vulnerabilities rather than just mental health. Therefore, being young, homeless and depressed does not bode well, even in the presence of decent service systems. The increasing recognition of valuing 'service user' perspectives is promising in that it is beginning to involve parents and youth, although meaningful participation that goes beyond tokenism has not yet been achieved.

This 20-year period that is under scrutiny is relatively brief, so it is difficult to judge its wider and long-term consequences. Regional conflicts remain or are transformed into global terrorism with new boundaries and no rules; as such their implications are difficult to read as yet. Inequalities have grown in recent years, despite a phase of economic growth. Sadly, this gap in population wealth and all its correlates has been prominent in new economic powers that seek a share of the world's wealth, only to offer its benefits to 1 per cent of their own people. States that have enjoyed a more prolonged post-colonial stability in Africa and Asia are beginning to grapple with social issues, although corruption and the authoritarian swinging of the pendulum give us reason to be cautious in our optimism.

Although economic growth and urbanization have brought opportunities for young people, they have also disrupted their natural family and social support networks. Globalization and technology have paradoxically encouraged both integration, through exposure to new ideas and ways of living, and racism and discrimination as natural forces against population movement, whether for economic or political reasons. These forces have risen in recent years in the face of the economic downturn, even in stable European states with strong welfare principles. Non-statutory organizations have grown to fill regional or global vacuums, together with a fundamental shift in the philosophy of aid to developing countries aiming at strengthening local capability and leading to sustainability – in contrast to early monetary aid lost through bureaucracy or corruption. Children always offer the face of good causes. However, deep down children often remain powerless within their disadvantaged communities, as these causes fail to generate sustainable benefits.

Advances in practice and therapeutic approaches

Over these same years, we have witnessed substantial advances in child mental health and welfare practice, also in the diversification and specificity of interventions, through a phased process. The psychotherapy tree initially consolidated its three main branches of social learning (behavioural), psychoanalytic theory (leading to various psychodynamic approaches) and cybernetics (leading to systems and family therapies) in terms of theory, professional training and accreditation, but less so in terms of evidence and application to specific groups. Then their offshoots gained enough strength to grow in their own right. Some of those, such as parent training, had to start from universal programmes whilst others, like cognitive behavioural therapy (CBT), developed from applications closely linked to their original theories (in that case, depression). Then they were applied, whether theoretically driven or not, to different problems and groups; thus leading, for example, to trauma-focused CBT or interventions for young offenders.

Other modalities, although broadly based on existing frameworks, were specifically developed for victims of trauma such as narrative exposure therapy. Their influences were theoretical, evidence-based and pragmatic. Our better understanding of the impact of psychological trauma has been informed by attachment and other theories, as well as by supporting research findings. Children's unmet complex needs and service gaps indicated that we can no longer rely on the same modalities for all those presenting with child mental health symptoms.

Unlike other programmes, namely CBT, trauma and attachment-focused therapies were not initially evidence-based, but rather adaptations of original modalities developed for generic population groups. Many practitioners who trained in these approaches returned to their jobs or moved on to more challenging positions such as working with homeless youth or children in care, where they had to innovate and remain flexible whilst retaining their therapeutic fidelity, in order to engage children and young people exposed to almost daily life upheaval. In that respect, therapists re-wrote the rules, and attempts at evaluation followed. There were examples of the opposite process too, where the first application of a therapeutic modality was developed by a research centre, followed by the challenge of rolling it out in the real world.

Overall though, in recent years there has been a plethora of training and interventions available for therapists working in a particular field; generic mental health practitioners such as community psychiatric nurses applying and extending their therapeutic skills; and frontline practitioners in contact with vulnerable children and their families, schools and communities. The indications for and boundaries between these fields are not always clear, but this is a promising baseline for the future.

34 Looking for answers

Service models: the weakest link

Developments in support for vulnerable children have largely been practice-driven, with a helping hand from policy and research. However, these have rarely been informed by a service approach. The reasons have not necessarily been due to lack of resources as, even when there has been a flow of designated funding in high-income countries, this has not been allocated on grounds of evidence, but rather on a 'bottom-up' good and innovative practice basis.

Health and welfare systems struggle to determine how interventions should be linked to policy, evidence-based data and a range of indirect staff activities (such as consultation, liaison and training). Better formulated models emerge from the more costly and often easier to define acute health care. Despite developments in establishing care pathways, outcomes and treatment guidelines, the perception that mental health is difficult to define persists among a large proportion of policy-makers, commissioners and practitioners alike. For the former there is an anxiety that detailed service models will expose unmet needs, hence cost, whilst clinicians may fear that certain interventions and ways of working may not be as effective as perceived, in terms of children's improvement and the resources used. This fallacy is reinforced by the frequent re-organization – consequently short-term outlook – of health, social care and education services; also, by the short-term funding of many non-statutory agencies.

Even when there is an injection of funding based on the well-documented evidence that vulnerable children are bottom of the priority pile, there is uncertainty, beyond agreeing some shared principles, about how to use it. This means missed windows of opportunity for sustainable input during favourable policy periods in some countries (e.g. the UK in the previous decade) and hesitancy in moving beyond the implementation of single interventions in other western countries. Yet, some innovative programmes have managed to see the light of day, with professional networks (like psychologists for looked after children in the UK) and practice innovation with vulnerable groups beginning to interact with emerging evidence of success. We will discuss these principles of inter-agency commissioning and planning, joint care pathways, wrap-around services, outreach and consultation later in this chapter.

These observations should lead to the logical conclusion: 'If high-income countries cannot agree and evidence their payment and service systems, why bother with societies where there is so much less? Let's just wait until they have more resources . . .' This is another myth, based on the false assumption that service models only apply to the relatively wealthy systems. In reality, a service model informs those who pay, deliver and use that service how the allocated funding can be best utilized to achieve its objectives. In that respect, when our partner charity in Pakistan took over the care of an orphanage, the first step was to agree a child-centred care model, which took into consideration the available resources. I would actually argue that the less resourced a service is, the more pertinent it is to have a clear rationale on how to make the maximum possible impact. Policy-makers, operational managers, practitioners and organizations that make such decisions with clarity and transparency are thus the likeliest to constantly adapt and evolve.

Why hard-to-reach groups are also hard to research

There are strong parallels between policy, practice, service and research. Ideally they all feed into one another, and this tends to happen to a limited extent. There are similar challenges though for researchers engaging, understanding and addressing the needs of hard-to-reach groups such as homeless or refugee youth. Why? Because they are more difficult to define, heterogeneous in their profiles, difficult to find as they are often on the move and equally difficult to engage. Their mistrust of research is often founded on their previous experience and conviction that nobody can help them. These barriers are particularly pronounced in establishing the effectiveness of new interventions. The main challenge is how to disentangle, thus measure, the impact of an intervention or service, from the constant 'noise' (or confounding factors) in vulnerable children's constantly changing environment; for example, distinguishing between the effect of a trauma-focused intervention and the quality of the child's foster placement. Experimental designs such as randomized controlled trials are faced with these hurdles, plus the ethical reservations of depriving children of available help or of their right to choose. Although there are methodological ways of working around these dilemmas, studies are further constrained by the relatively small numbers (sample size) at any one time or over a defined period. The range of research method options has helped in seeking evidence through qualitative means such as narratives, case studies, observations, service activities, analysis of naturally occurring data or mixed methods of integrating qualitative and quantitative datasets.

In that respect, progress has been slow but solid. Descriptive studies have been consistent in establishing traumatized children's high level of complex needs, co-occurring problems and inter-linkage between different needs. Research on the impact of several risk factors on child mental health has led to a better understanding of the development and prognosis of different mental health problems, although longitudinal studies have been scarce. In recent years, research interests have shifted towards the protective function of resilience factors in the face of adversity, and findings are constantly influencing practice and services. Evaluation of interventions tends to start from research centres or from applying research paradigms in high-risk groups such as children exposed to armed conflict. Where findings still fall short though is in knowing whether these can be generalized in real settings, as the consistency (or fidelity) of interventions is more difficult to ensure. During the same period, there has been an expanding body of 'grey' literature on a large number of small-scale and not always well designed studies that, nevertheless, point out to interesting and promising lessons on innovative interventions for vulnerable groups.

Principles and components of high-income countries' service model for vulnerable children

Despite the patchy evidence and inconsistent policy, a number of service components have emerged in recent years, which have variously been wholly or partially implemented. Ultimately, they are all driven by children's multiple and complex needs, by acknowledging that no single agency will respond adequately in isolation, no matter how skilled and well resourced it is. Consequently, the principles of integration, wrap-around, inter-agency partnerships and joint working come to mind. These are not consistently defined and are often interpreted loosely in terms of their principles rather than their operational implementation with various youth groups.

The word 'joint' should move to the very top of this principles ladder. When government departments and ministers recognize the reasons and potential benefits of integration, this resonates strong messages all the way through to frontline services. The philosophy of the UK education department 'for School and Families' had a broader mission than the subsequent, more traditional and narrow department 'for Education'. It is, therefore, not a coincidence that the most influential policies and initiatives followed suit from the former rather than the latter. These policies acknowledged the importance of integration for the neediest children, and consequently set the agenda and conditions for release of funding. The next level, usually regional or local level, should follow this lead by formulating local policies, joint commissioning and planning groups in response to specific population needs; for example, young offenders, homeless or children in care. It is true that these layers can add bureaucracy and slow the process down but, unless organizations are signed up to this philosophy, agencies on the ground will struggle to set up and, crucially, sustain partnerships.

If we draw a parallel with a research methods term, then service integration shares many similarities with mixed research methods, in that it is not merely about adding existing resources to the same pot, but rather qualitatively viewing services through a new 'multicolour' lens. Not everyone can take such a stance or manage a process that involves different groups with conflicting pressures and priorities. Leadership to drive such forums through and transparency in allocation of funding are essential at policy and senior level, if they are to give a consistent message to practitioners on the ground. Ultimately the drive should be to make the most of infrastructure, people and skills to help children and families break their interlinked cycles of mental health, social care and education deficits – not in parallel, not in turns, but *concurrently*.

If this approach is reflected in policy, funding and planning, then the next two levels of local policy and service implementation have an easier task. Practitioners should take over the implementation with the same drive, but with children and families in close proximity. Clear funding conditions and expectations can facilitate this process, by freeing managers' hands and minds in not only allowing but also encouraging a different, albeit potentially messy, way of working.

What does implementation mean in practice? Joint protocols, care pathways and guidelines should not be just a paper exercise. Their real purpose should be to provide seamless help for children who are likely to need different agencies at different points, without their carers and key workers (usually social workers) having to navigate through the system each time. For a start, what each agency can and cannot do with the level of resources they have should be clear and transparent. The challenge here is to avoid duplication, meetings and referrals that do not add anything to the life of the child and their parents or caregivers.

When there is a psychiatric emergency, social services should have the confidence that there will be a swift and direct response; on the other hand, the term 'psychiatric emergency' should not be used to compensate for placement issues. For example, a young person who has had a row with their foster carer and is refusing to go back to their home and is threatening to harm themselves will only be encouraged to do it again if s/he is automatically admitted to an in-patient unit. At the same time, it can be dangerous to 'cry wolf' and assume that the threat is not genuine without liaising with their social worker and foster carer, before assessing both the situation and the young person's mental state.

The principles of *seamless* and *comprehensive* provision could (or, rather, should, resources allowing) prevail both *within* and *across* agencies. Even when the UK mental health team for vulnerable children was at its peak, it was a constant battle to remind the rest of the mental health service that basing primary mental health practitioners (usually of social work background, and providing direct input to children's homes and foster families) in the same building with the psychiatrist or psychologist did not mean that they were fulfilling the same role. 'But they are tier 2 and you are tier 3 . . .' (at the time, tier 2 implied the interface with specialist services and tier 3 specialist input). 'Yes, they are different tiers, but isn't it nice that they work in the same building?' In reality, this meant that one could assess a crisis jointly (or in parallel) without stopping the ongoing support to the foster carers or adoptive parents, thus fragmenting the child's care with intermediate referrals and waiting. What mattered most was to keep all parties contained and engaged. This misperception took the opposite turn when resource cuts led to a dilution of roles. Those same practitioners who were meant to be operating on the interface were often asked to compensate for reduced capacity to respond to emergencies within the team – instead of changing the service model. Such default positions not only do not improve care, but confuse staff and clients alike, and can result in risky situations.

This leads to another key component of the model, its *outreach* nature. The term literally means 'reaching out', which is not necessarily the same as always 'going out'. It means being accessible and engaging by understanding vulnerable children's needs, as well as the need and constraints of their carers and the agencies involved (be it a homeless shelter or a community youth offending service), before adapting and working *through* them. Regular liaison and direct referral routes are a given. How these are set up will partly depend on the level of resources, hence the cost-effectiveness of the model. For example, whether one is covering one or four

38 Looking for answers

children's homes or special needs schools will determine the frequency and nature of meetings, but also the threshold of contact and cases taken. It will also usually mean physically visiting the settings covered, at least some of the time. This cannot be prescriptive. For example, not visiting children's living spaces, thus not getting a true picture of their milieu and staff dynamics can be as unhelpful as not giving them choice of where they wish to be seen, by ignoring their need for privacy and indiscriminately arranging appointments in that living environment.

The term *consultation* can be misperceived as one agency patronizing or being superior to another. Its real importance, whatever it is called, is based on the principle that, in order to help vulnerable children, one needs to work concurrently with their caregivers and primary contexts such as school, residential or secure unit staff groups. Consultation is a lot more than having close links or improving competencies. Instead it is more about knitting agencies together by developing an ongoing relationship within which the role of the caregivers can be improved in a different direction – in this case, by actively involving them in the intervention for an individual child, or regularly facilitating at a staff group level for all children in their care. As discussed previously, time and resource constraints need to come into the equation (who, how often, commitment from both ends), as do clarity on the function of the consultation process, and boundaries from other functions such as professional supervision and line management, which should usually remain within the staff line management structure and responsibilities.

Training is an extension of this philosophy, with a service context rather than theoretical teaching in mind. Its purpose is to complement and consolidate consultation, and to relate to the specific service remit and staff roles. We will consider specific issues and examples in Chapter 12. The same *joint* issues apply to service evaluation, outcomes and service user input, i.e. by not only incorporating evaluation in everyday practice and service monitoring, but by also approaching those questions from an integrated service perspective that ultimately reflects children's multiple needs. Given the extent to which individual sector services are still struggling with these challenges, one is less than optimistic that they can crack them together by agreeing common outcomes and measures, sharing data and information and accessing each other's IT systems. Nevertheless, there are successful examples for transient groups like homeless youth.

Why can't we just modify this model for low and middle-income countries?

The viewpoint that one only has to extend what we learn in the west to the rest of the world, i.e. by accepting that one has to wait for income growth and western views to be bedded in, is historically flawed. Such a political and economic stance left many countries and communities in tatters; and led to civil wars and military regimes in Africa and Latin America, and to increasing the inequalities and disadvantages of their people. Even the first few decades of foreign aid partly fell into the same trap. Why though? Because more is not necessarily better if it is of the wrong quality, or if there is a mismatch with local values, cultures and strengths. One cannot circumvent communities, systems and beliefs to impose inter-agency partnerships, child mental health services and interventions in a vacuum; even if there was enough money to support it – which there will not be in the foreseeable future. Accepting such a linear and rather arrogant principle makes any efforts to improve children's well-being in the largest part of the world futile.

But futile they are not. We have increasing knowledge and evidence of successfully marrying technological and scientific advances with traditional methods and old wisdom that led to self-sustained farming, small businesses and ecotourism. Translating those lessons to the less flexible and entrepreneurial fields of health, welfare and education has proved more difficult and the benefits have still to clearly emerge. Nevertheless, involving and training existing practitioners and, importantly, community volunteers such as parents has been shown to lead to better mental health outcomes for depressed mothers and growth for their infants in Pakistan; and has substantially reduced infant mortality in Bangladesh.

Perhaps there is more knowledge and experience at our disposal, but this is still rather fragmented between fields as diverse as international development, economics and social psychology; organizations ranging from large international structures to small charities, limited statutory services and theoretically driven academic centres.

Globalization, technology and instant communication through social media have brought some nightmares such as terrorism to humanity, but they have also brought huge opportunities. Suddenly one does not need to go through bureaucratic systems, governments or institutions to reach their target populations. Lessons of good practice and innovation can both be shared and initiated by groups and individuals, mostly young or youthful, without being held back by the status quo, consequently bringing freshness and energy to the situation. This will prevent many NGOs and statutory agencies around the world from re-inventing the wheel and wasting valuable time and resources. When they actually realize these commonalities, they feel ready to push on to the next stage.

Researchers have also been attempting to bridge different fields and have decided to take the plunge in the most challenging circumstances such as evaluating resilience-building interventions in areas of armed conflicts, including with ex-child soldiers – alluding to the inspirational but also robust trials of Theresa Betancourt in the US and Mark Jordans in the Netherlands, among others. Crucially, welfare and health-related inter-disciplinary groups have learned lessons from international development, economics, ethnography and anthropology, and innovated in improving, for example, as already stated, maternal and infant health in impoverished regions, by drawing on the natural resources and knowledge of their communities. So, maybe, just maybe, it is not impossible after all . . .

5

AN INTERNATIONAL PERSPECTIVE

The road to WACIT

Looking for a comprehensive psychosocial model

The tentative and limited evidence led to an exploratory phase or Trail Blazer. Taking existing knowledge into consideration, I set out to discover whether/how it might apply to child mental health in unchartered territories, at least in terms of conceptualization and connectedness. What systems could one build on? Are these engaging or engageable? If so, on what terms? Who are the key stakeholders, and what do they really think? How much stigma is attached to mental health? Is it taboo? Are societies as non-child centric as we might have been led to believe? Ultimately, how can we adapt interventions to children's and communities' needs? And how can we start building the evidence-base in those contexts?

It is important to acknowledge that this chapter, the most exciting of them all, largely lacks evidence. I would, however, bitterly argue that each step took existing theories and evidence seriously into consideration; observations and narratives were agonizingly thrown back into the mix until they made conceptual sense, hence informed the next phase; and pieces of evidence from inter-linked research projects were beginning to emerge and were tested against the theories and existing literature. The conclusions, therefore, led to a model that is hardly ground-breaking, whilst being at the same time consistent with Maslow's hierarchy of needs (1943) and evidence-based models being put forward by large international bodies such as the World Health Organization. The proposed six dimensions of the model will be taken apart and separately debated in the context of their own evidence in the next six chapters. I hope that the photos can be viewed in an analytical light, rather than as an indulgent trip or an adventure. I actually prefer the word 'journey' because it implies a continuous process with a destination, and because I was not as adventurous as I could have been.

A nearly impossible question, or just our own ignorance?

The overriding question was simple in all its complexity: How can we provide psychosocial support, or mental health interventions in the broad sense, for children who are exposed to complex and severe trauma in low and middle-income countries? Or, where trauma affects whole communities? Or, where there are no or very limited specialist resources? Can we? Is it impossible, pointless or are we asking the wrong questions? Maybe we are asking the right questions, but looking at them from the wrong angle, i.e. from an exclusively western perspective.

The journey had three phases. Initially, I set out to assess readiness, capacity, potential and challenges as defined by local communities, and to identify key agencies and stakeholders. Where possible, this was to be backed up by emerging evidence. This exploratory phase was followed by integration of observations and findings with the existing literature and policy direction, as well as consultation with international bodies, to formulate a psychosocial model. In the third phase, the aim was to build the components of the model, before moving on to implementation and evaluation. So, here we go . . .

Unless one adopts a 'top-down' approach through large, but not always flexible, organizations, there is no formula for how to start with virtually no funding. My conclusion was that people are worth more than money, for which reason I approached the 'trusted few', colleagues – and now friends – who had completed or were working towards research degrees, had visited me on sabbaticals in the past or had links with NGOs in their country of origin:

MYSELF: Who are the most vulnerable children in your country?
PARTNER: Those living on the streets, orphanages, slums or refugees.
MYSELF: Can you please take me to them?

In order to test the existing systems in practice, rather than subjecting them to voyeuristic observations, my trusted contacts agreed to target these vulnerable communities, work through one key agency whilst finding out who else operated in the area and bring them together in initial training and network-building workshops. These would be accompanied by visits to children's environments in conjunction with the training events. The training had to be focused, and constantly refined throughout the process. I initially opted for four key objectives:

- Overview of how trauma affects children, in order to demonstrate its complexity, but also multiple routes for intervention.
- Factors of vulnerability (or risk) and, crucially, resilience that participants could own.
- Formulation of a child's needs to help them focus and set goals (only much later this turned into a more purposeful child-family/caregivers-school-community model).

42 The road to WACIT

- Start thinking in wider agency and systemic terms about gaps, interprofessional networks and realistic options to address some of them in the face of overwhelming need.

So, roll on India, Kenya and Rwanda!

Exploring readiness of systems and communities, strengths and challenges

The magnitude of need and unchartered territories were overwhelming and exciting at the same time. We had to be realistic about what was possible within the time and resource constraints, whilst not letting those limited opportunities pass us by. Four groups of children were identified, because of their multiple, complex and often extreme needs: children in care (mostly living in orphanages in low-income countries), on the streets, refugees at different migration stages and children living in urban and rural slum areas. After identifying one target group per country, we moved on to liaise with the most appropriate – or, simply, enthusiastic – agency. As expected, these were largely NGOs. We subsequently got in touch with all the other agencies, whatever their names, structures and resources, in contact with children from the group at each participating site; and, crucially, locally defined stakeholders, predominantly community, spiritual and religious leads. We then invited them to a workshop organized by the hosting agency.

We faced several pragmatic challenges, as reality kicked in, and it was not always possible to keep to a protocol and maintain consistency in terms of participants' distribution, group size and allocated time. For example, the warm-up and confidence-testing first workshop in Mumbai was mainly attended by counsellors and psychologists, although other new agencies emerged such as an NGO against women's exploitation. Also in Mumbai and the surrounding rural areas, I tested the water with a large spiritual and religious organization, which ran an impressive network of schools, health and community centres. This could be an important model for the future, with widespread access to vulnerable groups. Initially, it was not easy to relate my rather vague goals to the religious leads. They looked rather puzzled to start with, but I was amazed by their open-mindedness to new approaches, as long as these helped children and families. We had interesting discussions on western and eastern approaches – which made me ponder on our excitement about and expansion of mindfulness in the west. One of the mediation centres I visited in Mumbai was over 100 years old.

Then came Africa with a different combination of coping with adversity through faith, music and dancing. Our target group in the Nakuru area of Kenya consisted of internally displaced families following ethnic violence, now living in peace but extreme poverty, usually in rural or inner-city ghettos without escape. Rwanda could not easily shake off the terrible history of its genocide, even 20 years later. Our target community care homes for post-orphanage children and young people with disabilities were, interestingly, staffed by several caregivers who had grown up and then worked in the orphanages that were hastily opened to accommodate

PHOTO 5.1   'What is this strange bloke doing here?' Children's polite puzzlement at the rehearsal for their national holiday celebrations at Ramakrishna Mission Centre in a rural slum outside Mumbai

300,000 children. During those fateful three months in the spring of 1994, one million Rwandans had perished . . .

The task was to balance maximizing a rare opportunity without overwhelming the participants. The overall objective was to provide a framework, whilst quickly adapting to capacity, culture and roles, in an iterative process with the participants. Providing key pointers and evidence without theorizing or talking at them had to be avoided at all costs; it was essential to adjust quickly, at least initially, since predictability bred confidence in the next phase. I was faced with several questions around similarities and differences; the ultimate one being, 'Can the workshop and its objectives relate to the participants' role within their sociocultural context?'

Turning point in Kenya

After starting with a relatively familiar group of professionals, and a couple of warm-up workshops in middle-income countries, Kenya was always going to be the first real test. The launch of a local charity was combined with invitations to all agencies and individuals relevant to the post-ethnic conflict urban and rural slum areas that we targeted. Around 20 people looked rather puzzled at the invitation. There was even a rumour that I was 'bringing money'. I liked the spread of disciplines, some being more familiar or anticipated (mainly teachers) than others (housing, community lead/elder, pastor/counsellor, probation officer). Still, these were not British foster carers or care home workers whom I had been used to . . .

The first 10–15 minutes were relatively smooth, albeit a stab in the dark, as it was difficult to tell if the child trauma framework made sense to my audience. I was also conscious of the difference between relaying clear and simple messages and being patronizing. Then came the question I had really come to test out: 'Tell us a

44 The road to WACIT

bit about your role; one challenge you have faced with children or youth, and how you overcame it.'

There are pros and cons to putting this question to a medium-size group such as this, breaking participants into smaller groups, having discussions in pairs or going around in turn. On that occasion, I took no chances and went round all the participants, despite the risk of them feeling inhibited in the presence of others. I was simply desperate to know . . . I have a vivid recollection of the first attendant, a young college tutor. There was a long silence . . . possibly only a few minutes, but it felt like an eternity. Self-doubt crept in, 'Perhaps I'm way off the mark, this is not gonna work here.' We stared at each other, I prompted but tried to resist the temptation to step in. Then:

COLLEGE TUTOR: When my students have a problem, but find it hard to share . . .
MYSELF: So, what you have found helpful in your experience?
COLLEGE TUTOR: My door is always open, they don't need to book an appointment
. . . we don't have to talk about their problem . . . they talk to their friends before coming to see me.

Then the floodgates opened. The examples related to tougher situations and the solutions offered were innovative. Because of the lack of available support staff, a teacher relied on peer mentors. A community elder connected with young people in his village when they were persecuted and internally displaced, 'This young man had an arrow in his head; it is miracle that he stayed alive; but he has never been the same since.' The dual role of spiritual support and counselling was clearly defined, along with the boundaries. Adopting a welfare approach within a punitive offending institution was hard, but was still championed by a probation officer. The biggest surprise though was the help service at the housing department for any problems that local youth wanted to share. Eventually the workshop facilitator had to intervene, as we had grossly overrun time before lunch. Nobody seemed keen to stop. Although the format of the workshop had not worked well, the substance of that natural experiment made lunch one of the most delicious ever!

Independent research interviews that followed captured and articulated better those first impressions:

> We try to let these girls come to us and we do activities which let them forget that they have experienced trauma from years ago or sometimes we give them activities or we give them something together we can have together and we can share experiences with them.
>
> *Secondary school teacher*

> We need to understand that people from these circumstances actually have serious problems and traumatisation, so it comes out very clear now that we need to look at it from a broader perspective than I used to initially.
>
> *Probation officer*

PHOTO 5.2 Breaking the ice: training turning point with community stakeholders at charity launch in Nakuru, Kenya

The encouragement I got from this workshop gave me the confidence to adopt a more assertive approach at the next workshop with care home staff in Rwanda. There was an additional challenge – an interesting combination of devising behavioural strategies for young people with disabilities (such as ABC observations, followed by goal-setting), whilst taking into account their upbringing in orphanages, hence a trauma context. Seeing this group of staff, some of whom had been children of the genocide and raised in the local orphanage, flourish over the course of three days was the most gratifying experience I have ever had. Level of education, background, language and culture were some irritating nuisances along the way – ultimately, none mattered a single jot!

To give some context to interactions with participants, once more I started from positive examples of solutions to a problem defined by the caregivers themselves. Then, we went backwards, trying to turn their intuitive responses to more salient and detailed explanations, and thus sharpen their future observation skills. This was accompanied by a brief theoretical justification. Like clients in therapy, it is much more productive for any human being to relax on the back of what they are doing right, before considering what they might have been doing wrong. Doing things in the opposite order would have got their defences up in the first place. The message was that these adults were as responsible and intelligent as anyone else in any other field of life or part of the world, and that they would have to work out some

46 The road to WACIT

implications for themselves. Obviously, this is where supervision and ongoing training need to take over, otherwise training benefits cannot be implemented and, crucially, sustained. Nevertheless, here is a real example:

Q: (through interpreter): Could you give me an example of a challenge you faced when you moved (six months earlier) the young people out of the orphanage (four to each of the four care homes)?

A: N (17-year-old girl with learning disability, who had been aggressive to staff, residents and neighbours in the past, but who now appeared content enough to take me by the hand and show me around the grounds) would not go to the toilet . . . she refused, and became angry.

Q: What happened then?

A: She is going now.

Q: What did you do to help her?

A: Nothing, she just did it.

Q: Hmm . . . difficult to believe that things just changed . . . something must have happened.

A: (another member of staff stepping in): We were taking her by the hand to the toilet, rather than telling her to go.

Q: Ah, that sounds more like it. But *how* did you take her to the toilet? Like *this* (not waiting for the interpreter, so as not to lose the moment – gently holding a participant's arm and smiling at them encouragingly); or like *this* (pretending to impatiently grab the participant's arm)?

A: (laughter)

Q: So, your body language and caring attitude to her seemed to have turned a previously unpleasant task to a positive need. But, do you remember what you were saying to N at the same time?

A: That she needed to go to feel better, so that her tummy would not hurt.

Q: If you look back, why do you think that N did not like to go to the toilet before? (This pattern had apparently set in at the orphanage, where multiple caregivers had responsibility for a large number of young people.)

A: Because the other young people teased her.

Q: So, what did you do about it?

A: We told them to stop teasing N, and we told N that nobody would tease her again for going to the toilet.

Q: It seems to me that you worked out the reasons, and tried out a number of strategies. But when one is in the middle of the action, it can be difficult to realize why you are using them.

Overall, it is possibly simplistic to think that the training components below were fully formed at that early stage, but certainly all these ingredients were variably used, and were further refined in the next phase.

PHOTO 5.3 It is often more difficult for care home staff to address emotional needs if a child does not cause any trouble

---

COMPONENTS OF CHILD TRAUMA WORKSHOPS

Child mental health awareness, constructs
How trauma impacts on child mental health
Risk and resilience factors – related to one's role
Recognition of common child mental health problems
Formulation of needs
Goal-setting
Therapeutic strategies – in relation to one's role and existing agencies
Assessment of capacity and gaps
Interprofessional network-building
The future: challenges and realistic potential for improvement
All case material was provided by the participants, whether planned or spontaneously.

Partnerships, evidence and the preliminary WACIT model

There is often a fine line between observations, innovation and evidence which, if broken, tends to result in the collapse of promising ideas and projects. Hence, each physically active WACIT phase has subsequently been followed by a period of calm, reflection, feedback, challenge and conceptual testing. At that early point, feedback from international organizations – initially professional and subsequently increasingly more NGOs – and consideration of the still limited but interesting evidence were invaluable. There is nothing new about Maslow's hierarchy of needs, which drives agencies in contact with vulnerable children all over the world:

> One has to be fed and sheltered in a safe base before moving up the therapeutic ladder.

The only difference in our case was the focus of the preliminary model according to various sources (policy, research, case studies and grey literature such as reports) to children in low and middle-income countries, particularly during and post conflict. The graph below is thus not substantially different from those endorsed by international organizations, but is possibly more focused and detailed in terms of psychosocial/mental health input at different levels. Other generic models originating from humanitarian work tend instead to combine the school/community and therapeutic applications and the psychological and mental health services levels. We will devote a chapter to each of these levels, as they are far from exclusive to non-western systems.

FIGURE 5.1 WACIT model of resilience-building, particularly in low and middle-income countries

Building the model: the second WACIT phase

The next aim was to refine the training and network-building events using the experience and evidence gained, albeit in a clearer direction, and with the above theoretical framework in mind. In doing so, I looked up to colleagues and agencies who had developed expertise at each level. The centres that were willing and able to participate in this experiment had grown by now to include Turkey, Pakistan, Indonesia and Brazil, before returning to Kenya for a regional rehearsal. Although conscious that it was not as yet possible to implement and evaluate the whole model, we focused on the exploratory evaluation at the end of this phase.

The safety and nurturing levels often looked inter-linked. Where some relationship had been established already such as state orphanages in Indonesia and slum schools in Pakistan, environments appeared more child-centred, even if often intuitive. This may not have been the norm, as there were units that we could not access even through our networks – such as hearing accounts of punitive practices in Brazilian care homes while being driven around the favelas. The positive role of education and community activities appeared obvious rather than 'therapeutic'. Yet, there were exceptions such as the school in the middle of the Karachi slums that functioned very much on social enterprise lines by using differential fees to support the poorest children, and providing learning in conjunction with family support. Not surprisingly, in an area offering little hope and plenty of violence, children could not wait for school to start during their festive periods. Another exception was the NGO that re-united street children selling water and tissues in Istanbul with their families, where possible.

Many interventions could be applied in these contexts, and with various objectives. Some of these came closer to matching and fulfilling needs because of their framework. Theraplay was certainly in the latter category, despite being in an early evidence phase at the time, because of a range of applied programmes for frontline caregivers and teachers (namely 'Sunshine Circles') that had already been used in similar cross-cultural settings. The network of locally trained therapists was the ideal choice to demonstrate techniques to frontline practitioners (see Photo 5.6 from Istanbul). Creative approaches appeared popular too, possibly because they also transcended language barriers. Music and art were constant tools across the therapeutic spectrum, in our case emotional recognition or anger management techniques offered by the US-based NGO Invest in Children Global. Options became more limited on the ground as we moved up the model pyramid and specialists became scarce. There was certainly potential, predominantly from a psychology and counselling background, but not usually available unless employed (and their role defined) by larger international organizations. The statutory sector could sometimes be accessed in middle-income countries, for example one child mental health team went into the Brazilian favelas (although this was clearly an exception). Academic centres offered more potential than originally envisaged, in terms of some clinical skills, training, volunteering (which in some countries was still an alien concept) and providing generalizable skills like farming.

PHOTO 5.4 Babies abandoned in plastic bags in Jakarta, but living in a nurturing orphanage environment

PHOTO 5.5 Warm welcome in Pakistan orphanage, but children's numbers have risen because of sectarian violence

PHOTO 5.6   Theraplay training for staff and volunteers in Istanbul

It was important at that stage to test the water to see whether we were moving in the right direction, through an independent evaluation with stakeholders among participants from six countries, representing managers, practitioners and caregivers. The emerging themes were interesting and reassuring, but not surprising. Interviewees valued a multi-faceted assessment of children's needs, overcoming stigma, engaging children and particularly parents, understanding cultural and contextual factors, and adapting interventions accordingly whilst dealing with limited resources and lacking in competencies. The key objective was to develop an inter-connected model that could concurrently deal with all those challenges:

> For me, psychosocial support is more about casting a wide net. There are many aspects . . . It involves security, leisure, access to education, health, etc.
>
> Here in Brazil, for instance, they may not face war zones or natural disasters like in other parts of the world but they do face other traumas like . . . drug dealing, violence, sexual abuse etc. Many young people join gangs.
>
> Psychiatrist, Brazil

I also started testing the six-dimension model in different circumstances around that time. One example was the refugee crisis in Greece. There were several levels of

PHOTO 5.7 Story-telling with Aboriginal children in Australia: a tool for both cultural continuity and resilience-building

contact with refugee families and unaccompanied minors, varying degrees of readiness and response and access to financial support, usually from international sources. One refugee camp I visited had no structure whatsoever, with families finding their way in and out of the camp at will. This did not fulfil any criteria, with structure and safety as the priority, and was rightly closed a year later. Two more camps had mastered that first step, and were beginning to make plans for in-camp education and leisure activities for the children. Nurturing and therapeutic direction seemed a long way off at the time though. The largest camp in the Athens area had taken some time to evolve, but was beginning to introduce creative activities and access to counselling, initially for adults, and subsequently for children. In contrast, several new centres for unaccompanied minors attempted to provide all six levels of support, despite the haste in setting them up, recruiting and upskilling staff over a short period.

Testing the model in six continents

Was it lack of fulfilment because I didn't take a gap year in my youth? Who knows . . . but there was certainly a temptation to test the model from east to west, across systems and cultures. The non-stop 12 workshops in eight countries were a unique opportunity to focus on the next course rather than returning home straightaway, as in the previous year. Somehow, patterns began to emerge that had little to do with people's appearances and customs, and more to do with some deeper and common mechanisms of how children are affected around the globe, and joint aspirations of how they could be helped.

There are two ways of viewing this phase. Geographically, the 38,000 air miles took me to organizations working with unaccompanied minors in Greece, street and refugee children in Turkey, orphanages in Indonesia, Aboriginal children in Australia, homeless and pregnant teenagers in the US, children living in favelas in Brazil, victims of ethnic displacement in Kenyan slums and street children in

Tanzania. A more systematic way of viewing countries and services according to their income status gave representation of the full spectrum, from low to various high-income countries, with their own internal inequalities.

As anticipated, there was an almost linear association between service typologies and country income. Specialist services were in direct contact with the most vulnerable populations, but these were not a service priority (possibly even on the decline at the time) unless specifically funded and designated for these groups. In middle-income countries, there was an unbalanced mixture of some access to specialist services (usually for youth with more severe presentations) and support by a growing number of NGOs. In low-income countries, this role was almost exclusively taken up by NGOs, with their funding and mission being inversely reliant on the international community as the income status of their country decreased. Key themes when considering the eight countries from six continents as a whole were: the conceptual seamlessness of the model whilst adapting to national and local systems; constraints through service paucity and staff shortages; the consistent embracing of the ecological systems' resilience framework by practitioners and caregivers in formulating children's needs and goals at individual, family, school and community level; and the limited but encouraging reception of the six dimensions of the model across those countries, by identifying service gaps and setting realistic short and medium-term goals. We will consider each of the six dimensions in detail in the next six chapters.

Last, but certainly not least, there were 12 children's events that accompanied the training workshops. There were several reasons for the children's active involvement. I did not want to forget who this was all about, and not to capture – even in a minimal way – user participation. Asking children and staff through each co-ordinator to choose a resilience-building event was at least as powerful in putting across key messages through staff training, network-building and interventions. There was colour, intensity, plenty of dancing (Turkey, Indonesia, Australia and Brazil) and sport (Greece and Kenya).

PHOTO 5.8 WACIT 6 x 6 in the Australian bush with Aboriginal pre-school children: life here seemed a world apart from the tourist brochures

54 The road to WACIT

PHOTO 5.9 WACIT 6 x 6 with the girls' soccer team in Nakuru slum in Kenya: it all started so well, until I scored an own goal . . .

Overall, the objective was to instil ambivalence and ambiguity in the children, caregivers and staff – also in myself and you as reader:

This sounds great fun!'
Well, it was fun, but we are talking about the most disadvantaged and traumatized children on the planet . . .
Oh, how desperately sad.
Yes, but they seemed to enjoy themselves, albeit briefly, and their carers could see therapeutic implications well beyond that short-lived enjoyment.

So, it was both – despair and hope all along – possibly reflecting children's and communities' internal struggles and strength to move forward.

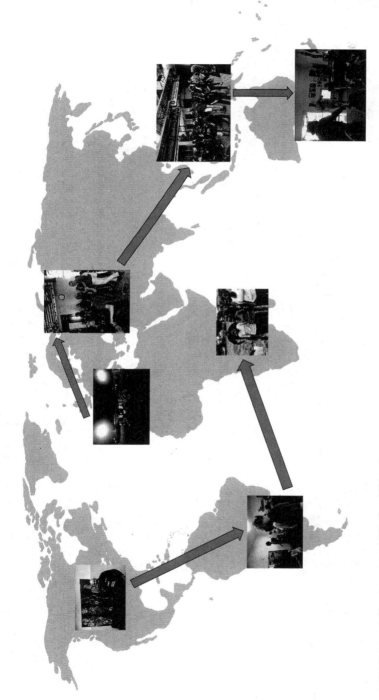

FIGURE 5.2 6 Continents in 6 Weeks children's events

6

CHILDREN'S SAFETY SHOULD PERMEATE POLICY, ATTITUDES AND ENVIRONMENTS

Levels and thresholds of safety

The first lesson one learns during one's child-related training is that 'the child's safety is paramount'. This is pretty obvious in extreme situations of physical and sexual abuse, but less so in grey areas of recurrent risk, emotional abuse, rejection, harsh parenting and negative attitudes. Legal thresholds keep changing, indeed variably across the world, they influence and are influenced by public and media views, are subject to interpretation and their engrained implementation involves a great deal more than reading the letter of the law and attending training courses.

Clearly human and children's rights principles have been the driving force behind child protection policy and practice. Yet, even those are not automatically linked or translated into specific policy objectives. Some societies may have become more child-centred in valuing children, but they still often define them as future adults. Other states may be proud of their child friendliness but endorse (overtly or otherwise) torture and other abuses of human rights. The line between an autocratic regime and the evolution of public attitudes can be very fine and in continuous conflict. Gender issues and acceptance of diversity are directly relevant too.

Examples of positive campaigns to stop child trafficking and exploitation have already been mentioned in relation to low-income countries. However, one should not forget that the same societies may not condemn, or at best tolerate, gender inequality and domestic violence, construct bullying as part of toughening up, penalize homosexuality and hide people with disabilities and mental illness behind closed doors. This is not a far cry from many western countries, which have their own contradictions. One can admire the quality of policy documents, procedures and training in many high-income countries; but these can be contaminated by indirect messages that incite discrimination and hatred. Is it acceptable for a white western child to be protected, but for a refugee child not to be because of their proxy connotation of faith and skin colour? One can never be complacent, as the ultimate goal is for child safety to be imprinted in practice and public mind sets, and to keep re-inventing itself within a wider sociocultural context.

Policy and legislation

In some ways, key child protection principles are not negated once they reach a legislative stage. Yet, their implementation can easily be diluted or lost, unless there are a continuous and active political will and supporting processes. A stand-alone national policy on children's rights and safety is essential, but it then needs to cut across all child policies in the welfare, health, education and judicial sectors. Is, for example, a new education policy compatible with safety standards? Is a policy on young offenders or immigrants only preoccupied with sentencing and length of stay, as the rest 'has nothing to do with me'? That policy and government department cannot then claim to aspire to children's rights and protection.

Ideology and political priorities can quickly undermine advances within the same government, by shifting between narrow objectives ('education is only about learning') and a broad mission ('education is about holistic development and maximizing potential'). Such changes can cause confusion within the next (local) level and to frontline practitioners, who have to reconcile impossible contradictions ('sort out a young offender's life without access to education and employment').

National and local policies are not necessarily linked either. Principles have to be translated into standards. This is not easy, as it is often constrained by an implicit or explicit threat of exposing unmet need. For example, children's homes and prison inspectors need to be equipped with more than broad guidelines in order to do their job effectively. They need to ensure that environments are safe, procedures are in place and are being implemented (with evidence) and, crucially, that staff competencies can be demonstrated by more than ticking the mandatory checklist.

How culture-specific should policies be? Child rearing styles may vary between cultural groups, even within the same society. Yet, the real challenges begin in either justifying or condemning physical punishment. Notwithstanding the lack of evidence that such approaches benefit children, ultimately one always has to comply with the legislation of the country of residence. How this is applied is a matter of skill though, in combining engagement and boundaries in setting up a child protection and family support plan. Enforcement is never sufficient, but this applies to all cultural groups. The additional – and extremely challenging – requirement is to work with existing beliefs and practices within the country's legal framework, until these are deemed safe for the child.

The national body responsible for child protection and its local providers should hold responsibility for all safeguarding aspects, including monitoring, staff training and review of procedures. Unfortunately, these lines of accountability are still not clear in many countries, where, for example, an independent agency might be set up without any links to other government departments or authority to act on recommendations. This creates confusion on the ground, and usually ends up in defensive practice, as professionals avoid referrals in the knowledge that they will

58 Children's safety

not be backed up by the system . . . or, until the next tragedy happens. Even when the state has clear responsibility at a high level, roles can be diffused between agencies. To my surprise, in many European countries the line of responsibility does not follow social services and social workers throughout all stages of contact with a child and their family, often because of lack of resources. An NGO may thus be handed responsibility for a child's care by the courts, but with loose or no connections with social services.

Implementation of child care practice

How legislation and systems are set up and become inter-linked will automatically affect practice and, ultimately, children. The same applies to the extent to which policy departments communicate and liaise with each other, as otherwise it is difficult to develop an inter-agency approach and culture on the ground. It is also important to connect parallel systems of safety. For example, what happens if there are concerns about a foster carer's style, as they will have a different organizational line of management from that of the child in their care? Or, what happens if a visiting health care professional or social worker feels uncomfortable about a residential school or care home? (See exercise at the end of this chapter.) Fragmentation and lack of communication in this area compromises children's safety and can prove fatal.

A social worker is constantly faced with difficult judgements in the course of their job; but, at least, this profession is identified in most people's minds as the children's primary safeguard. Policy implementation is really tested in how other practitioners, carers and communities incorporate child protection principles in their roles and attitudes. When a social worker is faced with a black-and-white choice of whether a child should be removed or not, or whether a family should return home with their child after attending a hospital emergency department with suspicious injuries, hard as these dilemmas might be, it is relatively less difficult to focus on the protocol, supporting evidence and balance of risks. In contrast, recognizing and responding to signs of potential child maltreatment can be more diluted, thus challenging, for practitioners whose primary role is to teach or to provide therapy.

We could extend these requirements to protect children to sports coaching and other community activities. Cases of historical sexual abuse in English football were going on under people's noses for decades, but were somehow ignored or covered up. So were scandals of abuse in religious care homes all over the world, as was the extensive network of sexual exploitation of girls in care in the English city of Rotherham. Surely, more than one professional, friend or neighbour would have picked up the signs in all those recurrent horrors? Undoubtedly they did, but this is where policy, implementation and attitudes come into play. If adults feel implicitly (or explicitly in some cases) threatened if they reported signs of abuse, what chance do children themselves have?

On other occasions, people either do not know where to look, intuitively see but cannot interpret the signs, record disparate observations without connecting them or do not corroborate with others. During a visit to a multi-cultural and impressively run primary school in a deprived Athens suburb, I spotted this African boy, who was sitting on his own during play time and was supervised by his mother. He was gradually finding his feet in the area and the school, but was described as still being 'out of control'. On closer discussion, I discovered that the boy was not fazed by adults (teachers) and would attack them despite his small stature. This looked as if it was a case of him being a direct victim or witness of violence at home – or both. When we explored his family situation and the aggressive stance of his mother's partner, it emerged that his behaviour was underpinned by domestic violence, which changed the teachers' whole approach to his management. This behaviour was no longer viewed as just a case of social and educational re-integration, but rather as an obligation to protect the child and his mother from forces that transcend cultural barriers.

Perhaps the hardest dilemmas face practitioners and communities when there is no policy framework to implement or, if there is a policy, the extent of vulnerability in the population is so widespread that it drowns those few who stand up against the tide. In countries with thousands and thousands of street children, is there a single street child among them who could be deemed safe? Is it safe or acceptable for any child to work in the streets, or to wander in bars and tube stations at night to make a living? Or, in worse situations exploited by gangs, and family poverty? Policy on its own will not solve the problems, as this needs to be complemented by alternatives, in terms of safety and opportunities, nevertheless it is a conditional start.

Shifting attitudes

Public attitudes can be both the cause and the effect of policy. They may become entrenched over time, be subject to inter-generational change, external influences, political exploitation, emerging evidence, the expanding role of social media and, of course, culture. The latter is too broad for simplistic interpretation; take, for example, middle-class families in Mumbai who were amenable to, at least some, western psychological interpretations, hence help-seeking patterns, but seemed a world apart from families in the slums or rural areas not that far away.

It is also dangerous to place oneself in a position of superior knowledge, thus defining progress in terms of one's own values. Some lines can be drawn in terms of child safety, and they may not be as difficult as they seem. The core human characteristics of nurturing (see next chapter), warmth and growth can be traced back to historic times to ensure survival, and have never been altered by culture. Unfortunately, the same could be argued about abuse and violence. Values can be genuine or distorted ('abuse does not happen in our culture'). If a teenager is the family's breadwinner, condemning their work as child labour (which it is) will not help them out of the cycle unless they are also offered social, education and employment skills. In the extreme, ex-child soldiers, whether viewed by society as perpetrators or victims or both, need more than usual life skills for a new start; fortunately, there are several positive examples and supporting evidence of such interventions.

60 Children's safety

In contrast, collusion with abuse in the name of social cohesion and faith (which are usually well-evidenced protective factors in their own right) are not only misguided, but can increase suffering by scapegoating the child. This is the powerful mechanism of the abuse and *not* the culture. I vividly recall such a case in the UK where this girl was not only not believed (and not protected) by her mother (which is a common mechanism that maintains the abuse across all cultures), but was subsequently ostracized by her close ethnic community for 'bringing them shame'.

Thinking 'child', 'vulnerability' and 'mental health'

Different groups of vulnerable children are exposed to multiple types of stigma. Tackling just one of them will not suffice. Many experienced organizations have first-hand experience of deprivation, conflict and humanitarian disasters, but are unable to think of people as parents, not even of adults as parents. I have seen the same pattern in homeless shelters, but this can eventually change, albeit with perseverance and a range of strategies. In contrast, some children's agencies may have experience in relation to children's and parents' needs, but only for families living in relative stability; they therefore struggle to consider the distinct needs of foster carers, residential staff or NGO workers. Thirdly, mental health and illness are still scary and misconceived by the caregivers and professionals alike:

RESIDENTIAL CARE WORKER: This is not our core business.

WORKSHOP FACILITATOR: Sure, but you can't avoid it altogether, and you probably do a lot more to help children than you think – you just call it something different.

RESIDENTIAL CARE WORKER: Yes, but we are not specialists, we are not trained to treat trauma.

WORKSHOP FACILITATOR: Do you mean PTSD? Trauma is an experience, so anyone in contact with a child who went through that experience is an expert on merit.

RESIDENTIAL CARE WORKER: Maybe we can help, but we don't do therapy.

WORKSHOP FACILITATOR: Maybe not, but I would argue that what you do is *therapeutic*; if you consider that all children need it, that some will not want therapy, and that many cannot have it anyway, you are making more direct impact in that way.

And so dialogues go up and down local services and countries, indeed across the globe. These are valuable arguments and concerns, which need to be understood before they are clarified and reframed. Not all mental health practitioners will share these views, because of the 'risk of making more harm by not being trained'. This is valid, and can only be addressed by defining roles and levels of input, and by balancing intervention against the 'risk of doing nothing'. When these different positions and constructs are understood (sometimes these are merely territorial excuses for professions or organizations; or, alternatively, reflect competition for funding), then policies, strategies and campaigns can become more targeted, hence more effective.

Children's safety **61**

> [T]hey will come to you and say mad, mad, mad woman. They talk about this mad woman . . . take them down to the shops, the market . . . and you'd be amazed how many people come and stand to watch these people that have been hidden away . . .
>
> *NGO Manager, Rwanda*

Views of children as vulnerable are dependent on several factors, not just cultural ones, but also real ones in the face of poverty, that force families to take more risks:

> [I]n one of the families we are currently taking care, mother wants her child to work . . . she does not believe the necessity of support.
>
> *NGO Manager, Pakistan*

Identifying the underlying reasons is important in informing interventions. This is, however, not a linear process. In other words, it does not automatically follow that A will lead to B, and B will lead to C, without working hard at tackling A. The case of child protection is a good example. Attitudes do not change overnight to lead to policies that will change practice. In contrast, all three of these factors are continuously in play, and it is this dynamic relationship that explains setbacks. We came across such unsurprising evidence when we interviewed practitioners in Saudi Arabia who had attended the National Family Safety Programme on child protection and domestic violence two years earlier. Although they were broadly positive about the training itself (indeed they wanted more), the chief obstacles in implementing what they had learnt were societal attitudes and organizational uptake, particularly inter-agency working. Child abuse and domestic violence were particularly enmeshed and rationalized by distortion of family values (it is worth stressing here that rationalization and distortion are universal characteristics of most crimes and have no cultural exclusivity):

> The police usually receive abuse cases, they said these are hit by their husbands or beaten by his/her father, and they are free to raise his child in his own way, or to deal with his wife.
>
> *Social worker*

The subtleties of child safety and child-centredness go beyond core policies and mandatory training. Underneath, one needs to ascertain the views of children as human beings in their own right, support these views with training (largely based on child development), then consolidate and sustain them through supervision and an ongoing support system. Some orphanages I visited in low-income countries (see next chapter) came across as caring but rather regimental. I did not get the impression of lack of safety, but rather of lack of engrained child-centredness in different aspects of everyday life. Opting not to offer unprompted advice to staff on what needed to change (which does not work anyway, if people are not ready!), instead I tried to indirectly make a few points after the training. For example, when

62 Children's safety

I was asked to visit the children's bedrooms, I would ask to talk to the children first: 'Thank you for letting me visit where you live; would it be OK to show me around, since this is your private space?' I was conscious of the children's blank looks, but the message was really directed at the staff.

Following one of these visits, there was an interaction between network members on Facebook (this is a reality, with both benefits and risks, which will be considered in Chapter 12). A very creative teacher I had previously met, asked me in public within that network:

TEACHER: Can I ask you a question mister?
AUTHOR: Of course, nice to catch up.
TEACHER: This child in my class is lazy (no name given), he will not do his home-work – what can I do?
AUTHOR: Maybe we need to discuss in more depth, shall we do so privately?
TEACHER: (in private message) Why in private?
AUTHOR: We need to protect the child's privacy, even from me; so, maybe we could just discuss the issues and concerns rather than the child?

. . . which we did, without identifying the child.

AUTHOR: Have you talked to him about it? Why he does not complete his home-work? In case he finds it hard? And/or is anxious?
TEACHER: Not yet, I will do, thinking about it, I will talk to him on his own, without anyone else present.
TEACHER (NEXT DAY): I talked to him mister, all sorted!

I still don't know what this was all about, and it might not have been appropriate for me to do so. The relevance to the training was, however, reinforcing child autonomy and safety, by adopting the same principles that we would routinely use with a middle-class family in a high-income country. Once adults start looking at children as equal humans, whilst maintaining the adult-child relationship, they can go a long way in protecting them.

Physical environments and people cannot be disentangled

A child-centred setting is usually reflected by equivalent staff attitudes. This is sub-sequently translated into children's attitudes and behaviours towards each other. A family *homeless* shelter that aims to be as home*ly* as possible is more likely to contain mothers' (usually victims of domestic violence) anxieties, thus promote their parenting skills. In contrast, an institutionalized children's home with long corridors, lack of personal space and only behaviour-oriented staff is likely to encourage bullying among young residents, and thus victimize further the younger and most vulnerable children.

However, neither settings nor staff reach a particular state by chance alone, con-sequently ethos and attitudes will not change overnight. After I had been generously shown around a residential school in Pakistan, a close colleague asked for my impressions. I replied that the place came across as safe and caring, there was structure and children seemed to enjoy activities and have fun in their learning; nevertheless, the building was rather impersonal, particularly children's bedrooms which, together with the daily programme on the walls, indicated a rather regimental approach. It would be nice if there were more colours, toys and private space. These might make the staff feel more relaxed and informal too in their interactions with the children.

NGO PSYCHOLOGIST: So, did you tell him (the headmaster)?
AUTHOR: No, not yet.
NGO PSYCHOLOGIST: Why not?
AUTHOR: I did not feel he was ready; he was proud and trusting, but did not ask me what I thought . . . this is maybe your role, next!

In other words, there has to be organizational readiness for change (or external pressure, when this is resisted), otherwise premature attempts can backfire, as they would indeed with parents in cases of child protection. On other occasions, unless key structures are put in place, marginal work with the staff is unlikely to have much effect.

Changing attitudes can, of course, not be disentangled from available resources. In cases of refugee influx, the states that have to take the burden are usually faced with economic challenges of their own such as Greece and Italy in southern Europe, Turkey and Lebanon in the Middle East or Uganda in eastern Africa. When a young person with disability went missing (thankfully not for long) from a care home in an African remote area, the hosting NGO revised their monitoring procedures, staff supervision and checks. Looking at different options, the preferred one was to instigate a book for staff to sign when a young person left or returned to the unit, together with the protective actions they were implementing. Needless to say we then spent some time debating how soon a few books could actually be sent to them! So many things that we so easily take for granted . . .

Interprofessional training means interprofessional care

Perhaps not automatically and certainly not always, but these two functions are closely associated. Learning procedures in relation to one's role are essential, but new knowledge and skills are really put to the test in relation to other professions, disciplines or agencies. It is nowhere near good enough to implement child protection in silo from other policies. As a result concerns can be lost in a vacuum or lead to circular tensions. International and national organizations, local implementation bodies and training programmes should ideally constitute a natural continuation of a common philosophy and a seamless process.

Like other types of interprofessional training, the benefits are immediate in understanding the strengths and, especially, the constraints under which other professions and agencies operate, in terms of both their remits and resources:

64 Children's safety

CHILD MENTAL HEALTH PRACTITIONER: While I am stuck with this risky case, I get no response from social services . . .

SOCIAL WORKER: My caseload has doubled in the last year, and this case would never stand up in court, not without a prolonged parenting assessment and family support; child mental health services used to do that . . .

TEACHER: Nobody is listening . . . it is not my job to counsel on parenting.

PARENT: We had three meetings and nothing in-between . . . bla bla bla, and no help.

Some benefits are obvious in terms of joint planning and (unlike that last example) joint action. I would argue that interprofessional training goes well beyond this, in promoting critical and systematic thinking when considering risk and safety, anticipating situations better and not raising expectations that cannot be met. One does not necessarily always need to physically meet with other professionals to make a multi-context assessment, or to incorporate safety in their goal-setting.

Resources will never match children's needs, as thresholds will keep being lowered and shifted. But natural resourcefulness and networks can adapt and be pro-active, even in the most adverse circumstances. During my second training event in Kenya, it was a pleasant surprise when the local child protection officer attended. She was overwhelmed with demand, but appeared clear on roles and procedures. When we discussed a young person raising safety concerns:

Teacher (addressing me): I wish we had more time, maybe next time you come back . . .

Myself (looking at the child protection officer): Why do I need to come back to train on child protection?

Child protection officer (nodding): I can organize the next training.

CASE SCENARIO 1

You are a health care professional visiting a recently established children's home in a high-income country for a routine health check with a 15-year-old girl who moved in two weeks ago. The staff are friendly but no one seems to be in charge: 'We are all new, finding our feet at the moment.' This is your second appointment, and the young lady is not around again. 'We rarely see her these days, she tends to go out in the evening, sometimes she stays out all night, then goes straight into her room to sleep; heaven knows what she is up to. We are, of course, worried, but what can you do? After all, she is 15 . . .'

Questions

1   What potential concerns should you be formulating in your mind regarding:

   a)   The young resident?
   b)   The children's home as an organization and a staff group?

2   What steps would you follow to evidence or alleviate these concerns?
3   Who would you talk to and in which order?

   a)   Your line manager
   b)   Child protection officer within your organization
   c)   The girl's social worker
   d)   The children's home staff
   e)   The children's home manager

4   *How* would you talk to these people, both to ensure that your concerns are heard and that the young person is safe (and, indeed, the other residents), and that you maintain an engaging relationship with the staff?

CASE SCENARIO 2

You are the project manager of an international NGO operating in a low-income country. You have just secured a considerable grant to support and expand three orphanages. Following a few visits to an existing local orphanage which has expressed an interest to act as a provider, you are still concerned about their regime and potential to change. The children are clean and well fed, but they seem to fend for themselves a lot of the time, with fighting often breaking out between the teenagers. Staff told you 'not to worry, this is how they learn – it is common in our culture'.

As you debate your decision and the next step forward, some potential markers for consideration could be:

1   What is the legislative framework in this country?
2   How do other units compare in terms of standards?
3   How is the unit managed?
4   What is the potential for staff training and change?
5   Ultimately, if you were to proceed, what conditions could you determine, and what parallel supports for staff and children alike?

7

NURTURING ATTITUDES AND APPROACHES

When one looks at different hierarchical needs models, this level is missing, possibly because the models were originally developed for adults. When we consider 'little people' though, the quality of their immediate and wider care is crucial, and consequently merits separate attention. It is also difficult to disentangle the previously discussed topic of safety from concepts such as awareness, attitudes or child rearing style. By now though it should be apparent that these should not be mechanical classifications but rather integral components in policy, service and practice thinking. In particular, regarding vulnerable children, primary or main caregivers may consist of the child's immediate family, extended networks and kinship care, foster carers, adoptive parents or residential staff in various types of settings. Advances in evidence and practice have followed parallel paths in recent years. Programmes were usually initially developed for the general population, before being tested, then extended and adapted to different caregiver groups. In the process the programmes were often influenced by trauma and attachment-focused frameworks.

Parents and extended family

This is probably the most difficult and heterogeneous group to define, as parenting and caregiving difficulties can range from rejecting attitudes to their children to being removed because of abuse and neglect. Nevertheless, the qualitative difference between trauma and attachment-focused programme and universal or targeted parenting approaches based on social learning theory, and which predominantly aim to enhance positive parenting skills, is the negative emotional relationship that can be viewed in traumatic terms from a child's perspective and upbringing.

In that respect, the widely established parent training programmes such as the Incredible Years developed by Webster-Stratton and her group, were initially designed for universal purposes. It would be simplistic though to assume that these

Nurturing attitudes and approaches **67**

are not appropriate for families who experience trauma, for two reasons: a) facing trauma does not mean that parents would not benefit from broader, and often more normalizing, approaches at some point; and b) these programmes have been adapted for high-risk groups, and their current underpinning is not as clear-cut as it was at the outset. The Triple P parenting programme started from a broader base by providing different levels, from prevention to management of more severe parenting and child behavioural difficulties. This has also evolved by adapting to particular needs. Preliminary findings from the US and Canada thus indicated that access to the programme contributed to the reduction of child abuse rates and to costs associated with child behavioural problems.

The increasing interaction between attachment and trauma theory and research has led to an expansion of interventions such as theraplay that aim to enhance the quality of the parent-child relationship. These are predominantly used with adoptive parents and to a lesser extent foster carers who look after children with histories of abuse and neglect. Evolving programmes incorporate different components, from the enhancement of positive parenting skills through to attachment relationships, but also target different cultural and vulnerable groups. The ACT Raising Safe Kids programme developed by the American Psychological Association is such an example, and faces challenging implementation in such cases as the prevention of violence in Brazil.

The flexible use of these programmes with vulnerable parents should be balanced against the temptation to 'mix' approaches without a clear conceptual guide, and consequent lack of clarity on goal-setting. Similarly, the importance of ensuring fidelity through appropriate training can be negated by the cost, hence their lack of accessibility to small agencies that support the families most in need, particularly in low and middle-income countries. Overall, there is plenty of scope for cultural adaptation, as parenting itself is especially subject to cultural values and societal norms that constantly change.

Compared with these interventions which originated from relatively structured packages developed within research centres, the term 'family support' is widely defined and used in practice. But what does it really mean? Family support is indeed wider than a specific psychological intervention, often encompassing more than one approach. It implies flexibility and 'real life' application when the previous interventions have not been successful. It may involve variously children, parents and other caregivers. It also implies that this may be the interim stage between relatively brief parenting interventions and the need to involve social services – although this is probably an interpretation of its current position rather than of its original development.

Family support encompasses engaging, practical and relationship-changing strategies, often through community meetings and home visits. Its broad objectives and value should not be undermined by the danger of becoming a 'by default' option when other interventions have failed. The principles of being needs-led and flexible are not mutually exclusive with following a clear framework and goals, nor with being regularly appraised rather than open-ended (which is not viable in public

68 Nurturing attitudes and approaches

services). Such appraisal of goals and response by the family have another important consequence. At the end of a planned and relatively intensive input, one would usually expect the family to generate enough change to revert to a more focused and less costly community intervention. Alternatively, the reasons for non-response should be examined carefully. It could well be that the family justifiably require more time. A not uncommon scenario could be parental non-engagement which should be balanced against evidence of the impact on the child. Some difficult dilemmas might thus follow on considering child protection action. If there are no child protection grounds for action, these should be explicitly articulated, shared and agreed; and expectations or goals should be adjusted accordingly where there is not sufficient risk for the 'no change' option.

Another chronic pattern that can be similarly difficult to define, tackle or alter can be a looked after child's contact with their family of birth. At least here there is a statutory precedent and baseline. The plan should be time-limited assessment, with either a view to returning home which is supported by clear evidence, or to remaining in care – with a variable level of contact – which is also backed by evidence. The ultimate principle that the 'child comes first' should guide these difficult processes. Evidence needs to be corroborated from several sources such as records, assessments, participating agencies, outcome of previous interventions and children's and parents' views. These cannot be simplistic wishes for reconstitution or regular contact (which most families want), but rather exploration of reasons behind why a similar intervention did not work in the past and, crucially, why it should work this time. On the whole, where there are ongoing tensions, regularity and predictability of contact, as well as clear goals and boundaries, can protect parents and children alike. In other words, if contact is proving to be enjoyable and constructive, whatever its parameters, for which reason it should continue, rather than the reverse principle of prolonging a negative experience for a child on the basis that 'it must be a good thing'?

Kinship care: within family or external placement?

If none of the above interventions are effective, and a child cannot remain with their family of origin, it is a logical and natural decision to seek alternative carers within the extended family. There is no need to rehearse the benefits of continuity and identity for the child, nor for relatives' wishes to compensate for previous adversities within their own resources. From their point of view, each decision should consider the particular child's needs, their family context and supporting evidence. The natural extension of the child's care to a relative should not be automatic though. Instead, it should go through the same thorough assessment as for an external placement, to prevent painful breakdowns later on.

For those reasons, kinship care should first be guided by policy and legislative frameworks and safeguards for carers and children. It should not be driven by the ideology that 'any relative is better than a foster carer'; or on economic grounds that it is a 'cheaper' option. The problem is that most countries that widely use kinship care do not have these systems in place. In the majority of cases where, for example, a parent is struggling, possibly because of mental illness (with child protection consequences such as lack of supervision), but still cares for their child, the family boundaries may be clear enough for the child to be placed with their aunt or grandparents. There are, however, many 'grey' situations where relationships are ambiguous and fragile, be it between birth parents and kinship carers and/or between birth parents and child. Relying on reconstituted families to define their new roles of their own accord may be too risky, no matter how good their intentions are.

For that reason, both the kinships carer(s) and the birth parents context should be assessed over an extensive period, and support should not be withdrawn at the point of placement. If anything, this is where input and support mechanisms are likely to be most meaningful. Paradoxically, it can often be easier for foster carers to access financial incentives, having their own social worker, access to training and informal peer support, than kinship carers who tend to be left to their own devices on the premise that 'they are family'. This may well be sufficient in most cases, but needs to be demonstrated rather than be left to chance.

Emotional reasons for taking over a child's care are also usually genuine, but kinship carers may need time to re-define their new relationship with the child, and to disentangle their motivation from drivers such as guilt or self-blame. These can prove poisonous, unless they are worked through when kinship carers and child are ready to do so. A useful parallel would be to consider what supports we would be providing to foster carers and adoptive parents with similar needs, rather than to start looking for such supports when the placement is at risk.

Adoptive parents: from assessment to permanency

The balance between thoroughness and efficiency is extremely hard. This is not about 'finding a good home for someone who needs it'. It is rather about making difficult judgements on the needs of a child who has already been through many life mishaps, and whose development cannot be predicted with accuracy; then matching the child's needs with the wishes and needs of the potential adopters, whilst being mindful that wishes and needs can change when under strain. And, as is often the case, this is not about summing up these needs, but instead trying to anticipate the new chemistry between child and adopters. Against this lies the risk of missing a window (or *the* window) in a child's life by not acting decisively or sitting on the fence indefinitely, hence prolonging foster placements that can lead the child to a different life course. And this is just the start of the family's journey! The whole adoption process is not just about a positive start, but rather about continuously and sensitively reading signs, gathering evidence and making informed decisions.

Not all assessments will prove correct, but the proportion of those which lead to painful adoption breakdowns should steadily decrease with experience and improved procedures and skills; and the indications are that there is improvement across the adoption world. One cannot, of course, predict the course of a placement or subsequent events and transitions, e.g. during the difficult move to secondary school

70 Nurturing attitudes and approaches

or the later teenage years, during that early assessment. This can only be as effective as the availability and quality of support systems when needed. These range from universal support to targeted interventions.

Preventive measures for all new and evolving adoptive families include sensitive but realistic preparation, information resources of different formats (including recent examples of web-based tools), an allocated social worker and peer support. The nature of targeted interventions on the whole can be distinguished between those that are 'adoption-specific' and those that could apply to any family. Adopted children and their parents have distinct characteristics and needs, whilst they are also 'just children or adolescents' and 'just parents'. It should not automatically follow that, just because the parents have adopted, at least in later years, that either they themselves do not require booster parent training input or that the teenager does not require similar types of help to their peer group. This can be a difficult demarcation, simply because it may take time for the family to work out the answers, which they can only achieve through trusting relationships with the agencies surrounding them. An initial reaction such as 'it is because of his history' can prove equally misleading as 'we put all this behind us years ago'. Crucially, adoption-specific and generic interventions are not mutually exclusive. Both can prove valuable for the right reasons at the right time.

Nevertheless, if we briefly refer to interventions developed for adopted families, these largely target attachment difficulties by focusing on the quality of the child–parent relationship through joint or intermittent sessions of theraplay or other approaches such as child–parent relationship therapy, the child's emotional dysregulation or, involving just the parents, through attachment-focused groups, adaptation of parenting programmes, or psychoeducation.

No intervention can be viewed in a vacuum from the legislative and policy framework of each country. As many adoption systems are still in their infancy, often because of stigma and fear, neither assessment nor support will be boundaried and protected enough to enable any therapeutic input to be embedded. This can be more complex in the case of inter-country adoption, where three systems (child, parent and international) can potentially interact. Encouragingly, there are increasing safeguards which, whilst not depriving children of opportunities, are not as openly accessible as they may have been in the past; as countries (e.g. China or Eastern European countries) have placed restrictions on or prohibited inter-country adoption. There is also more awareness of the need to address the child and family's evolving cultural identities.

The wide spectrum of residential care staff needs

One could not ask for a more diverse and fluent group of workers and roles than in residential care. Their remit might primarily be welfare (orphanages, children's homes or other residential units), education but with a strong caregiving role (residential schools for children with learning, developmental, emotional and/or behavioural problems), temporary protection (homeless hostels, shelters for victims of domestic violence, reception centres or hostels for unaccompanied minors) or judicial (secure units, again of different primary objectives and admission criteria). Their underpinning national systems, policy, legislation and standards also vary enormously.

Rather than starting from systems where standards and safeguards are in place, let us approach residential care the other way round, i.e. from the basics to the specifics. Substitute care of any duration, even short-term, should always be guided by key child protection and nurturing principles, in addition to the specific role of each setting. These principles should not be theoretical or desirable, but be backed up by legislation and authority for action. Their serious implications trespass the suitability and child-centredness of environments, staff recruitment and retention, the expected levels of competencies and skills, training and support and the mechanisms of inspection and monitoring that standards adhere to.

Scandals of abuse in children's homes go back in time among 'respected' organizations and layers of society, otherwise caring religious groups and well-meaning innovators. Sadly, it is highly unlikely that these have ceased. The nature of child care and the vulnerability of these youth are always likely to attract some of the very same adults that care homes were set up to protect children from in the first instance. Being mindful, having a policy framework and regulations in place are a start, but nowhere near enough.

So, where does one start in countries and settings without a legal framework, or without specified bodies and procedures to implement an existing framework? Although the objective should always be to work with government authorities in that direction, this can take a long time, with no reassurances in the interim. Organizations, usually of international origin, can and should adopt available international principles when they commission new providers to look after vulnerable children. These should start from child protection, as discussed in the previous chapter but, crucially equip, and thus empower, staff with nurturing and therapeutic skills. In other words, firm and tightly acted guidance should be combined with training and supports in place.

Punitive and negative attitudes usually reflect wider societal views, fears of stigma and misperceptions of what works. These are not likely to change overnight, whatever the staff potential at the time of recruitment. Knowledge of child development, the impact of trauma, risk and resilience and key strategies are a few of the recommended topics, as will be discussed in Chapter 12. Their uptake and application in practice require ongoing training and supervision; both of which are usually glaringly lacking where needed most. This knowledge then needs to be translated, practised and modelled, before it is really embedded in the ethos of a care home or other setting. Often the turning point in this process is when staff start looking at (hence seeing) children as victims:

> [It] was wonderful to see these carers who had never really shown any interest at the orphanage, all chatting together, exchanging stories of each of the people they care for.
>
> *NGO Director, Rwanda*

> After attending this workshop, now we had theoretical background of trauma, and we know how it affects children. It is important because some of us, as staff and volunteers, were unaware of trauma.
>
> *Educationalist, Turkey*

Promoting nurturing relies on multiple strategies. Ongoing training, supervised practice and psychoeducation are key components. As will be discussed in more detail in Chapter 9, adapted therapeutic strategies also have a large role to play, in this case based on attachment theory and resulting techniques. One notable example arising from the original specialist theraplay approach is the programme Sunshine Circles, which was developed for teachers, social workers and other professionals to help promote vulnerable children's social and emotional development, in particular emotional regulation. This provides participants with key principles and a rationale followed (or precipitated) by simple and practical strategies on how to relate to children who have suffered abuse and neglect through games, singing or other activities. Its bottom line is building trust, based on which other interventions can follow.

Where policies, structures and processes are in place, mainly in higher-income countries, a more systematic approach can focus on sustaining benefits – a not negligible challenge, considering the staff turnover of residential units. Engaging unit managers is crucial, as any ambivalence on their behalf will reflect on their staff. Where a number of settings such as care homes belong to a large organization, a child-centred ethos instilled from the top (instead of a solely business-minded or detached style) will also give the right signals. New units provide opportunities but can equally be rushed through because of economic pressures; as will staff recruitment when a new source of funding needs to be processed quickly. Certain residential contexts such as youth secure units and refugee reception centres are usually harder nuts to crack because of potential philosophical viewpoints on their primary role, which can be traced all the way back to the relevant government department. A nurturing culture is much easier to embrace from the outset, i.e. at planning stage, rather than be parachuted in later through time-limited training for the staff.

Inspectors and other external evaluators are no exception, particularly as they need to know where and how to look, beyond glossy brochures, activity patterns and minimal data. The subtlety of assessing organizational ethos, staff attitudes and skills, but also the functionality of spaces, requires training and competencies in their own right. If one strand of the system does not function in tandem with the rest, children will inevitably be affected somewhere down the line.

Community practitioners' multiple roles

One of several major contributions of attachment theory and subsequent supporting evidence, about which I never tire of talking during workshops, is children's ability to form multiple attachment**s** (stressing the letter 's'). Many children who have suffered trauma find that their fortunes begin to change when they enter a classroom, youth or sports club, and encounter a role model who turns rejection into acceptance, whilst instilling firmness and boundaries. Teachers are more likely than most to offer that new life blueprint, although schools can also mirror placement breakdowns and societal exclusion. They are also faced with the need to send consistent messages and strategies across different classes and activities. One teacher who responds to a child's aggression in a trauma context can easily be undermined by another who falls into a negative transference trap. Having to alternate a trauma-focused style for one child in a class with universal approaches for the remaining pupils is extremely hard and stressful, so is the additional dimension of the relationship between the traumatized child and their peer group. Therefore, both individual and system supports are as important as in a care home. Health care settings, both community and hospital-based, face similar challenges. One should not forget or neglect either the reinforcing/destabilizing role that all adults such as administrators, catering staff or volunteers can exert, so they should be brought into the equation, their contribution valued and training extended to them. There is no such creature as a 'fly on the wall' as far as a vulnerable child is concerned. I try to make this point by asking to meet and spend time with cooks, other kitchen staff or coaches whenever I visit places like orphanages (Photo 7.1).

PHOTO 7.1   With kitchen staff, a teacher and a young resident and two massive papayas at a Jakarta care home

74 Nurturing attitudes and approaches

REFLECTIVE EXERCISE 1

Jocelyn, a nine-year-old girl in foster care, has just moved to your school. You know little about her, other than that 'she has been moving around because of her behaviour'. She first came with her foster carer and looked polite, if rather anxious. She has since been in your classroom for two weeks, but nobody 'can read her'. Sometimes she is quiet and keeps to herself, and sometimes she stares at you and the other children, which rather unnerves you. Then she can 'flip' in an instant. There seems no clear reason – it could be because you asked her to fetch something or because another child asked her to play.

Other teachers seem equally confused about Jocelyn. Some feel sorry for her and think she needs time, whilst others think she needs boundaries and a behavioural programme. Nothing really seems to be getting through to her. She just shrugs her shoulders that says 'she doesn't care'.

Questions

1   How does Jocelyn make you feel? Why?
2   What are the triggers for your feelings and responses?
3   How do your colleagues react to Jocelyn?
4   Who could you talk to about Jocelyn?

REFLECTIVE EXERCISE 2

Karubo is a nine-year-old girl in a Kenyan orphanage that you manage. She was found wandering in the street and was picked up by the police three months ago. You have tried to find out about her background, but still know nothing about where she came from.

Karubo does not speak much. You are not sure she understands. She likes eating – or rather 'stuffing herself' – but does not show any interest in anything else. She can sit and stare at people passing by for hours. Sometimes she looks sad, sometimes 'evil'. When staff, particularly males, try to talk to her, Karubo starts screaming. She may then attack them with a vengeance. I have not seen such strength in a child before. Some people think she is 'possessed'.

Questions

1   How does Karubo make you feel? Why?
2   How do you think she is feeling?
3   What responses does she evoke from your staff?
4   What mechanisms do you have to share these observations, support the staff and help them to respond consistently to Karubo?

8

BUILDING RESILIENCE AT SCHOOL AND IN THE COMMUNITY

Life never stops in the therapy room

There is often a false dichotomy – and false economy – between therapeutic approaches: 'either or, wait until, get more stable, then . . .' Perhaps because we like neat solutions, perhaps because agencies prefer to focus on what they are good at, irrespective of anyone else, perhaps for financial reasons in the short term. The reality is that children function at several inter-related levels; this functioning constantly evolves and interacts with their environment and their needs are broader than their mental health status at each level. Being in therapy does not stop them from going to school or living in the community; on the contrary, their adaptive capacity should be enhanced in both contexts, whilst parallel – and ideally integrated – supports in these settings will increase the likelihood of them making the most of their therapy input. I am stressing the term 'therapy' rather than 'therapeutic', which applies to all agencies involved with a vulnerable child.

These arguments can be multiplied for vulnerable children with complex needs. The more concurrent problems a child has, the less likely they are to respond to a single intervention. Additionally, the more inter-connected these problems are, the more difficult it will be to tackle them with a single approach, no matter how appropriate and effective it is. Vulnerable groups like children in care and young offenders often find it hard to engage with one intervention and, even if they do, there is a high chance that this will be disrupted by changes in their immediate and wider environment such as family turbulence. Vulnerable groups such as homeless families and single homeless youth will not be strong enough to utilize and sustain an intervention, if interventions are available anyway. In refugee camps and war-torn societies, the school and/or community may be the only opportunity to start breaking the cycle.

This is a logical conclusion arising from evidence on the nature of vulnerable children's characteristics. It is also backed up by evidence of the protective effect of

76 Building resilience

peer relationships, social networks and supports and, especially, school-related factors such as attainment. These factors were initially seen as a reversal of the more researched risk factors, before being framed in their own right under the increasing influence of positive psychology. Resilience theories are currently influential but are not particularly new. They originate from different – if not disparate – fields such as economics, biology and psychology. In mental health, resilience research originally focused on the children's individual attributes, whether inherent or acquired, to overcome stressors. The gradual broadening of the conceptualization of resilience as applying to each stage of a child's life was in turn influenced by the ecological systems theory.

Interestingly, researchers have integrated previous theories into current ones, although their psychosocial implications have not as yet been tested. For example, Folke proposed four resilience types: speed and ease of recovery to an equilibrium (which was referred to as 'engineering' resilience); ability to maintain goal-focused behaviours (ecological resilience); predisposition to adapt (adaptive capacity); and ability to shift developments into new pathways (transformability). Such a framework is particularly important for vulnerable groups, although one first needs to understand the conflict-related systems (factors leading to conflict, challenges and risks, strengths and potential) before determining the requirements for adaptive or transformational behaviours within those systems; hence the developing interventions and services. These issues apply to a range of groups and communities, but in the context of this chapter the focus will be on their relevance to psychosocial support for children who experience trauma.

Emotional literacy, and 'directed' or 'therapeutic' education

As already discussed, adopting a whole-school approach and endorsing emotional (or mental health) literacy at school often is a reflection of government ideology and priorities on whether education is 'only for' or 'more than' learning. Inevitably, the former will create societal divisions that will predominantly affect those who are least equipped to 'learn' (whatever that means) in those artificially defined terms. The lower down the social ladder they are, the less likely children are to find their way through barrier after barrier. Notable exceptions of achievement against all odds deserve nothing but our wholehearted admiration; however, they also confirm the grim prospects for the remaining vast majority of children and youth.

Adopting a school culture and supporting approaches that view the child in a holistic way is thus important for all children. Inevitably though, those children who are less well equipped socially and emotionally are the ones most in need of that integration. To start with, disadvantaged communities are likely to have large groups of children with multiple needs, unstable home environments and, particularly in urban areas, fragmented social networks. Consequently, the most inspiring school models of integration and inclusion tend to originate in such areas of disadvantage, which often attract teachers with a particular resilience of their own.

Vulnerable children, such as those in care who have suffered abuse and neglect, are the most likely to lack the emotional and social foundations to mobilize their

Building resilience **77**

academic capacity, and consequently to drop out because of challenging behaviours and emotional dysregulation that stop them in their tracks. For many of these children, school will be their main opportunity to turn their life around. For children who have fled domestic violence, it will be their haven and a chance to savour a positive experience of adults. For refugee children or those living in slums, it might be the *only* option at this point in time. Where trauma is collective such as in war zones, teachers themselves will be affected, and will thus be caught in a double bind of being both victims and carers. Many teachers in Pakistan had stories of personal loss during our workshops. In a study with health care workers in Gaza, traumatic experiences in their civilian life were stronger predictors of post-traumatic stress symptoms than what they had witnessed in their professional capacity.

One can turn similar adversity on its head so that it becomes an opportunity, for example, for cultural integration from a very young age. This seemed to be the case with Aboriginal and other cultural groups in Australia, as well as between several ethnic groups in a large refugee settlement in Uganda. Children ended up choosing their friends because of their joint interests rather than their religion or skin colour. Unfortunately, tolerance often stopped at the school gate, as parents and other adults in the community brought to bear their own experiences and prejudice, hence the need for extensive awareness and integration programmes.

What does this mean in practice? First, it is about viewing traumatized children differently, understanding the context of their behaviours and recognizing triggers in the classroom, playground and social activities. Second, it highlights the need for the adaptation of individual strategies in all these contexts. This requires investment in both teacher training and allocated time, as these children require structure, individual input and patience in their expected academic and social growth. These are not automatically available in large and target-driven mainstream schools. There are also indirect requirements in guiding them through peer relationships, which they often find hard to initiate and sustain; consequently, in sports and other group activities. The interplay between social, emotional and academic learning is always important; though crucial albeit slow in this group of children.

Third, it is important to note that these objectives are unlikely to be achieved without additional supports, and preferably structural changes such as by providing nurture groups for younger children. By running in parallel with usual school activities, these groups can provide both a booster and a 'safe return' from ordinary stressors. Nurture groups have been shown to enhance children's emotional regulation, social empathy and communication. Finally, all the above goals should be regularly reviewed with adoptive parents, foster carers or other caregivers, as well as key agencies involved, predominantly the child's social worker, so that these goals are consistent with interventions at home and in the community. In systems and societies where emotional literacy is not widely endorsed, attempts should start at policy level by demonstrating the strong links between social and emotional learning with better academic outcomes, before filtering down to individual schools.

78 Building resilience

School-based interventions

The evidence is mixed, both in methodological quality and specificity in relation to vulnerable groups. This is often due to a number of reasons such as interventions not having been adapted for these children as yet, or vulnerable children being unevenly distributed across school settings (i.e. not enough numbers per school for a targeted programme). Paradoxically, it is easier to plan such targeted school-based interventions where whole communities have been affected, namely from war exposure, displacement or natural disasters.

Universal promotion of mental health is becoming increasingly accepted and requested, although its applications vary enormously. Examples include a single psychoeducation session, building on existing health programmes such as nutrition and sexual health or being dispersed across different parts of the curriculum, which, to date, is the least likely option, but will gradually increase in the near future based on emerging reported programmes. Reasons for the inconsistent adoption of mental health promotion include ideological doubts about its contribution to learning, conflicting teacher commitments and resource constraints on its delivery. It is also still hindered by lack of conceptual grounding, fidelity in its implementation and conclusive evidence on its indications and effectiveness. Nevertheless, its value in tackling stigma and fear of mental illness is widely recognized. Such focus can be nicely complemented by similarly stigmatizing topics like disability, gender and cultural diversity. Integration with protection and anti-bullying programmes fits well within a broad mental health promotion strategy.

Targeted school programmes tend to be originally developed for research purposes, which are not immediately contextualized in real settings. These are either geared towards at risk groups such as children with aggressive behaviours or exposed to war trauma, or those who may have already developed a degree of mental health problems, namely anxiety, depression or post-traumatic stress disorder (PTSD). Although the modalities described in the literature do not differ greatly, their objectives and outcomes are often not sufficiently distinct, hence the lack of conclusive evidence. Interventions for children at risk, like those who have suffered trauma, predominantly have a preventive role. Goals can include developing adaptive coping strategies for various (often ongoing) stressors, safety planning, normalizing experiences when the stressors have ceased, adaptation to loss, regulating emotions, understanding how stressors may lead to mental health problems (psychoeducation), acculturation and developing social and life skills, or a combination of all of these. Approaches used (which will be considered in more detail in the next two chapters) are based on behavioural, interpersonal, cognitive and creative expressive (writing, drawing, play, music, drama) frameworks. The lack of clear evidence in the literature on the impact of several innovative resilience-building programmes can be partly explained by the lack of sensitive outcomes that directly reflect the approach used, as these are often evaluated only in terms of mental health symptoms. Expanding research in the construction and psychometric evaluation of resilience measures that mirror intervention goals will hopefully help bridge this gap.

This is less of a challenge for first-line programmes targeting children who have already developed mental health problems of mild severity. Their underpinning frameworks are more closely matched to evidence, whether for children in the general population or within affected communities. To this effect, school-based programmes adopt relaxation, cognitive-behavioural or mindfulness techniques for anxiety, cognitive-behavioural of interpersonal strategies for depression and verbal or creative trauma re-processing (cognitive-behavioural, narrative exposure, trauma systems or eye movement desensitization and reprocessing (EMDR)) for PTSD. These groups of studies have largely been developed for refugee and war-affected children, as school is the most economical and often the only option for collective interventions. So far, there is limited knowledge on the use of attachment-informed approaches, although the gathering pace of nurture groups for younger children should lead to a supporting evidence base.

The challenge for programmes primarily targeting mental health problems should not be confined to symptomatic reduction (which in this instance is rightly the primary outcome), but also to reducing functional impairment, whilst replacing deficits with quality of life skills. The reasons for this mismatch go back to the separate trajectories of risk and resilience philosophies in practice and research, although these are increasingly being viewed in conjunction with each other. All types of school-based programmes should ideally be complemented by parent and caregiver involvement. Reframing children's stigmatizing attitudes, promoting tolerance and integration, strengthening their resilience and improving their mental health will be difficult to sustain without reinforcement at home. Parental engagement, the type of agency involved and the resulting costs are not negligible factors, consequently these need thinking through from the outset.

Involving communities: exciting but largely untested opportunities

'Community' can have many different connotations. It may refer to the extension of a child's life outside school and their immediate environment, their peer group, purposefully structured or unstructured activities or wider groups with their own attitudes and beliefs (macrosystem). All of those components have a part to play, but can also be subject to the same trauma exposure as the child. Ideally, these should not be fragmented, instead they should be incorporated into the child's care plan and into strategic organizational objectives in order to produce more fertile and conducive environments for individual interventions to stand a better chance.

In many ways, community-based programmes share several principles, as well as conceptual and therapeutic characteristics, with those discussed in the previous section on school-based resilience. Sometimes their differences are practical or artificial, hence difficult to disentangle in many available studies. The school setting could be a focal community point, both for engagement and delivery. For example, developing a relationship with two Syrian schools for refugee children in Istanbul naturally led to approaching families, engaging them and involving them in an

80 Building resilience

attachment-focused intervention (theraplay). Other similar vulnerable groups would not have otherwise engaged if approached directly. Changes can be parallel and gradual across both systems, with teachers being exposed to the philosophy of an intervention and complementing it with training, and communities initially becoming more tolerant of the approach, followed by curiosity and hopefully endorsement of its principles.

Tackling the stigma of mental illness, disability and vulnerability can follow a similar course of structured awareness programmes and practical demonstration of usefulness to the community. Opening a community centre for children with disability in Rwanda to local youth for after-school groups appeared to achieve a lot more than a formal lecture in the local population co-owning the centre, embracing the pupils and ultimately challenging their own beliefs on disability. In general, the more different children's groups mix, the more likely their parents and other adults are to follow suit. In most countries, organizations for children in care hold a strong belief in children attending mainstream schools, even if this sometimes results in relatively long commuting. Seeing a group of local nursery children visit an orphanage in Jakarta was a breath of fresh air. Regular music and dance activities for child mental health service attenders in Brazil were not only organized at the local community centre, but were equally attended by any interested children and teenagers in the neighbourhood. I was not able to tell who was who, largely because nobody seemed to care.

Admittedly, bottom-up innovation will not be effective without parallel policy endorsement and key stakeholders being on board, be it local government managers or community leads. The most comprehensive initiatives for homeless youth and families reflect housing departments and directors who truly believe that 'housing is more than a roof', and thus work closely with health and social care agencies, sometimes against the tide of targets and narrowly defined budgets. When the Father who hosted my visit to a large refugee settlement in Uganda greeted me in public with an unequivocal statement that 'we have a large mental health problem in our communities', the first battle had been won, as he had set the parameters in no uncertain terms for me to then deal with the specifics. For similar reasons, innovative health projects in India and Bangladesh trained young people or parents as health care assistants, whom they retained to engage their own communities in attending immunization and other clinics. Because of this community ownership, they were able to confront previous strong taboos like gender-based violence and family planning/contraception. Why not mental health next? Similar examples have emerged in Africa to promote safe sex and HIV prevention. The intelligence of these initiatives lies in developing local skills and expertise, providing employment, retaining those skills and finding a way through the most deprived – but often also least trusting – parts of the population. Such solutions are more sustainable than continuously relying on external experts.

For programmes to be needs-led and cost-effective, they should be adapted to address the specific characteristics of vulnerable children and communities, after taking their views and perspectives into consideration; consequently they require users' active involvement throughout planning and delivery. This relies on community engagement and tackling negative attitudes, for example, by accepting a children's home, juvenile hostel or reception centre for refugee families in their locality. Involving such youth groups in community activities necessitates a fine balance of accepting them as the same as one's own children, whilst at the same time understanding their specific needs. For example, teenagers in care should be accepted without prejudice (which usually reflects fear), in the same way as their peers, by a local drama, arts or sports group. However, group leads should also understand that these young people may not be able to attend regularly, nor may they be able to cope with usual stressors and expectations. A more tailored approach is often enough to help them belong rather than excluding them for not conforming.

The role of mentors

None of this is going to happen overnight. Young people who have suffered abuse and rejection, and who may have been out of school for a while, are not likely to fit in straightaway. A vacuum in their social development means that they may avoid peer pressure by playing up, thus miss out on fun and friendships. In turn, lack of self-confidence is likely to prevent them from exploring their potential: 'I am worthless, what's the point?' This is where mentors can bridge the gap between upbringing and external or specialist help. For a young offender, this could be the first role model who does not judge them whilst setting boundaries and taking no nonsense from them either. Consequently, this could be a turning point for them to gain enough self-control and confidence to access education, employment or therapy.

This sounds too easy in all its complexity! Unfortunately, organizations often neglect those bridging roles, or they simply fall between different funding strands, with no agency taking ownership. They are, nevertheless, crucial as the alternative assumption that a traumatized young person will find their own way through life transitions in the same way as someone enjoying continuous family and social supports is flawed, as demonstrated by research on the reasons for placement breakdowns, school and social exclusion and crime recidivism. In conclusion, bridging mentorship roles should be defined positively, hosted within welfare agencies (whether statutory or NGOs) and funded properly; otherwise the previously mentioned disruptions increase societal and public sector costs. Mentors need a professional identity, training and supervision, support mechanisms and career prospects, rather than being a by default selection of passionate individuals who will move on just as they have required sufficient skills. Learning what not to do can be even harder, hence the need for direct links with therapeutic and other services that they can access in their own right.

Peer mentors add another dimension, i.e. relating to young people both because of their age and their relevant experiences. Street credibility is (literally) important for particular groups like those living on the streets and drug users who do not trust authority, because of its real or perceived links with the courts and the police. Such posts are central to many homeless and drug use services in, for example, Australia, the US and the UK. To my surprise, I discovered more peer mentors than I expected in low-income countries. To a certain extent this compensates for limited resources. The peer mentors at a drug rehabilitation centre in Jakarta had escaped both the drug gangs and the streets, and were now employed by the state (Photo 8.1). They seemed to be the only ones whom the current street kids appeared to trust, even if some of their techniques still smelled of 'roughing them up'. In Kenyan schools, peer mentors were described as an innovative solution to help pupils, as their teachers were overwhelmed. Refugee mentors also fulfil those criteria, but there are also reasons for caution, as they may also represent intra-ethnic, cultural or religious conflicts from their countries of origin which persist in their new communities.

PHOTO 8.1 Do these West African refugee lads in Athens know how talented they are?

A new experience of belonging

For children and young people who have not yet had many opportunities, if any at all, of interacting with their peers outside their immediate environment, at least for lengthy periods of their young lives, expecting them to slot in is a big ask. If there has been a vacuum of enjoyment and a gradual strive for independence, from children's parties and sleepovers to teenagers' sports and music camps, these experiences will be scary, therefore avoided. Changing attitudes and enhancing youth leads' understanding and sensitivity, as already discussed, are the first steps. These should be followed by opportunities, related financial support and easy access. As sports and out-of-school clubs are likely to be hard for children in care, because of known emotional dysregulation particularly in social contexts, they should be eased in with planning, some individual input and structured activities, before the real test of unstructured and spontaneous joining in. Even this should be introduced gradually. Team sports are highly desirable because of the team benefits, but may be unrealistic for some time because some children may not be able to handle peer pressure. Individual sports can instead purposefully aim to instil confidence and exposure to other children without having to interact with them initially. Pets, farm animals and nature activities are other introductory outlets that do not cause social anxiety.

The value of integration on self-worth and positive functioning has been shown in studies on the acculturation of young refugees. Integration denotes embracing both the new and the host culture, in contrast to assimilation to the host/dominant culture, segregation or marginalization. This has been found to be strongly mediated by peer acceptance and support. Indeed, this feeling of belonging was young people's (predominantly Afghani youth) priority and longing in a study following attendance at a designated mental health service in England; not surprisingly, mental well-being was further down their list. This was apparent in their appearance (clothes, hair style and mannerisms) when they came for appointments, particularly when their English began to improve. For those reasons, many programmes, especially in multi-ethnic areas, target children from as young an age as possible. The school and community intervention with young Aboriginal children in Australia, which has already been referred to, was such an example, particularly as there was a sense of (hopefully temporary) impasse between mutually mistrusting adults.

I would argue that the same principles and evidence should be applied with other vulnerable and potentially marginalized groups of young people and families, be they raised in care, coming off the streets or going through the juvenile system (sadly, many young people may have experienced all those experiences). The likelihood of segregation and exclusion are equally high, with both the apparent (drug use, unemployment, street culture) and less overt characteristics (not coping with peer and other social pressures, no one to turn to when it matters most) playing their part. The mechanisms and risks of living in silos or ghettos, which often creep across generations, are strikingly similar for refugee vs host, care and street vs mainstream and indigenous vs dominant culture or all the previous being summed up as living in extremely poor communities vs children raised with multiple opportunities, including access to services.

Obviously, this is a wider ideological, policy and public welfare/health debate; nevertheless, there are locally driven initiatives that have been shown to bring together youth and families on the edge with the rest of society. Where possible,

PHOTO 8.2 With refugee graduates from different communities in Uganda: the training certificates were only the beginning

cultural integration should start even in acute frontline settings such as refugee camps, children's homes, domestic violence shelters and secure units, environments that have repeatedly been shown to be fertile grounds for bullying, abuse and other forms of violence. The positive experience of children's integration in United Nations High Commissioner for Refugees (UNHCR) primary schools in a large Uganda refugee settlement was in stark contrast to adult attitudes in the disparate (albeit not hostile) communities that interestingly took the names of their countries or cities of origin such as New Congo or New Kigali (Rwanda). For this reason, we decided to mirror children's acculturation in our training and network-building programme with refugee graduates (largely victims of political persecution themselves) from those communities to act as catalysts between children and their parents (Photo 8.2).

Linking emotional literacy with a business nous

All the previous principles need to be endorsed in providing further education, vocational training and employment opportunities to young people who have worked through adversity and are relatively ready to move on. This is another and longer battle to fight, as they are now virtually on the cusp of real life where they have to fend for themselves. And on this cusp is where many contradictions lie.

Young people living in stability and with plenty of emotional and financial support often struggle, and may need a couple or more attempts before they find their way. Yet, we often refer to 'care leaving' and 'independent living' as discreet transitions for the most vulnerable in our society. And these may even be the better examples of some options and supports, as most countries do not have exit routes from the care system, and there are few examples of initiatives for young people coming off the streets, secure establishments or refugee centres (assuming that the latter have cleared their legal status).

The more successful examples of such initiatives combine a number of ingredients. Providing opportunities is a start, but is unlikely to be taken up and sustained if young people's emotional and social fragility are not understood, as we discussed in previous sections, hence these are not incorporated in the format and culture of their learning and employment. The ways in which they adapt to their strengths, flexibility and needs-led stepped progression have been identified as good predictors. On the other hand, employers being sympathetic to young people's hardships does not resolve the problem if there are no economically viable training schemes and jobs. Incentives for employers and links with colleges and universities are getting harder to come by in increasingly individualistic western societies, where access to higher education is becoming a privilege; or for low-income countries where short-term survival takes precedence over sustained growth and reduction of inequalities.

If one temporarily tried to forget the predicament of the African refugee graduates in the previous example, their potential and intelligence were second to none. These were young adults with training and qualifications in social work, law, health and education, but who had since been persecuted, usually for civil rights issues. Yet refugees all over the world are likely to be penalized for a second time, as they provide easy prey for politicians in the host country to fill their own vacuum whilst depriving their own society of new energy and skills.

When there are no primary caregivers to immediately step in, building a network of supports around the young person is essential to see them through inevitable setbacks without them having to go through another cycle of rejection and end up homeless or in prison. Inter-connected affordable and supported housing, sports and creative activities, community networks, technology and social enterprises in emerging economic fields can both help to create a protective multi-layered shield for vulnerable young people in transition and to actively demonstrate the socio-economic benefits to their immediate and wider communities. These communities should also be engaged at an organizational, public health or welfare level throughout this process by feeding back evidence and information, mobilizing natural resources and involving them as co-partners in service planning via genuine empowerment. Such an approach has been followed by several health programmes in low-income countries, and I witnessed its benefits in an African region through a UK-based NGO that set up an impressive local child protection team of professionals and volunteers through sheer engagement with local communities in order to eliminate incidents of child sacrifice.

86 Building resilience

The power of religion, religiosity and spirituality

The protective effect of religion, the broader religiosity (which encompasses beliefs, dedication and activity) and spirituality (personal quest for ultimate meaning, peace and fulfilment) arising from or independent of religion (often referred to as secular spirituality), has been demonstrated in several studies with at risk groups. For example, we established such an association in analysing data from the UK child mental health surveys. The mechanisms underpinning these findings can be difficult to unravel. The reality is that it can play a major part in both individual and collective contexts if it helps a child, family or community draw strength and resources to process and respond to adversity. For some it is another contributor, along with ethnicity and culture, in forming an identity. For others it can be a way into services as a first trusting step, or the only source of help-seeking. These mechanisms can obviously also have the opposite effect if religious leads and parents dismiss mental health suffering and reject other forms of concurrent or sequential help.

This was not my experience of religious leads in any of my visits – although the point has to be made that they were open-minded enough to invite or accept me in the first instance. Many had a broader leadership role than narrow religious practice, and worked closely with external agencies (sometimes employed by them in a dual remit) and local groups, thus forming a strong link for the cross-fertilization of ideas and approaches that initially seemed incompatible. Most were unprejudiced in mixing local or national culture with western psychological approaches, and this openness seemed to instil confidence in their communities.

The influence of religion and/or spirituality appears to have grown as other life values and safeguards have diminished. Across Islam, Hinduism, Buddhism or Christianity, the mosque, temple or church often becomes the focal point of drawing strength, rejoicing or mourning during Friday prayers or Sunday mass. Perhaps inner strength is all that war-torn and extremely poor communities can hold on to, a simplicity lost in materially affluent societies which are, in consequence, seeing a rise in different expressions of spirituality. The protection of Christ The Redeemer in Rio de Janeiro, the muezzin's mosque prayers in Gazza, the contented joyfulness of East African churches and the sacred water of the Ganges in Varanasi all had the same impact on me by reflecting the human need for seeking solace, forgiveness and salvation; they also all appeared to exert more powerful effects on the most vulnerable and neglected on this earth. It is no surprise that traditional resilience mechanisms periodically resurface in refined forms adapted to current life, as for example the re-emergence of mindfulness, which we will consider in the next two chapters.

9

APPLICATION OF THERAPEUTIC APPROACHES

'Therapeutic': a widely used and often misunderstood word

'But I am not a therapist!'

How many times have I heard this response during training or informal conversations with highly experienced caregivers and practitioners? This usually follows a simple question about a recent therapeutic activity with the children, their therapeutic skills and aspirations or the therapeutic strengths of their setting. Even large organizations are sometimes as keen to dissociate themselves from the term 'therapist', as they are to avoid the use of the related concept 'psychological trauma'. The connotation can be that both terms potentially imply competencies they do not possess, or are not meant to be part of their core remit. In some western countries, it may be a denouncement to avoid litigation if something goes wrong. All these examples are based on the assumption that 'therapeutic = therapy' and, more often than not, 'therapeutic = individual psychotherapy'; thus implying a specialist approach that requires lengthy training with specific requirements and guidelines.

These assumptions are partially both false and true. Reducing all interventions, supports and types of help for a vulnerable child to one type, no matter how valuable it is, is a simplification that undermines all those equipped to support the child, and which deprives the child themselves of multiple modalities that have been shown to contribute positively to their mental well-being. Equally there is a risk of undermining interventions and their required competences by adopting a low denominator, whether for economic or other purposes. There is clearly a reason why it has taken a painfully long time for different frameworks to evolve from their original underpinning theories, training programmes, boards, curricula and monitoring to be established, programmes to be implemented in real settings, particularly with vulnerable groups, and evidence to emerge, before feeding back into the loop. Diluting the fidelity of an approach would thus diminish its potential

88 Application of therapeutic approaches

efficacy, especially for children with complex needs, who require a high level of staff competencies.

This evolution and breadth of therapeutic options, with their continuously emerging evidence-base, has offered therapeutic tools not just *between* or *across* interventions, but also *within* interventions. This has been made possible for a number of reasons. First, although each framework rightly started from a sophisticated point of purity, and was originally only meant to be used by adequately trained therapists, different professional disciplines increasingly sought the application of related skills as additional ammunition to their existing role. This process usually started with mental health practitioners, for example within the rapidly expanding nursing profession; before more recently being transferred to frontline staff in education, social care, physical health care and a variety of community roles, both statutory and NGO-based.

Second, policies are increasingly acknowledging all these staff groups as making a contribution to children's psychosocial needs. This has consequently encouraged and financially supported the relevant upskilling of existing staff, as well as the establishment of new posts. Third, even when resources were available, the paucity of professionals adhering to the ideal requirements led to a 'bottom-up' implementation and experimentation, which was not without its risks. This experimentation is gradually leading to a better understanding of how applications of certain approaches can be utilized at different service levels and settings.

Unfortunately, we are still early on in this exciting process, which will undoubtedly continue to expand in the near future. The downside is that there is still limited evidence or consensus on what it really means. How could or should a particular therapeutic framework be applied by different professional groups and in different contexts? Where do we draw the boundaries between these levels? Do they operate on a continuum with specialist provisions? What are the training, service and supervisory requirements for each professional and service level? What are the risks of crossing boundaries? And when may resource-effective competencies become diluted, and consequently clinically non-effective? These are important debates to consider and test in practice. However, in the absence of substantive evidence, some suggestions made in this chapter may still be more pragmatic or preliminary than fully formulated.

Inevitably, they will also pose overlap within our psychosocial model under consideration; that is with the previous two chapters on parents, families and caregivers (Chapter 7), and on school and community involvement (Chapter 8). Nevertheless, the main debate will relate to the next chapter, Chapter 10, on the boundaries with the 'specialist' implementation of interventions, ranging from the original psychodynamic and behavioural therapies to the more recent targeted approaches for children who have experienced trauma such as narrative therapy.

Psychoeducation

For lack of a better term, psychoeducation denotes more than advice. Rather, it implies reaffirming what carers and some children may already know, whilst

Application of therapeutic approaches **89**

providing a missing link between trauma and behaviours, confirming that this is not an uncommon pattern and providing an explanation for the first time. If young people and their parents or carers are not ready to make these connections and to use their own coping strategies (i.e. subconsciously repressed rather than consciously suppressed), this approach will not suffice. The objective of this first-line intervention is to help manage symptoms and distress without prolonged input or attempting to process the child's experience. Such packages or brief courses largely target PTSD symptoms, but can equally apply to other concurrent presentations such as mild anxiety and depressive symptoms. Specific aims include engagement, symptomatic control, understanding of emotional responses and related behaviours and development of adaptive strategies.

Different means can be used, whether verbal, written or creative. Nevertheless, there is some overlap of frameworks, for example, the Writing for Recovery programme, which has been widely used with positive evidence of its effectiveness after war conflict and natural disasters, incorporates both cognitive and behavioural activities. Inevitably, the line between directed structure, self-regulation and generalization of strategies is very fine indeed. This may be challenging to define on paper, but is also somewhat refreshing in its unpredictability in response to children's individuality. Although these techniques may be considered the least difficult in terms of staff training before they can communicate them to children, over-reliance on manuals without being convinced of their merits, understanding the context of their application, making some individual judgements such as on the child's developmental capacity or state of distress and resisting the temptation to respond to trauma-related material are not without risks.

Behavioural strategies

I feel rather sorry for behavioural therapy! Although one of the oldest and most widely used approaches (after all, we all knowingly or not regularly apply behavioural strategies in our everyday lives, whether at home, at work or with friends), it tends to receive little credit, plenty of misunderstanding and, crucially, decreasing opportunities for proper training. The result is that strategies are often used ad hoc, in isolation and not consistently, hence they do not work or fizzle out. It is beyond the remit of this text to defend any modality or try to understand the reasons behind its applications. In relation to behavioural therapy though, perhaps training programmes take for granted the false premise that it is easy to use because of its long history and substantial theoretical background.

It is more important to consider its relevance – or not – to children who experience trauma. Naturally, behavioural strategies do not target trauma-specific problems, and were never meant to. Often the behaviours they need to target are secondary to the child's vulnerabilities. Consequently, one could mistakenly follow the 'either or' path of framing approaches as mutually exclusive rather than needs-led and complementary. As already discussed, the implementation of behavioural programmes often leaves a lot to be desired, particularly when

90 Application of therapeutic approaches

multiple staff and caregivers try to tackle multiple problems. This can be a recipe for disappointment.

The baseline is to define and establish the child's needs, before tailoring an intervention, with clear goals, a target period and a monitoring process. Behavioural strategies can be applied sequentially or in parallel with trauma-focused interventions, as long as their distinct therapeutic criteria are met and all caregivers, staff and especially the child or young person are clear. What is more difficult a lot of the time is not so much defining these boundaries, but rather shifting between different approaches when these are implemented in parallel. A common example is of an adoptive parent or foster carer instilling behavioural boundaries without taking into account the child's history, hence the importance of concurrent nurturing and avoiding the threat of rejection: 'I don't like what you've just done, because . . . but I love you the same and it will make no difference to living with us.'

What are the indications for instigating behavioural programmes with vulnerable children? Hierarchically, high risk behaviours such as aggression are top of the list. All come with the above proviso that they will not be resolved with behavioural strategies alone; instead they first need to be contained and manageable, and thus allow the child and their carers to pursue other more long-term solutions. The same could be said of self-harm behaviours, where behavioural strategies can be viewed as superficial. However, if some residential staff respond with sympathy, others opt to ignore the incidents and a few even conceptualize them as 'attention-seeking' and respond negatively, it is highly unlikely that the young person will be able to access an emotion-focused intervention. The same applies to drug use, running away or sexual vulnerability. It is thus difficult to distinguish between staff or carers' behavioural responses and their established, often subtle, attitudes. It is also important to understand the context of any behaviour and whether it is learnt or understood as part of underlying attachment difficulties. Stealing can be such an example, with one adolescent copying their peers and stealing in public places; and another stealing insignificant objects such as sweets at home, without even trying to hide them.

Moving on to trauma-related symptoms such as nightmares and flashbacks in post-traumatic stress disorder (PTSD), these tend to respond well to targeted interventions which will be discussed in the next chapter. However, sometimes such symptoms can become entrenched, and, therefore, less responsive, or the young person may not as yet be amenable to a psychological interpretation – this is rather common with refugee youth. A behavioural approach will give the young person mastery over their more debilitating symptoms, and consequently of their life. In turn, this will bring their arousal levels down to enable them to reflect and accept an alternative approach to induce sustained change. Even when such a trauma-focused approach is acceptable to the young person and takes effect, their carers, teachers and other important adults need to reinforce this improvement with clear and consistent responses. Similar principles apply to panic attacks and other expressions of anxiety. Behavioural strategies can be combined with cognitive techniques (the letter 'B' in CBT), as will be discussed later in this chapter.

Application of therapeutic approaches **91**

Without going through behavioural techniques in detail, it might be more useful to list the key principles in relation to vulnerable children, and where these tend to go wrong. The priority is for carers and all staff involved to agree goals, remain consistent and involve the child throughout, without shifting the goalposts. Multiple staff groups with a recurrent turnover and shifts at children's homes can find it particularly hard to maintain consistency. This is where the child's key worker and unit manager need to take the lead and drive the programme, particularly as behaviours and circumstances are likely to fluctuate. Vulnerable children often present with multiple and inter-linked behaviours, for which reason it is important to initially identify and target one behaviour (or group of similar behaviours), usually starting with the hierarchically most challenging or risky one. For example, physical outbursts will have to take precedence for a while over the child swearing or not completing their homework. This does not preclude the staff from continuously engaging the child, explaining the reasons and instilling wider principles for them to generate improvement in other aspects of their life.

For younger children, behaviours, goals and reinforcements need to be simply defined and in developmentally appropriate language. If a child has learning difficulties or functions within the autism spectrum, these strategies should be adapted according to their functional rather than their chronological age. General expectations should be avoided. What does 'be good' really mean? Is anybody good all the time? Involving children in defining goals and rewards gives them some control within pre-defined boundaries – i.e. not 'What behaviour would you like to change', but rather 'How would you like us to change this (specified) behaviour together?'

Rewards are preferable to negative reinforcement, and negative reinforcement does not equate to punishment. Goals and rewards need to be achievable. Moving from multiple outbursts a day to none is unrealistic. In contrast, achieving a realistic number of outbursts per day in the first instance, followed by setting, for example, three outburst-free days per week at the next stage is more likely to work or at least come close. Otherwise, the child and carers will lose interest and morale pretty quickly. Rewards do not need to be material such as gifts or money, but rather a target that is meaningful to the child such as a joint and enjoyable activity, and should *always* be accompanied by verbal and non-verbal reinforcement. Absence of negative behaviours should be rewarded too – these are easy to forget but mean a lot to the child! The older the young person, the more complex the reward should be, in which case tokens to gain a privilege, outing or small monetary target may work well. Ultimately, what really matters (and works) is the emotional tone of the reward, which constitutes the *real* reinforcement. After all, don't a warm smile, gentle nod and kind words mean the world to all of us?

How about negative reinforcement? To this day one can still hear statements like 'getting some stick when I was younger did me no harm'. First, we cannot assume that it did you no harm – even if it didn't, it certainly did you no good! There is no evidence whatsoever of any benefits from harsh or physical parenting, irrespective of culture. It is true that in some countries the boundaries between physical

92 Application of therapeutic approaches

punishment and physical abuse remain fine, but child protection legal frameworks are rapidly moving beyond narrow cultural interpretation. Instead, negative reinforcement can be defined as either not gaining privileges or losing some, but not being punished. There should be careful thought about how far withdrawing privileges should go. If a young person has been deprived throughout their life and one takes away their only source of enjoyment (e.g. listening to music), this can be construed as punitive or cruel, and is likely to aggravate their behaviour. Instead, the young person could temporarily lose the opportunity to buy more music (OK, they may be downloading it for free anyway – just making a point!). On the other hand, if the same young person maintains all their privileges, they will remain confused and unlikely to change. Even in those cases, negotiating with them what is a fair reward or loss can maintain their sense of control during difficult times.

When a child or young person is very distressed or violent, there needs to be a pre-determined plan and response, which should be brief – usually to keep them safe – without reasoning extensively during the crisis. The next stage should be to comfort the child, and only later, when they are settled, to re-visit the behavioural plan and ask them to reflect on their behaviour. Behavioural strategies are particularly difficult to implement with traumatized children who may pass on their experiences and guilt to their carers ('I hate you', 'you are all the same'), and tend to process behavioural strategies disproportionately, by perceiving them as yet another rejection. Consequently, carers can be left blaming themselves and mirroring the child's anger. These complex interactions demonstrate why it is a fallacy that behavioural strategies are simple, and do not require training or supervision.

Family and attachment-based approaches

This section particularly overlaps with Chapter 7 on family and attachment-focused interventions. These may vary widely from approaches to prevent one young person from going into care to facilitating another young person's contact and communication with their birth parents whilst in care. Family frameworks, certainly at this level, are likely to borrow principles and techniques from both behavioural and family therapy (largely systemic) models which we will discuss in the next chapter. So, what are their distinct features and indications for their use?

Virtually every children's practitioner will have contact with the birth or other parents, relatives or caregivers; whether working individually with the child, within a care setting or in a school. Their time capacity and the nature of their role will determine both their input and relationship with the parents but, either way, they will require some training and to adapt their role according to the circumstances. In the context of vulnerable children, their family – whatever the status – are likely to share similar characteristics such as exposure to trauma. Therefore, staff will require additional competencies to those dealing with parents and families in relative stability.

For this reason, and because of the potential for family interventions not to be integrated in the child's care plan, and thus be side-tracked, a holistic assessment and

Application of therapeutic approaches **93**

goals should be pre-requisites to any action. Where is the child living at the moment? Who are the primary caregiver(s)? What is a realistic short and long-term objective (e.g. remain in foster care or return to their birth family)? What is the legal context – if applicable? Should child protection procedures be considered, and, if so, how? Who are the important family members or other caregivers? What are their views and wishes? Are these compatible with those of the child and agencies involved? Are there agencies in contact with those important adults? Is their goal to help them in their own right, such as through counselling or mental health treatment, in which case there should be liaison with the agencies for adults? Is there another agency involved with the family unit, and in what capacity?

It is crucial to address all these questions before initiating any intervention as, otherwise, there may be a mismatch of approaches and goals, and they are therefore less likely to be effective and to sustain change. Defining a goal can be hard enough, but doing so across systems that involve several adults, often in the presence of ongoing conflict, is extremely challenging. Below are some potential 'family' goals for children who experience complex trauma:

Past traumatic events may have been important, but are no longer present, and there are no major concerns in relation to the immediate family, other than the need for support in relation to their social circumstances such as housing. This scenario could apply to some refugee families. In a variation of this, the child's presenting behaviours may be related to external factors (like community violence or bullying), and not primarily to family issues. Here reassurance, empowerment, involvement and consistency may be sufficient.

If there are some parenting difficulties, but no conflict or primary trauma exposure within the family, parent training and/or related behavioural strategies could be the way forward. In the same situation, but when a parent additionally suffers from a mental health disorder, adult service input should be provided in conjunction, but also in regular communication with child care agencies. In all the scenarios so far, such liaison and regular communication, by whatever means are most resource-effective, should be extended to school and the other child care agencies involved.

Alternatively, there may be no immediate placement or child protection concerns, but there is sufficient impairment in the parenting capacity and/or the parent-child relationship to indicate future risk. One of the approaches discussed in Chapter 7 could be provided by the key agency, usually social services, although an NGO or other designated agency may be the most appropriate provider in some countries. Family support and parent training could be the core remit of this agency who routinely provide the programme. Lack of response could require an additional attachment-focused approach by a more specialist service.

In the case of a kinship, foster or adoptive placement, one should establish and evidence which concerns are related to the child's past experiences (usually in helping the child develop secure attachment with their current carers), and which are related to 'here-and-now' difficulties in caregiving/parenting. These can be difficult to disentangle, with a lot of circular and confounding factors; especially

94 Application of therapeutic approaches

when both aspects need tackling. Nevertheless, goals and solutions are entirely different for these two issues, with distinct skills and clarity required, i.e. attachment-focused for the former and behavioural strategies for the latter. These are not mutually exclusive, and can complement each other well, but it can be tempting to either miss the past trauma (in many contexts where children's behaviours are managed indiscriminately); or to miss routine struggles with parenting, for example in instilling boundaries, by being too distracted by the child's past history.

Therapeutic goals should always be adapted to the care plan. In a short-term foster placement, the priorities should be safety, containment and some return to normality, to provide the child with a relatively positive experience, considering the circumstances. In a medium-term foster placement, in contrast, the child may be left in limbo without a clear decision on their future, hence such clarity would be required to break the cycle of insecurity and resulting behaviours, before enhancing the quality of the attachment relationship. In a more desirable long-term foster placement, interventions should aim to consolidate, strengthen and prevent relationship and behavioural difficulties, whilst providing the child with enough breathing space and unequivocal statements to convince them that they are staying with their new family. All adults should unconditionally be in agreement with this commitment. The two latter scenarios and their constraints need to be multiplied in the challenges they present for residential placements, where both containing behavioural and resilience-building attachment interventions require consistency, good communication, similar skills and an amalgamation of different attitudes among the staff.

Moving up the severity and complexity continuum to immediate concerns about the child's safety (including emotional attitudes and risks arising from unsupervised parenting), approaches need to be closely linked to statutory requirements, in line with the legal framework of the country. The goal should not be 'let's try and see what happens', but rather the opposite in framing the intervention in a legal context: 'let's try this to avoid escalation of risk, with clear monitoring criteria and evidence of whether/why it has/has not worked, and a resulting next plan, depending on the response'. This means that, if there are child protection concerns and the family intervention has not led to change, one should never solely revert to preventive or behavioural strategies without consideration of safeguarding consequences, no matter how unpalatable these might be – ranging from the child's formal registration to removal. If, in contrast, there has been some demonstrable improvement, one would hope to empower the family to generate further change with less support. However, having been on the verge of a child protection decision usually means that monitoring should be de-escalated gradually, and not withdrawn overnight.

When family input is mandated within a statutory plan, then the opposite rule should apply, in that the intervention should be framed in that context and feed into the legal process. This raises issues of engagement with families and young people, as indeed when working with juvenile offenders, drug users or refugee families. One can only be clear and transparent about their therapeutic role, and where it may or will cross over to the legal process. Examples of goals in this context could include a 'parenting assessment to inform a court decision' (which is different from a routine assessment following a family request), or a 'specific course of family intervention to inform the courts'. At some point the legal and therapeutic process will hopefully be disentangled, or at least run in parallel, but until that happens, agency roles and goals should be crystal clear to avoid enmeshment, waste of resources, family disengagement and, crucially, adding to children's existing distress.

Even in the most difficult circumstances, for example when there is no prospect of the child returning to their family of origin, family input has a role to play; again with the proviso of clear goals being defined and agreed with all parties involved, and these being communicated in a developmentally appropriate language to the child. Contact with a birth parent is a common example where a judgement needs to be made whether this should be informal, relatively boundaried or supervised. The next question is whether the birth family seek and need support and, if so, what for? The approach will be substantially different depending on whether the objective is to help them re-define their relationship and enjoy their contact, as in the case of older adolescents, to overtly (but not covertly) aim to enable them to live together in the foreseeable or distant future or to formulate a tangible plan to do so relatively soon. Family therapy strategies in enhancing communication and helping family members reframe their relationships and expectations could be appropriate.

Trauma-focused strategies: usually expected, but where does one start and stop?

We all want to help children, particularly those who have suffered a great deal. For many practitioners, this is the main reason that attracted them to their career choice or current post. In that respect, getting 'tucked in' to relieve distress is both tempting and welcome, particularly as many of these practitioners will find themselves in the position of making a connection for the first time with a traumatized child who has previously only suffered rejection. This is not just altruistically welcome, but also relevant to whatever role one has. Practitioners have many more therapeutic tools in their locker, albeit with variable evidence of their effectiveness so far, than they did 5–10 years ago. The difficult question is, how should they use them? And what are the challenges and risks in perhaps going a little too far? As therapeutic applications are often (wrongly, in my opinion) equated to individual trauma-focused modalities, these dilemmas are at the heart of ongoing debates.

Let's start with everyday roles in making that connection therapeutically meaningful for the child. One could argue that any positive relationship is of benefit to a child who has experienced significant trauma. This is possibly true, but the benefits will be more pronounced and sustainable if we are conscious of which aspects of the connection and relationship are important, and how to avoid potentially troubled waters. Traumatized children are neither scripted in their interactions nor static in their behaviours. Any relationship, no matter how positive, will draw them to reproduce unwanted experiences in order to unconsciously test out whether this new adult is any different from what they expect. This testing will involve

96 Application of therapeutic approaches

aggression, avoidance or displacement of distress that well-meaning but not adequately trained and supported caregivers and staff may fall for ('After all, I am only trying to help you, why do you hate me?'). Therefore, retaining one's role whilst viewing the child slightly differently, thus making pro-active adjustments, largely depends on integrated training and support mechanisms. If these components are in place, this reprocessing of the child's experience outside the therapy room may well make all the difference between a sustained and a disrupted placement. However, because it is more difficult to define these therapeutic elements than, for example, a time-defined course of therapy, it is harder too.

Although the principles of observing, making sense of the situation, linking and reflecting the child's experience, needs and behaviours are similar to those required in the therapy process, the objectives, strategies and competencies required are vastly different. Building some level of trust based on safety but without expecting too much reciprocity, at least at the beginning, can be sufficient for the child to share their distress in their own time – be it in the car, walking to school or in the kitchen. Absorbing and reframing needs in the context of normal everyday life is hard, but a chance not to be missed if the child is to reap the benefits. The difference from being in therapy is that the caregiver, volunteer or practitioner reassures, contains (verbally, non-verbally and occasionally physically), reflects back and ultimately shares the distress at *that* moment; but stops short of opening up a process that cannot be managed by either themselves or the child, for example by making interpretations. It is a big ask of a teacher to concurrently treat a child as both the *same* as and *different* from other children in the class. But this is exactly what vulnerable children need.

If we confer the specific (rather than specialist) trauma-focused interventions to the next chapter, there is plenty of ground to cover in this chapter between adopting a therapeutic role and being a therapist. Although, admittedly, this is an area we still know little about, there is huge potential for a range of professionals to extend their skills and to purposely apply therapeutic principles and techniques within their agency remit. Such new competencies can take one's role a step further, and thus hopefully also bridge the gap for the child.

As we will be discussing in the next chapter, there are several theories and resulting modalities aimed at helping children re-process their traumatic experience. The means vary, depending on the child's capacity and preferences, being verbal, play or creative. The focus of this section is on the objectives of applying some of the principles discussed above, without the objective of re-processing trauma. In a similar manner to behavioural strategies focusing on symptom management, here the equivalent would be the understanding and management of emotions (emotional regulation), which can be particularly problematic for this group of children and youth who have missed out on natural developmental processes, and have instead experienced a negative and punitive distortion of human growth.

Some strategies can be used within everyday frontline roles, to initiate or reinforce more self-control. There are also more structured programmes, delivered individually or in groups, to help children explore, understand and express

Application of therapeutic approaches **97**

their emotions in a more adaptive way, and thus start reversing their life script. The challenge here is that, in doing so, children will spontaneously introduce difficult experiences which the practitioner needs to confine to the defined goals, and thus avoid the temptation of delving into the child's past or inner world.

Cognitive-behavioural and other applications

Similar dilemmas will arise related to cognitive-behaviour therapeutic techniques of variable combinations (Cbt or cBt or CBt) and objectives. These are increasingly popular, but run the risk of being perceived as 'easy' to apply without specialist training. Learning to view oneself positively in the face of adversity and recurrent trauma is a lengthy process, which requires more than encouragement and setting simple tasks. The first step for the practitioner is being aware of these constraints, before helping the child begin to challenge negative thinking patterns, usually at an everyday coping level ('How do you know the other kids don't like you? What's the evidence?'). This can lead to sharpening their ability to observe, 'catching' their negative thinking patterns and making links with events, feelings and behaviours. What we may perceive as sudden and unexplained aggression is likely to have obvious explanations, as long as our mind and our eyes are trained where to 'look'. These strategies are not specific to conditions such as depression or PTSD, but are valuable nevertheless. A number of new CBT training courses designed for this purpose are helpful in addressing this therapeutic, albeit non-specialist, level.

One could propose similar examples and arguments for using anxiety management, relaxation or meditation techniques. Their underpinning frameworks vary between behavioural, cognitive or a mixture of both. Crucially though there is a difference between employing meditation techniques to sleep better (e.g. by detaching oneself from troubling thoughts and 'noise') and adopting a different attitude to life ('I can't control what my friends do at school, but I can control my own mind and how I feel') and applying this attitude to the context of traumatic experiences. Here, the confusion lies primarily with the practitioner or caregiver in determining what their approach should be and how to share it with the child. Training and supervision, in whatever capacity, are essential to make the most of valuable modalities that are implemented within a particular agency remit, rather than as originally intended and developed in the first place, albeit without losing their fidelity.

CASE SCENARIO

Laura (15 years) ran away from her parents' home about six months ago and ended up in a children's home, and still does not want to go back. She still lives at the children's home, as both Laura and her family have agreed that 'it is best if she stays there for the time being'. Laura goes to school and has stayed in touch with some of her friends, but tends to keep to herself at the home. She

98 Application of therapeutic approaches

finds it difficult to open up, instead she tends to follow the residential care staff and her teachers around, often scratching herself with sharp objects until she bleeds. When encouraged to talk, Laura screams and walks off. The staff and teacher groups are split over how to respond to Laura. Some think it is a cry for help and ask her why she is doing it, others try to stay with her until her wounds have been cleaned and Laura looks calmer, but without talking, and a few staff think she should be ignored, as too much attention 'will only reinforce her behaviour'.

Questions

1   How should the staff respond to Laura's needs?
2   Should they set up a behavioural programme?
3   If so, what should this involve?

Some points to consider:

- It is important to have a shared understanding and a consistent approach in understanding Laura's needs, before agreeing the most appropriate way to respond.
- Laura's key worker should take the lead in setting up a staff group discussion. Other important adults such as Laura's school tutor should be actively involved.
- These important adults should remain in close communication with each other, irrespective of Laura's behaviour, and Laura should remain aware of this, as a sign of caring, wishing to help her and being consistent.
- Before any behavioural programme is set up, staff need to share observations on factors that precipitate, sustain or improve Laura's behaviours.
- During the first discussion, views, attitudes and perceptions should be spelled out ('I feel sorry for her', 'she is manipulative', 'she needs time'), so that staff can also begin to notice how their responses perpetuate or alter behaviours, particularly when they are conflicting, thus confusing Laura further.
- The next step is to define a realistic goal. In this case, the priority is to reduce Laura's self-harm behaviours, and to gradually replace them with functional communication with the staff, whether verbal (sharing what distresses her) or non-verbal (such as being unable to talk, but tolerating their presence in silence, thus gaining comfort without self-harming and/or sharing an activity).
- There has to be a clear definition of which behaviour is to be targeted. For example, if the goal is to stop Laura self-harming but only in front of staff, she is likely to continue to doing so in her own room. Instead, her change of behaviour should be seen as an opportunity for change, which can be worked through between Laura and the staff, rather than being ignored.

Application of therapeutic approaches **99**

- If there are secondary and/or intermittent behaviours such as Laura being angry or running away (as long as she is safe), there are decisions to be made whether to adopt the same approach (see below) for these behaviours because they are inter-linked, or to concentrate on the primary one for the time being.
- There is no prescriptive answer, but some strategies that could be used include: making sure Laura is safe; showing empathy, without either collusion or confrontation; being emotionally and physically available, even if Laura cannot talk to the staff; using both verbal and non-verbal means to comfort Laura and contain her acute distress; following her clues, if she shows signs of alternative and adaptive communication, and responding positively accordingly; not trying to reason or seek reasons for the self-harm during the incident (although there are always exceptions!). Instead: use other opportunities to help Laura reflect when she is settled, preferably with someone she feels close to, such as her key worker or school tutor; make sure that other young people are not present or do not make matters worse by teasing Laura; regularly monitor Laura's progress rather than waiting for more incidents before calling a staff meeting; do not forget to praise Laura (verbally and non-verbally) for the absence of self-harm attempts, particularly if she is under stress.
- The young person's age, developmental functioning and preferences and the nature of the target behaviour will determine the choice of goals and reinforcers. In Laura's case, this is more about employing emotional rather than material reinforcement, which is more difficult both to define and to implement! It also disproves the myth that behavioural and emotion-focused strategies are mutually exclusive.
- Introducing creativity into these principles, and involving the young person, can make a behavioural programme more personal, thus more empowering.

REFLEXIVE EXERCISE

You are a volunteer with a psychology background in a refugee camp in southern Europe. You were not given much training or guidelines when you started this new role, but you were encouraged to keep younger children (of primary school age and below) occupied through 'creative activities'. Children have nothing to do in the baking sun, as there is no schooling as yet in the camp. You have some ideas for games, and the children add their own ideas too. They seem to be having great fun.

100 Application of therapeutic approaches

Your initial anxieties have subsided, as the children seem to like you and their parents are happy for you to keep them busy. After a lot of negotiation with the camp authorities, you have just managed to get some crayons and paper, as well as access to a cooler container on the edge of the camp. You ask the children to draw something that is important to them. You are surprised how well they can concentrate and focus, coming up with all sorts of drawings. Some are fun, just bright colours, some look dark. When you ask them to tell you what each drawing means, some children tell you that they are 'memories (good or bad) of home'. You make no comment, just nod sadly.

After the end of the activity, this little girl follows you around, holding a drawing. You stop and smile at her, she smiles back. Then you carry on and she keeps following you. In the end, you decide to wait for her and see what happens. The little girl comes to you and hands you her drawing, her eyes filling with tears. It is obviously a crowded boat, with some faces in the water (swimming? drowning?). Suddenly, it dawns on you, you thank the little girl for her drawing, and take it with you. You feel increasingly distressed on the way home. You wish you could throw the drawing away, but you just can't . . . you put it upside down on your desk so that you won't look at it . . . when you turn it over later, it is you who bursts into tears . . .

Question

How can you best handle the situation, by defining the boundaries of your role, seeking appropriate support and ultimately making an impact on the children?

Again, there is no clear right or wrong answer, but the following are a few *organizational, professional* and *personal* pointers:

- There is no such thing as an easy placement or post that involves contact with children who have suffered trauma, all the more so in the absence of support services, and/or when little is known about the children. Any organization or agency arranging voluntary placements or employing staff should, therefore, be clear about the employee's remit, boundaries, skills they should bring to the role, risks and, crucially, the support systems required.
- When there is clarity within the organization, this should be shared with the new volunteer or employee, and appropriate induction training put in place.
- A regular supervisory arrangement should remain throughout the post and placement, to enable volunteers to offload, reflect and adapt to their role.

- One challenge in such training is the unpredictability of whether, when and how traumatized children will communicate their distress. One might expect them to share experiences when asked questions, hence keeping some safe distance; but this is rather unlikely to happen, at least not until a relationship of some sort has been built. As in this case, children will follow triggers in different ways and when least expected.
- Staying with our volunteer, her remit is clearly to engage and stimulate the children. Both the building of trust and the mode of interaction (games or drawings) are likely to lead to similar responses from the children. This is not a reason to avoid them, as they can be therapeutic in their own right, by giving the child a positive experience; moreover, avoidance does not take distress away, it merely distorts it. Rather, the objective is more about anticipating the disclosure of distress, and being able to close it within the defined boundaries.
- The volunteer or practitioner's style will determine the nature of their response, i.e. what they are comfortable with. In this scenario, one could have anticipated the outcome, and either been prescriptive with the drawings ('something important' is likely to have emotional connotations for the child), or acknowledge at the outset that 'you are aware that they have had a difficult time, and that there could be memories that make them sad, no matter how fun the game or drawing is'.
- This, of course, can take human interactions only so far. Some children will manage to boundary the experience for now, others will give signs of sharing their experience and some will be desperate to pass some of their emotional weight to 'this nice person'. One has to judge how to react. Acknowledging and sharing children's sadness during or after an activity is a therapeutic response, as long as this is not open-ended. Otherwise, this could spill over rather quickly without access to a trauma-focused intervention. This would be unfair to both the child and the volunteer/practitioner.
- Even the best possible response will leave some remnants of horror with the (particularly sensitive) volunteer/practitioner. This is where internally or externally arranged supervision kicks in to process the child's negative energy and transference.

10

THERAPEUTIC INTERVENTIONS

A plethora of interventions to choose from, but need for clarity and integration

The next level of the intervention for consideration is what we have come to expect when working with children and adults who have experienced trauma. For those practitioners who are entering the field now, it is exciting to find out about the range of approaches available, emerging evidence, the training programmes for different levels of competencies and, crucially, the application of most of these approaches in challenging circumstances and with difficult to reach groups such as refugee and homeless youth. It is true that these programmes are largely practitioner-led due to the complexity of research designs and multiple factors involved in the planning of randomized controlled trials, but smaller-scale and equally valuable research is gradually building a picture on a range of factors related to the feasibility and fidelity of new interventions in real settings.

Many questions remain to be addressed such as the specificity and effectiveness of these interventions for different conditions. As discussed below, some interventions like narrative therapy have been designed to target trauma-based emotional processes and/or symptoms; others, notably cognitive behavioural therapy (CBT), have evolved to offer trauma-specific options and a core range of disorder-focused or resilience-building options; whilst a few such as family therapy do not claim to target trauma, but are nevertheless indispensable in targeting primary or secondary difficulties which either lead to further traumatization or hinder its resolution.

Setting goals that mirror both the child's needs and the tailored intervention are clearly imperative; but so are the chosen research and service outcomes. These are made more complicated by ongoing debates related to theoretical, measurement and clinical issues. Are counselling and psychotherapies meant to relieve symptoms, and thus follow a disease-driven health/medical model? Or re-process dysfunctional emotional processes, i.e. be more aligned to their psychoanalytic origins but sometimes in tension with resource-related expectations? Or promote well-being, which is philosophically different from the mere absence of symptoms, and has largely been influenced by positive psychology? I would argue that all three objectives are important, but we are still constrained by suitable and sensitive outcome measures in terms of the last two categories, i.e. the detection of therapeutic change other than client satisfaction, and the demonstration of a direct impact on the child's behaviour. More importantly, we lack the integration of these three models that often still remain rather uncomfortable in each other's company. As children's needs cannot satisfactorily be met by an 'either-or' philosophy, one would anticipate more convergence in the near future, thus cross-fertilization of theoretical and practice perspectives.

Other challenges include the cultural adaptation of interventions in relation to the constructs of trauma and mental health, the incorporation of user perspectives, connection with wider public health and natural community systems and being more attuned to vulnerable children and youth's lifestyles and other characteristics. We cannot assume that intervention x can automatically be transferred from a western out-patient mainstream clinic to a service for young offenders in the same country, and even less so to a low-income country and resource-limited setting. On a positive note though, it is currently a question of *how* rather than *whether* these interventions could be transferred in different contexts.

As already discussed, there are also some difficult boundaries to acknowledge in relation to the previous chapter on therapeutic applications, i.e. on the adapted use of therapeutic frameworks and techniques for frontline practitioners and caregivers. This is a better way of making the distinction than between specialist vs non-specialist interventions, as it is based on children's needs, and consequently service objectives. This is the reason for viewing therapeutic approaches in their totality and through a service lens, rather than in individual detail, which can be supplied in more detail by targeted texts. When considering interventions in a bigger picture, their common origins, complementarity, indications and, crucially, limitations become more apparent. The following list is not exhaustive, but rather a practical and critical contextualization of interventions to be used in adverse circumstances, and for vulnerable children and young people.

Making sense of traumatic memories

Taking a historical overview, it can be difficult to distinguish between the evolutionary stages of a therapeutic modality. A range of approaches have been specifically designed in the course of the last decade to help children (and, indeed, adults) re-process their traumatic experience. Even this concept can occasionally cause confusion, as trauma can refer to primary or secondary experiences, or to the symptomatic presentation of post-traumatic stress disorder (PTSD), which is a rather narrow perception of the effects of trauma. But if one goes back to the very beginning of therapy and Freud's psychoanalysis, some of the objectives and terminology were not that different. Recent interventions are really targeted off-shoots,

104 Therapeutic interventions

which have been tested with vulnerable groups of children who share certain characteristics.

What does re-processing the trauma really mean? It implies making sense of the experience, re-writing the script, developing a variable degree of understanding and ultimately being able to move on with life, or, put simply, re-telling the story to oneself through different therapeutic means. The resulting broad term 'narrative therapy' can be applied through various techniques based on common principles. Trauma is viewed as separate from the child, whose memories, beliefs and values are the key tools for an alternative meaning. The client is perceived as capable of using their own skills through conversations with the therapist to reconstruct their reality. They are encouraged to use their own values and knowledge to solve future problems. Needless to say in many cases even young children may intellectually know the answers but, without help, struggle emotionally to make sense of their experiences until they reconstruct them in a coherent script.

In light of the available branches of narrative therapy, it is interesting to consider a few interventions as a demonstration of their origins and evolution, as well as their increasing adaptation for vulnerable targeted groups. Narrative exposure therapy constitutes such a modality. This is a short-term intervention based on testimony, CBT and emotion-processing therapies. The child's fragmented memories are testified, linked to sensations or other experiences and re-processed into a coherent narrative through a range of techniques and materials such as paint, flowers, stones or rope (the latter as a lifeline). Narrative exposure therapy was specifically developed for children who have experienced complex trauma such as abuse, gender-based violence and war conflict. It has been implemented and evaluated in partnership with NGOs in pretty 'tough' contexts across several African countries.

These challenging applications of narrative exposure therapy can be traced back to some of its origins. Testimonial psychotherapy was developed as a brief psycho-social cross-cultural approach to trauma. The child is enabled to map their fragmented memories of trauma, before recovering their emotional and social resources. This cross-cultural origin made testimonial therapy more accessible to children from diverse backgrounds, often escaping from war zones through migration.

Eye movement desensitization and reprocessing (EMDR) therapy is another example of an evolving modality that integrates different approaches. In addition, it has a physiological basis in the way it tackles the processing of information by the brain. Its aim is to build new connections between traumatic memories and adaptive information through recalling images and beliefs, while paying attention to external stimuli guided by the therapist, then discussing what was brought up in the course of the exercise. In this way, the same material and experiences can be viewed in a less distressing manner by disentangling the effect of sensations and feelings. Although EMDR is widely used with victims of abuse, most of its indications are problem or symptom-focused (predominantly PTSD and a variety of stress-related conditions), and this could be a factor in its choice by both client and therapist.

CBT has several indications, supporting evidence and misinterpretations. A variation of CBT programmes may specifically target underlying anxiety, depression, aggression or offending behaviours, enhance coping strategies and, more recently, trauma-based symptoms. The latter has been used with abused or refugee youth. Like parent training, the structure, expansion and availability of CBT can result in false expectations that it can 'easily' be applied or used indiscriminately to achieve multiple outcomes. To avoid dilution and loss of fidelity, training, clear goal-setting and sharing information with the young person and their caregivers are all essential. In a sense, cognitive restructuring has similarities with narrative approaches in rewriting the child's script, albeit through beliefs which may have a secondary impact on emotions.

Interestingly, the majority of psychodynamic or psychoanalytic-based approaches would argue that, although they originate from children and adults who have suffered trauma, this was not their primary objective, at least not symptomatically. Instead of being reconstructed or directed, semi-conscious or unconscious experiences are released through free associations in the therapeutic space and re-enacting them in the client-therapist relationship.

The child or young person's developmental capacity, means of communication or simply preference can indicate the choice of tools, i.e. using play or a range of creative modes such as music, drama or art. These can be particularly useful for children or young people who cannot easily articulate their inner experiences, like refugee children with learning difficulties. Goals and expectations should be clearly defined and communicated respectively, as emotional regulation is a different objective through a different process from re-experiencing trauma, or making links between the past and the present. Therapy duration and therapist competencies vary accordingly.

Client-centred or humanistic counselling has common factors in relation to the process of therapeutic change with other approaches. Again, there is variation in terms of goal-setting and duration, with examples being targeting bullying or dealing with grief – an interesting concept in itself of trying to compartmentalize traumatic experiences. This could be more manageable for some young people and restrictive for others, whilst part of the therapeutic journey for the majority.

The integration of trauma-focused approaches does not end at the crossroads of related theories and therapy schools. Individual and environmental paths are increasingly being crossed in involving caregivers (usually adoptive parents or foster carers) in different contexts. Theraplay has already been discussed in the context of enhancing the quality of the attachment in a parent-child relationship through play and other activities, with varying involvement of the adult. In child-parent psychotherapy, the focus is on the dyad rather than the individuals. This can be particularly useful when parent and child have jointly experienced trauma such as domestic violence or immigration, and/or where the trauma has affected the relationship. In addition to the trauma and attachment-focused aspects such as emotional regulation, attention is given to safety, daily living and reciprocity in the relationship.

Family attachment narrative therapy is an interesting combination of approaches with the parent or caregiver re-telling the story. It is the parent or caregiver rather than the therapist who helps the child reconstruct their narrative by talking through

106 Therapeutic interventions

the child's development from the beginning, as they would have liked it to have been had the child been living with them from the outset. This third-person narrative targets both the healing of the past and the strengthening of the present relationship.

Therapeutic relief given by touching upon the trauma

'Do children always need therapy to recover from trauma?' was a post-training question at a European workshop. My response was, 'No, people can use their own resources, or they may not be ready; importantly, it may not feel right for them, and they should have a choice.' My questioner was visibly relieved, 'I am not a specialist, but this is good to hear.'

Human pathways are not easy to predict, i.e. how and when a person is ready and prepared to tackle their painful past – assuming that therapy is available. Some children and their carers may seek symptomatic relief, as discussed in the previous chapter, predominantly through behavioural strategies, which may not at first glance be related to the trauma, although sleep disturbance or emotionally dysregulated aggression in a child with a known history of trauma should not be viewed in isolation. Nevertheless, the goals and strategies of tackling those symptoms are clearly different.

There are also 'intermediate' approaches, which primarily aim at enhanced and more adaptive coping, albeit by targeting signs or behaviours that are the direct outcomes of trauma. The reason I called them intermediate is because they do not avoid referring to those experiences and their links (as, for example, a behavioural regime to improve sleep routines might), but do not re-process the trauma either. Dialectical behavioural therapy (DBT), for example, integrates techniques from different psychotherapeutic approaches in regulating emotions, acknowledging and synthesizing different perspectives, breaking down and analysing maladaptive behaviours and enhancing interpersonal problem-solving, whilst encouraging the young person to accept themselves. Its indication primarily for young people with (often controversially defined) borderline personality disorders is not exclusive, but its primary indication is when a young person fluctuates between deliberate self-harm, aggressive outbursts and relationship difficulties that inhibit other therapeutic and more reflective attempts. Through DBT many young people, such as older adolescents in residential care or care leavers, can rediscover a sense of self-containment and control over this frightening cycle, and some may use this as a stepping stone to a more searching therapeutic attempt.

Motivational interviewing and its version of brief motivational therapy have been established in even harder to engage circumstances, i.e. with drug users, young offenders or homeless young people, on the assumption that this might be the only chance to transmit a glimpse of hope, trust and control in their overwhelming life circumstances. Both these lifestyles and their associated behaviours lead to mistrust of any perceived authority, for which reason conventional appointments are unlikely to work. So, opportunities for contact at drop-in centres, probation settings or on the street had to be seized. This non-judgemental, goal-directed type of counselling aims at changing behaviours by helping young people realize and work through their ambivalent emotions, and by unravelling their inner motivation for change through the release of their strengths. This has been found to reduce illicit drugs use and offending, equip young people to deal with anger and to protect themselves from domestic violence and sexually transmitted diseases, and encourage future therapeutic engagement. The nature of its clientele and provision, initially as a 'one-off' chance, is particularly suited to mentors (including peer mentors), youth workers and practitioners within homeless, drug and alcohol, juvenile and mental health outreach services.

A range of anxiety management and relaxation techniques variably include breathing and lessening muscular tension. These techniques which may go beyond symptomatic relief to include cognitive reframing, whether formally structured (through tasks and diary-keeping) or spontaneous use by the young person when practising the exercises. Such programmes may also 'touch' upon traumatic experiences by targeting directly related anxiety (or PTSD) symptoms such as somatic or sensory presentations precipitated by reminders.

This leads us nicely to versions of meditation and mindfulness techniques, which help the young person concentrate, regain self-control, master anxiety symptoms and prevent the intrusion of distressing stimuli. Their increasing popularity, whether for therapeutic, well-being, spiritual or religious reasons, is interesting in that they are also among the oldest ones! These constitute good examples of body–mind integration, as well as east–west rapprochement. It is interesting to note the emergence of combined approaches that involve parents or by adding CBT techniques. This bodes well for the future, as such programmes will inevitably be used with more vulnerable groups and complex problems, as long as they are not diluted, and do not lose their fidelity and distinct strengths.

The involvement of parents and caregivers in relation to trauma has already been discussed in Chapter 7 in the context of enhancing their nurturing qualities in universal or targeted programmes. In specialist settings, interventions such as theraplay are increasingly used with adoptive parents and foster carers of children with a range of attachment difficulties, usually emotional dysregulation. The extent of the child, parent/caregiver and dyadic involvement in sessions varies, depending on the weight of concerns in a given family, as much as the length of input. In that respect, attachment theory has been incorporated in different approaches such as play therapy in this framework, parent training in the development of training programmes – as we will discuss in Chapter 12 – and a range of family therapies.

The influence of family therapy, largely – although not solely – of the systemic model, has both generic and specific implications. Adoptive parents, foster carers or families of young people who offend (predominantly teenagers) may face the same relationship and communication difficulties as any other family that would indicate referral to a family therapy service. One needs to remain conscious of not being unduly pre-occupied with the impact of trauma, and to establish when problems and behaviours are in the here and now. Even when trauma has affected relationships in the past, the focus of a family therapy course might still be on such current stressors.

108 Therapeutic interventions

Systemic training offers a valuable perspective in viewing complex needs, which are common among these groups of children and young people, both in terms of the sub-systems surrounding the child (family, school and community – thus consistent with the ecological systems framework) and the agencies involved. As the complexity of needs is acknowledged to increase both the indication and the fragmentation of the services involved with the child, distancing oneself from the case and adopting a systemic lens to consider what drives, pressurizes, brings together or pulls apart agency sub-systems can offer a different perspective and unlock difficult situations. This can be particularly important to professionals working on the interface of different agencies such as social workers. Another valuable contribution of systemic theory is in approaching staff groups or units that are central to the care of vulnerable children and youth such as refugee children (reception or other centres), children in care (different types of care homes), offenders (secure units, legal or community teams) and homeless youth (shelters, community centres or teams). Skills can relate to developing operational criteria, consultation, liaison and training, in addition to individual contact. Moreover, different family therapy models and attachment and trauma-focused therapies have crossed their own borders in coming up with combined approaches. These skills are still to be applied more effectively with multi-need groups such as refugee or homeless families, i.e. outside specialist clinics. There are also emerging examples where family therapy or family support combine theoretical fidelity with pragmatic implementation, in order to prevent family placement breakdowns or to reintegrate children in care to their families of origin.

Indications and misunderstandings of medication

Pharmacological treatment is not directly indicated for trauma-related conditions, at least as a first-line evidence-based intervention. Instead, this has a rather by proxy association with – not uncommon – concurrent disorders, i.e. attention deficit hyperactivity disorder (ADHD), depression, severe anxiety, obsessive-compulsive disorders (OCD), sleep problems and psychosis. With the exception of psychosis, where medication is first-line treatment, this is not the case for mild presentations of ADHD and depression, or for the majority of children with anxiety, OCD and sleep problems.

The particular challenges with vulnerable groups relate to appropriate assessment and diagnosis, clarity of goals, understanding of the problem by the child and adults involved, safety, compliance and monitoring. Assessment can be constrained by the lack of detailed history (such as with refugee children), consistent observations among carers (e.g. in residential settings), and disentanglement from attachment-related (especially difficult for ADHD) and other behaviours. The impact of such behaviours may be greater for carers and staff, and therefore lead to expectations that these behaviours will decrease or subside with the use of medication, with inevitable disappointment and lack of compliance when such is not the case. This is particularly hard for children on the move, and those living in chaotic and constantly changing environments. If one adds the impact of such a lifestyle on monitoring and providing clear feedback on the child's response or, crucially, side-effects, it is extremely difficult to reach an evidenced opinion on the appropriateness of medication, the risks involved, the need for change or discontinuation: 'It hasn't worked, she has run away from the care home . . .' Lack of adult supervision and safe keeping of medication and inconsistent dosage pose their own risks. These problems do not apply only to individual carers but to institutions as well. Again, staff groups can be particularly anxious about reducing or withdrawing medication in the absence of response to a specific mental health problem, in the hope that it might help improve the child's behaviour, which was not an indication in the first place.

Multimodal programmes and principles

Certain intensive programmes have been designed to reflect children's and young people's complex needs, non-response to single interventions, risk and the escalation of problem behaviours which result in either incarceration or accommodation into care. The most widely known and evaluated programme is multisystem therapy (MST), which predominantly targets such groups of young people. Its principles are based on combined input at individual, family, school and community level (here comes the ecological systems framework again!), and intensive application for a defined period. It may be costly to provide all these facets and at such intensity, however some evaluation studies have found the outcomes to mitigate high-cost residential placements. As the developers of the programme quote the danger of losing fidelity by diluting it, and consequently not reaping the expected benefits, the adoption and implementation of MST and similar approaches requires policy and funding commitment, at least for a period of a few years. Similar characteristics apply to Treatment Foster Care, although possibly with less expansion and evaluation than MST. Some findings are inconclusive, but they suggest that this could be indicated more to children than to adolescents in foster care. Irrespective of the issues of cost, fidelity and training implications, the wider lesson of these programmes is that complex and entrenched needs do not usually respond to a single agency or intervention; even if they do in the short term, they are likely to recur. The irony is that multimodal programmes were set up in the US, where it is more difficult to implement them in the public sector, because of insurance barriers; whereas countries with a reasonable level of statutory health, social care and education services, namely in western Europe, Canada and Australia, go through policy cycles and frequent re-organizations to control escalating costs, but which largely affect vulnerable groups who require consistency and commitment in any investment.

110 Therapeutic interventions

CASE SCENARIO 1

Ellie is 15 years old and lives in a children's home in a high-income country. She has had previous placements in foster care, which usually broke down because of incidents of deliberate self-harm and running away. Ellie was sexually abused by an older cousin in her early teenage years while living with her mother and stepfather. Following disclosure to a teacher and a prolonged investigation, Ellie was eventually accommodated in care when she was 14 years old. Her mother washed her hands of her and said that 'it was all Ellie's fault' and that she 'wanted nothing more to do with her'.

Ellie developed a good relationship with her first foster carer, but her risky behaviours led to her move one year later. She has been living at the children's home for six months. Her behaviours have not changed much, it is more that the staff are used to them by now. Ellie has no close friends, and recently stopped going to school. She likes her key worker and often talks to her when they are on their own, mostly before going to bed. She tells her that she wants to talk, it is just that she doesn't trust anyone. Ellie's social worker has arranged twice for her to meet with a psychotherapist. Ellie tends to go for a few sessions, then drop out: 'It's too painful, I can't do it.' Then she cries, apologizes and asks to go back.

The staff are split on how to respond. Some think that Ellie should have therapy to 'get it off her chest', but no one helps. Others think she is not ready. Ellie's social worker finds herself in the middle, and under a lot of pressure when Ellie ends up in hospital after taking an overdose.

Questions

1　What should the staff and Ellie do?
2　How should they engage Ellie?
3　How should they relate to external agencies?

Crucially, how should they reach a decision?

Some thoughts for consideration

- Ellie appears ambivalent towards therapy, which is reflected in her high-risk behaviours of acting out her distress, rather than being able to articulate and process it. There is little point in pushing Ellie to attend sessions or to continue indefinitely, in the hope that she will manage to attend. This does not mean that she cannot receive therapeutic help or that interventions are mutually exclusive.

Therapeutic interventions **111**

- As Ellie appears to form some relationships, building her trust in adults, followed by her peers and hopefully her return to school should remain a priority and not be put on hold until Ellie engages in therapy. All levels of engagement (individual, care home, school, community) should be maximized to strengthen Ellie's resilience.
- Behavioural approaches can help manage risk, while ensuring consistency between caregivers and other professionals.
- Trusting relationships offer good opportunities for Ellie to decide what type of help she wants.
- Depending on availability, brief therapeutic approaches could be appropriate in helping Ellie to manage her acute distress and behaviours, and to develop alternative adaptive coping strategies. These could include CBT or DBT (without implying by using the latter that Ellie has personality difficulties, as this is not possible to assess from the above information, and Ellie is relatively young for such a conclusion).
- Trauma-focused therapies or psychodynamic psychotherapy to help Ellie address a number of experiences and vulnerabilities would require a degree of readiness and capacity to process. This readiness will have to be judged and discussed openly with Ellie before further attempts are made to re-engage her in such a modality.
- It would be both confusing and inappropriate to initiate different types of interventions at the same time 'just in case one of them works'. This would disengage and alienate Ellie even more. Instead, a sequential plan from resilience-building to therapeutic exploration is more likely to succeed, again by defining and monitoring goals and expectations.

CASE SCENARIO 2

A new care home for refugee young people has recently opened in a middle-income country. The manager has approached you, as the clinical psychologist at the busy local child mental health service, to offer input. The request is to help these young people in much need to 'get comfort from talking'. A colleague suggests that you find out which is the 'most appropriate therapy', then perhaps 'start a group'.

Questions

1   How would you respond to this request?
2   Which factors would you consider in your caseload, service duties and expectations?
3   Which challenges would you anticipate before deciding on a resource-effective model?

112 Therapeutic interventions

Some thoughts for consideration

- You first need to step back and take stock of the situation across both agencies, before you explore options for their future links. Jumping in out of goodwill and external pressure to help through therapy can lead to messy situations later.
- Assess the young people's needs and duration of stay, staffing capacity and competencies at the care home and level of organizational commitment.
- Consider your own competencies, capacity and potential to accommodate additional caseload, and/or whether a financial agreement with the care home would be possible.
- If you have minimal capacity, the most effective use of it would be through consultation and training for the care home staff to enhance their skills, which would impact on the whole group of young people.
- Before deciding on therapeutic input it is necessary to determine the model (universal for all young people who all carry several risk factors, or targeted for those who develop specific mental health problems), the therapeutic framework and objectives and whether the treatment is to be offered individually or in groups (while balancing the respective pros and cons).
- How will the service respond to psychiatric requests and emergencies, both in relation to refugee youth who receive therapeutic input and those who are not?
- Will there be special arrangements with the care home for direct referral pathways, or will the staff need to follow existing standard procedures? All these are important points, as any setting with vulnerable residents is likely to generate substantive additional service demands.

CASE SCENARIO 3

You have just been appointed as the senior designated mental health practitioner for a large international NGO. Your remit is to 'provide psychosocial support in a large post-conflict region'. You are trained in a particular therapeutic modality, which your organization favours to roll out among your teams of practitioners and volunteers. You are under some pressure to start soon.

Questions

1 How should you approach this challenge?
2 How would you define and distinguish between service, professional and practice issues?
3 What process would you put in place?

Some thoughts for consideration

- This is primarily a service, rather than a practice or therapy-related question. It needs a lot of consideration and discussions with key stakeholders, before reaching consensus on a number of issues.
- The different components of your new role potentially encompass management, development, training, supervision and direct therapeutic work.
- There needs to be clarity on priorities, expectations and a staged plan in achieving these, as it is unlikely that you can address them all in a short period of time.
- Organizational issues are likely to make more impact, so they need to be addressed first.
- These issues do not need to preclude direct therapeutic input, if anything this will be refreshing and keep your enthusiasm and influence alive. However, the choice of a therapeutic approach should not be driving 'bottom-up' such an exciting but also potentially overwhelming initiative. Perhaps you should think more after reading the next chapter on service aspects!

11

ALWAYS A SERVICE MODEL, WHATEVER THE CONSTRAINTS

Absence of service modelling

'But we have very little, we are not a service.'

I would argue that every provision to children and young people, whatever context, whatever the level of resources and wider systems, constitutes a service. Consequently, every service needs a philosophy and resulting model behind it. Unfortunately, a large proportion of our services remains largely driven by good theoretical underpinning and continuously improving clinical or practice thinking, but is often not set up in a rationalized, model-driven and evidence-based way. Unsurprisingly, the evidence remains weak on why we set up roles, teams, agencies, services or even organizations, the way we do.

When one traces back the rationale for setting up or running a service, the answers can sometimes be baffling: 'we always did it this way', 'other similar services are set up like ours' or 'the founder was very keen on this, somehow it has carried on without much change'. Large policy reviews are equally culpable of avoiding difficult questions that may lead to tough answers and choices, usually related to cost. For those reasons, policy and service reviews often become trapped in debating terminology (mental health, well-being or psychological well-being?), repeating literature searches or surveys on the extent of children's needs or being distracted by professional groups defending their territories.

A comprehensive, analytical and consequently productive process would be to tackle service questions such as:

Which is the target population?
What evidence can we draw on their needs?
Which of these needs are we going to address?
What is the available level of resources (not necessarily the same as the budget)?

Which competencies are best placed to fulfil these roles within the existing resources?

What is the evidence that drives the implementation of these service roles (therapeutic interventions as well as indirect activities like consultation)?

How do all these strands hold together?

Additional questions that are particularly threatening will not disappear by ignoring them, as these relate to: defining outcomes in demonstrating how children's needs are met (varying from symptomatic relief to improved quality of life and client satisfaction); setting up a monitoring system that regularly feeds into the model; establishing close and transparent relationships between those who pay for (commissioner) the service and those who deliver it (provider); and being open about which needs it isn't realistic to address, at least not at this point in time.

Improved tools, more sophisticated and targeted approaches, training choices for staff, public pressure to demonstrate the high quality of care as well as value for money have set some parameters in recent years to develop service thinking and justification for decision-making. These parameters should be the same for all agencies (or services), although the balance of choices might be different for systems primarily run for profit, where outcomes and clinical choices can be adjusted accordingly, whether deliberately or by default, thus resulting in the use of brief, symptom-driven and uni-dimensional treatment. In contrast, public sector systems have flexibility in setting their objectives in a broader context for children and society, but are under increasing pressure to slash funding in the face of increasing demand, an expanding aging population and new costly treatments such as in cancer care.

These are the general principles and challenges for all children's services. The examples above may be predominantly related to the health sector, but similar dilemmas can be construed for education (learning vs learning plus welfare), care systems (large vs small children's homes, minimal vs skilled and supported foster carers) and the juvenile system (containment vs rehabilitation). If one adds vulnerability to the equation, these difficult choices increase, and so are often 'best left alone'. The reasons have been well demonstrated, in terms of children's complex needs, lengthy and adverse backgrounds, multiple care involvement, high mobility and lack of advocacy, to name but the key ones. The challenge, therefore, is to concurrently address *both* vulnerability *and* service modelling at the same time. If you also consider the overwhelming needs and gaps of vulnerable children in low-income countries and conflict areas, you may want to put this book away now! And yet, as in the formulation of care plans for children with complex needs, the more testing a situation is the more focused and clearer the service rationale and solutions should be.

As the underpinning philosophy and principles are common to all, these are initially discussed across all societies and systems. Their implementation into service delivery though will subsequently depend on the system context of each country.

116 Service issues

For this reason, we will follow a rather artificial split between high-income and low-income countries in the consideration of service issues. Middle-income countries will inevitably need to borrow ideas from both, as statutory services are present and growing, but remain pretty stretched. It should also be acknowledged that training should largely be viewed in a service context, but for pragmatic reasons this will be addressed separately in the next chapter.

Policy encompassing vulnerability

As already mentioned, service considerations arise from a mixture of evidence on children's needs, theoretical perspectives which have not always been tested on the ground and bottom-up practice innovation. Hopefully, in a few years these components will filter across each other, and thus give us more confidence in setting up services for particular groups and in specific circumstances.

The main challenge is that one ideally requires related and fairly well developed sectors (led by relevant government departments), i.e. in welfare, education, health and youth justice, all of which should acknowledge the particular needs of vulnerable children and be favourable to integration across departments; and an overarching policy that cuts across and joins up uni-sector policies, thus giving leverage for funding and joint initiatives. This is a tough call, as it requires not only even development across sectors and departments, but also a government that ideologically embraces growth, rather than containment and crisis management. Unfortunately, many western governments are currently adopting the opposite stance, with vulnerable groups being left on the margins rather than troubling government thinking. It usually takes a disaster, which is more likely to affect such groups, and some public and media pressure for half-hearted and panic-driven measures to be put in place. The *Every Child Matters* policy in the UK in 2003 was a notable exception in approaching vulnerable children's needs from multiple and integrated policy perspectives (welfare, education and health). In most cases, an economic argument on the benefits of combining forces and resources is more effective than emotive pressure, with advocacy and user groups exercising increasing influence. These groups, together with non-statutory organizations, are also more likely to fill the void that governments may not want to touch. Consequently, this dynamic means that changes in ministerial direction do not necessarily demolish inter-agency initiatives on the ground, they just make them harder to sustain.

The more 'inter' the better, but without dilution

National policy will facilitate local implementation, although regional and local governments can follow their own paths, for better or for worse, notably when their links from the umbilical cord are weakened in favour of independent providers. There is purpose, theory, justification and cost-efficiency behind professions, disciplines, teams, agencies, services and organizations working together. Yet, this remains notoriously elusive, for a number of established reasons such as different cultures, competing priorities or simply tribal squabbles.

In the case of vulnerable children, it is essential that they gain maximum benefit from the complementary skills and input of practitioners (inter-disciplinary or inter-professional), agencies (inter-agency) and organizations (inter-sector). This philosophy should ideally transcend commissioning and practice. When such relationships and processes are sound, everyone enjoys the rewards and interventions become slick. At the same time, there is a risk of dilution of skills, repetition and waste of resources in endless meetings and circular discussions when the principles are in place, but these inter-agency interventions flounder because of lack of leadership at the strategic and operational level. Selecting and agreeing a lead organization to lead this process is a step forward, but can be a challenge in its own right.

There are parallels between interpersonal, therapeutic and organizational relationships. They are not built overnight, are hard work to establish and even harder to sustain, particularly in the face of ongoing government policy changes. Continuity at both the strategic and operational level certainly helps, backed up by clear processes and forums, where the inevitable tensions will be addressed rather than left to simmer. There should be clear demarcation of responsibilities within and across organizations and the formation of joint commissioning, planning and delivery groups. These groups have different roles, but still need to understand each other. If policy-makers or managers cannot apply principles to practice, and in reverse if practitioners are only interested in their narrow field, the vacuum between these groups will increase.

What does joint commissioning mean for vulnerable groups? It recognizes the importance of agencies collaborating to meet vulnerable children's needs, and goes beyond routine implementation by joining up staff resources and setting conditions on how the funding should be best used. This funding could be given to one of the collaborating agencies to deliver the service, could be shared by more than one agency, but with expectations of how the service should be run, or be given to a third agency to deliver the contract. Clarity on objectives and the whole process are essential where multiple stakeholders are involved.

Of course, the devil is often in the detail, and success will very much rely on personalities and collaboration on the ground. Nevertheless, transparent rules and expectations should be communicated from the outset. These may need time to be worked through within each organization, depending on staff readiness or resistance to change their working style. It is natural to feel somewhat exposed and threatened, whilst also excited to share new ideas and skills. Consequently, this is a process that needs to be led and managed pro-actively.

From joint care pathways to joint care plans

What does this all mean for children and young people? As demonstrated by a number of studies, there is a clear paradox in that the more needs a child has, the less likely they often are to receive timely and appropriate interventions. If they do, it may come from one agency, or sequentially, or in response to a crisis, when the child finds it even harder to engage. This means that the vulnerable child (homeless,

118 Service issues

in care or refugee) is not able to access the usual mainstream service pathways (or, in this case, barriers), such as through parent referral to a family doctor or via the child's school.

Joint care pathways and direct access can instead be tailored to the child or young person's profile and needs, rather than the other way round. Where or who are they most likely to live, trust or attend? This is where the entry point to the service should be. Examples include children's homes, refugee centres and related community agencies, community or residential juvenile settings, adoption agencies, shelters for victims of domestic violence and drop-in centres for homeless youth.

Next comes the challenge of services being accessed promptly and 'jointly' from that entry point. Different interesting models have been established such as wrap-around services, one-stop-shops and school health centres. Assess, engagement, efficiency and service equity can thus go hand in hand. A key worker or co-ordinator, with whom the child has a confiding relationship, can be the focal point of service activities, making decisions about how the child's needs are best met by suitable agencies. This may mean that more agencies are required in some cases; whilst on other occasions this can save costly duplication or agencies being added 'just in case', thus increasing the child's confusion and frustration. Ideally, mental health input should start here. If this is not possible, the next best scenario is to have a direct access route as part of this joint pathway, rather than initiating it from scratch, and thus slowing down the whole process.

The next stage of a jointly agreed integrated care plan will come naturally. 'Integrated' is more than the sum of the parts. For example, it may mean that individual counselling and a school-based programme are complementary and can be implemented concurrently, rather than sequentially. Or, in other cases, the key worker may judge that the child cannot cope with both the counselling and the school programme at the same time, and set priorities instead in the child's interests. What really matters is that the care plan is tailored to the child's needs and that agencies are immediately clear, rather than waiting for each other to make an assessment and (hopefully) let the others know. Systems should be flexible and responsive. If, for example, a child engages with a mentor and feels ready to see a therapist next, this small window of opportunity should not be wasted through cumbersome and time-consuming referral loops, by which time the child will have disengaged again.

No need for specialists, but rather for specialist competencies

All practitioners need to develop core skills first, through their professional and their service role. Within that capacity, almost all generic staff will come in contact with children who have suffered trauma. On the other hand, practitioners who predominantly work with a vulnerable group may still hold a generic caseload, or wish to return to a generic post in the future. Consequently, it is preferable to build specialist skills from a sound base of general knowledge and skills.

The significance of developing skills in trauma, attachment-focused or other targeted interventions has already been demonstrated. Training, for example, in

Service issues **119**

theraplay or EMDT would be highly relevant and generalizable in other areas of work. The additional skills acquisition to be considered here relates to the children's needs, systems and services context. It is not easy to put across such 'real life' messages without some 'hands on' experience. If not in a service post already, such training placements should combine visits to care homes and homeless hostels, and meetings with representative agencies with case-based experience, preferably over a sufficient period of time to witness changes, both positive and negative, and thus really grasp children's complex needs. It is also rather different to attend an inter-agency meeting as an observer compared to in a case-holding role, in order to experience the challenge of making difficult decisions amidst tensions and pressure.

The importance of indirect service activities

Agencies, staff groups and individual practitioners can fulfil their wider systemic functions in several ways. Planning, sharing, co-ordinating and integrating service issues (usually at management level) or children's care (usually at practitioner level) are central to this model. Other activities may have a more purposeful and ongoing function, without involving children. Consultation is particularly prominent in inter-agency contexts, even more so in relation to vulnerable groups, yet it is notoriously difficult to define, agree and measure. This can come across as deceptively easy, or be perceived as hierarchical between agencies. It can also be confusing in terms of responsibility, by misidentifying it with line management, which should be provided within the practitioner's organization; or with supervision, which should be provided separately, whether internally or by a designated external supervisor.

Consultation does not imply that one knows better. A children's home group will have better knowledge of the ground and of children in their care than the mental health practitioner. It is not about advice either, although some can be given. It is more about providing space to connect different philosophies, cultures and practices, to the benfit of the children. Its planning and setting up are worth sufficient time to get consensus among managers and staff, test commitment on everyone's behalf (no point in arranging meetings when staff will be constantly distracted by youth, crises or the phone), set a realistic level of input (perhaps target one rather than all children's homes in one area to start with) and define its parameters. Consultation models include discussing any systemic or child-related issues brought by the consultees, systematically reviewing all children, irrespective of their needs, and ad hoc discussion on a particular child that is causing concern. Because of the time and cost involved, it is important to formally include these indirect activities in service agreements, evaluate their value and impact in simple ways and monitor the need for re-adjustment of the model.

Genuine user participation

The increasing acknowledgement that it is useful for people who use services to have the opportunity to influence their quality is still going through the motions.

120 Service issues

Emerging ways appear to range on a spectrum from complete lack of awareness that clients, particularly children, have a voice, to a tokenistic participation, but also include some meaningful demonstrations that it can really work. In relation to vulnerable populations, we need to add a few dimensions of involving fragile parents and even more fragile children of chronologically and functionally young age.

Unsurprisingly, user participation started with adults, including powerful and influential examples of people with mental illness, followed by parents of children with physical health or developmental conditions like autism, who have demonstrated multiple ways of bringing change, through pressure groups, advocacy, policy and service input. Indeed, governments are often more inclined to listen to such groups or networks, although a vacuum still exists in the ideal triangulation of policy-user-service provision. Nevertheless, there are positive examples of parents attending policy and service forums, training programmes and even staff appointment panels. Threatening as some of these new processes might be, their dynamic can only challenge us all to try to grasp when interventions and services make a real impact on children, and to understand how to work through barriers of misperceptions, disengagement and mismatch of expectations.

The next step in user participation has been to involve young people, mostly older adolescents. Here, we are beginning to see direct relevance to mental health, with young people increasingly being prepared to speak up against stigma and adult-led service provision. This can lead to conflict with such adult-led practices and services that may not understand young people's needs as well as they should. Such boundaries should be disentangled and managed sensitively if we are to give young people a genuine voice.

In contrast, there have been almost no examples, never mind evidence, on how to involve children. The practical and ethical constraints are obvious, i.e. their lack of physical, cognitive and emotional capacity to replicate adult and adolescent participation. This is correct, but in no way does it justify the exclusion of those who primarily use services. It is simply terribly wrong! One could draw parallels with people with learning disability or dementia, where their carers act as their main voice, or where charity representatives fill that gap. These are useful, but only partial solutions. The main reason for which children are excluded is that we are scared of our lack of knowledge on how to meaningfully involve them, whether as researchers or service providers.

Answers possibly lie in the well-established therapeutic practice of directly assessing, getting information from and directly helping children from a very young age. Naturally, we do not expect them to turn up on their own or to complete lengthy forms. Instead, we can engage them as individuals in their own right, using developmentally appropriate techniques like play and drawing, but largely through trust building. Why can't we do the same in relation to user participation? Because of our inability to think beyond traditional advisory steering groups and to adapt accordingly. Also, perhaps because of our own cognitive limitation of equating user input to policy and service documentation and jargon. Or because of our social communicative limitation in translating what matters to children who use our services to policy and practice. There is evidence that, when all these factors are in place, children are perfectly capable of telling us in their own way what they have been told about coming to the service, how they have been prepared (or not), their fears and expectations, their impression of service environment and staff and, crucially, what would be helpful to them rather than to their parents or older siblings. Can we listen?

This may sound harsh, but it only gets worse when we move on to vulnerable groups. Do we really expect a homeless mother from a shelter for victims of domestic violence to turn up at a service meeting (even if driven there), read the technical agenda, understand jargon and feel confident to communicate how a service should improve? Or, in a similar scenario, a young care leaver or drug user off the streets? How about a younger child in foster care? They clearly can't, but they have no less right to express their opinion than a well-off service user living in stability. At least not according to the human rights book, although many decision-makers may not aspire to it. The answers are not simple, but there are a few. One needs to work around users' circumstances, adapt accordingly, relate to them individually or in smaller groups, seek their views outside traditional and rigid forums and, most importantly, respect them as equal human beings. Then they will have all the confidence and ability in the world to tell us what they really think and actually help us improve. I particularly witnessed this in participatory workshops with homeless mothers in the UK, as well as with parents, young people and community volunteers across Africa and Asia.

Are we making an impact? The ever-growing and changing role of service evaluation

Advances in service evaluation are driven by a number of factors, notably economic pressures to justify the use of resources and to demonstrate impact, improved options of methods and measures and a genuine need to know and improve what is on offer for children. There are also several constraints, predominantly the 'noise' of multiple factors (confounders) that are difficult to control for in real service research (contrasted with research centres), and which are compounded for vulnerable children and their constantly changing life circumstances. As with service users, these difficulties should not be an excuse for failing to address these questions.

Research will continue to improve, but services cannot stand still in the meantime. Incorporating an evaluative and critical ethos is a start, before putting IT and outcome measurement systems in place that put as little burden on practitioners as possible, albeit with the maximum return. In reality, the opposite pattern may be true at times, which results in some resistance to the whole evaluation concept. Another fallacy is that research can answer complex questions in a superficial way. Rather than hoping that the question 'Does it work?' can be answered in a short time, breaking it down into simpler but addressable sub-questions like 'Which outcome for which intervention/goal?' might be more realistic and effective in leading to the next stage of the evaluation process. Selecting sensitive and

122 Service issues

easy-to-complete outcome measures tailored to an intervention or service goal would help in that direction. Let us not underestimate the value of simple descriptive data that is already available, for example on referral patterns, help-seeking or service activities that can inform – rather than substitute – service decisions.

High-income countries

These broad groupings are, of course, pretty artificial in terms of welfare and health care systems. Overall, one could generally assume embedded child protection policies, relatively well-established care and juvenile procedures and settings, reasonably resourced multidisciplinary community and hospital-based teams and a range of competencies and training opportunities for practitioners. There are substantial differences too, largely on the extent of public sector involvement, which is in reverse proportion to technological and research advances in the US; and the variable strength of seamlessness between primary, secondary and tertiary services in western countries. Perhaps surprisingly, the level of resources does not necessarily imply well-established community services, as some well-funded health care systems are still rather overtly centralized and hospital-based. This is often related to cultural as much as economic reasons.

What is generally lacking is a systematic interface between existing child mental health services and other children's agencies, be it schools or social care settings. If one adds the variation in child policy (e.g. minimal age of criminal responsibility, admission to residential homes or responsibility to homeless youth and victims of domestic violence) and care systems (adoption, kinship, foster and residential care), not all that shines is gold for vulnerable groups in high-income countries. The weakening of links between central and local government, and between those and service providers, in countries like the UK increasingly affects the neediest groups, as they tend to fall off the radar. Non-statutory agencies and user-led groups play an increasingly influential role and can bring innovation, but their financially constrained initiatives are often short-term and not in tandem with other services.

Direction ideally needs to come from the top, with one overarching policy through a lead government department or ministry for children, and with sufficient clout. The next step is the identification of overlap, complementarity and gaps between sector policies, followed by a strategic plan to rationalize resources – naturally, also how to increase those, although one has to remain pragmatic. As repeatedly demonstrated throughout this text, vulnerable groups have characteristics that especially require inter-agency working and other principles of wrap-around services. If these principles are at least acknowledged and spelled out at national level, and are preferably followed by guidance, they can provide the impetus for local implementation. This will not automatically happen without financial and other conditions and parameters, but will at least encourage the initiation of local inter-agency dialogue and networks. This philosophy of child-centred inter-agency working tailored to the needs of vulnerable children should permeate different training levels, which will be discussed in the next chapter. Training though should

Service issues

be strongly linked to both policy and service development, rather than be developed in silo.

Low and middle-income countries

The priority should be to resist being overwhelmed by the discrepancy between the extent of needs and lack of resources. Both individuals and organizations should distance themselves even more than in high-income countries, define their target population and range of problems to tackle, map existing resources, set short and long-term goals and decide how to tackle these goals in an incremental way. There are different theoretical and organizational models for this, with Theory of Change being particularly popular in these contexts. Understanding the key stakeholders (local, national and international), their priorities and strengths and, particularly, their limitations and how to overcome them will be crucial. This may involve dealing with sensitive issues like corruption, autocratic regimes, tenuous relationships with the international community and negative attitudes (e.g. against mental health or women) among some of the main players themselves.

Attempts to influence policy should take advantage of critical incidents, increasing awareness and existing networks, in ensuring that key children's principles are in place, namely child protection, care procedures and access to primary and secondary health services. Naturally, opportunities to establish child mental health policies should be maximized, even if they cannot go beyond principles at first. These hurdles may have as much to do with mind-sets as with funding deficits. Embedding such documents with child-centredness and vulnerability, hence the need for collaboration between government departments as well as agencies on the ground, is ideal but may not be realistic to start with. Instead, implementation may follow slightly different paths. For example, concepts such as mental health literacy, emotional well-being or whole-school ethos may take time before they are endorsed by education authorities. For this reason, a more effective approach initially might be to demonstrate the benefits of psychologically supporting children's learning in order to improve their performance. If this principle is endorsed, its translation into guidelines that aim to incorporate learning and mental health approaches could form the next step.

The service map may be patchy and consist of different types of agencies. These include international organizations acting as both commissioners and providers, national or smaller NGOs which are either self-funded or dependent on external support (hence the need for a sustainability vision), relatively small and not consistently set up statutory services, universities and local government agencies or their substitutes (such as a charitable foundation acting on their behalf). Even if it is not possible to connect all those agencies in a short period, adopting this approach at a micro-level, for example building inter-agency and interprofessional networks around vulnerable populations such as slum areas or orphanages is possible, with the obvious initial objective of maximizing resources, before leading to more strategic partnerships.

124 Service issues

There should be clarity on staff roles, and a strategy for recruitment, development and retention, no matter (or rather especially when) practitioners operate in difficult circumstances. Induction, continuous training and supervision are all 'musts' for every agency. Similar principles should be adopted in the 'professionalization' of community volunteers and caregivers, irrespective of their financial or indirect rewards (ideally these should be put in place too). Upskilling, respect and input to service forums are examples of such, and should be implemented without losing their grassroots freshness and spontaneity. All these principles should be reflected in workforce plans, including the development of local trainers. Unfortunately, the inevitable drive for funding and the gradual increase in the size of both national and international organizations also increase the risk of distance between service users and their communities. Consequently, training strategies for policy-makers, senior and operational managers should aim at integrating policy, practice and user language and perspectives. There is no magic recipe for addressing the immense extent of children's needs, but rather a logical and systematic collection of inter-connected principles and approaches. If I had to choose one, it would probably be: 'No matter how small and challenging, every provision and initiative should *always* be underpinned by a service model approach!'

CASE SCENARIO 1

A recent service audit has confirmed your impression that your adolescent in-patient hospital unit admits a disproportionately high number of refugees, usually during a crisis. This seems in direct contrast with the well-documented high rates of unmet mental health needs for this vulnerable group.

Questions

1 What could possible reasons be for this finding?
2 Who else should you involve in these discussions?
3 How could you try to re-dress the problem?
4 Who are the important stakeholders within your service and externally?

Some thoughts for consideration

- In line with existing evidence on vulnerable groups, this possibly reflects the fragmentation of care pathways, in that refugee young people do not have easy access to community services and there is no continuity between those services and the tertiary (hospital) sector.
- It is worth mapping the key points in a refugee young person's service journey, then making contact and building relationships with service representatives who would be relevant to these key points such as refugee care homes, community refugee agencies, social services and community mental health teams.

- You are likely to come up with a disrupted line in this journey. What would it take to smoothen the line in establishing a network that could lead to jointly agreed care pathways in the future?
- If you achieve such a seamless care pathway for refugee young people, this is likely to be reflected in changes to your service user profile.

CASE SCENARIO 2

As the regional manager of a large international NGO, you have been asked to extend your organizational remit to also provide psychosocial care. No one is clear what this means yet in practice, but there is enthusiasm to move in that direction.

Questions

1. How would you approach this exciting opportunity within your organization and with external agencies?
2. Are there available models to use as a basis?
3. What is the existing evidence, if any?
4. What process would you determine in this direction? What pitfalls might you anticipate?

Some thoughts for consideration

- Checking and mapping these perceptions and expectations within your organization is a start, particularly if some views are conflicting.
- Are your core business and remit (e.g. humanitarian, child protection, primary health care or education) changing drastically, or do you want to maintain your core business but strengthen it with a psychosocial 'layer'?
- The resulting solutions and directions will be quite different. Adding to your remit will require new and different skills, some organizational redesign and a plan for connecting and integrating with existing structures and services.
- In contrast, strengthening skills with a 'p' (for psychosocial supports) will require adaptation of staff roles without substantially changing them, and this is not easy. Examples of similar changes were providing psychosocial training to a primary health care team in Bangladesh and to a child protection team in Uganda. One implication is setting boundaries and resisting the temptation to open new areas of demand that it will not be possible to meet, thus compromising or diluting existing strengths. Still, this is a nice dilemma to have!

12

TRAINING IN A SERVICE CONTEXT

Service connotations and principles

This may sound a strange heading. After all, isn't all child-related training relevant to practice? Psychotherapy, for example, has had enormous influence on how generations of practitioners in different settings approach their work with children, with a knock-on effect on teams, agencies and policy which now endorse a more child-centred philosophy. Yet, this has not often been service-driven, linked or implemented. Training choices tend to be influenced by individual preferences, career aspirations (whether in the public or private sector) or simply finding oneself in a working environment historically underpinned by a particular approach. All these reasons are absolutely fine, as they highlight initiative and they invariably match new skills with the trainee's therapeutic style.

However, the training process also introduces a strong element of chance, both for the practitioner and their agency. The increasing requirement to rationalize resources, develop and match competencies with children's needs and demonstrate their impact through client feedback and other evaluation means has begun to change our approach to training and education in general. Policy-makers, service managers and heads of professions can no longer afford to 'wait and see how the service pans out' or to hope that different acquired modalities will somehow fall into place. The evolution and expansion of available frameworks is also providing managers and practitioners alike with more choices. Overall they should try to balance emerging evidence, users' choices and children's needs in selecting the most appropriate intervention.

Client needs should frame the service objectives, which should in turn determine the relevant staff competencies. Consequently existing practitioners have to do more than just keep up with evidence and professional standards. Furthermore, staff recruitment no longer simply relies on criteria such as coming from a particular professional discipline and having acquired broad experience in the field. As children's agencies usually consist of small teams, diversity and complementarity rather than theoretical homogeneity are more likely to determine their sustainability and longevity. The question 'What type of service do we want to/can we provide?' will lead to what type of staff competencies we need, and not the other way round. On a larger scale, policy can only be implemented with a parallel workforce strategy. Service quality cannot be dictated, nevertheless it requires negotiation with staff on what skills are needed, how these could be acquired, the necessary service investment through time release and funding, how these skills will meet staff career aspirations and how this investment from both parties will have a healthy return and implementation with children and their families.

Inter-connectedness between training and service provision

We have extensively discussed why children with multiple and complex needs require inter-agency working, integrated approaches and clear communication. This would ensure efficient utilization of resources and improved user experience. It is only logical to extend this rationale to some aspects of training. Practitioners need a professional identity, focus and unique competencies to start with. These will enable them to function independently within their team and agency. The next step is not only to understand other team members but, crucially, to develop a common philosophy, just like a sports team. They will also be expected to operate in wider systems across different agencies, so it is important to establish a good understanding of their remit in terms of both strengths and limitations, create joined up thinking, set up networks and, ultimately, develop pathways and interventions to benefit children. For this reason, inter-agency training will have a direct impact on the nature and direction of the service; equally, an inter-agency service strategy will lead to and support inter-agency training. The extent and topics to be targeted within each profession or discipline, agency (interdisciplinary or interprofessional) and inter-agency grouping need to be thought through carefully in terms of staff time, funding and priorities. However, often the toughest challenge is the acceptance of the principle of interprofessional and inter-agency training, rather than agonizing over how to implement it.

For this reason, it is useful to consider the theories, applications and evidence arising from interprofessional education. I am embarrassed to say that I fully endorsed interprofessional interventions for many years when setting up programmes across health and local authority agencies and, more recently, in low and middle-income countries and conflict settings, without fully grasping their driving frameworks and principles. Had I done so it would have helped me address barriers much earlier, and thus facilitated the sustainability of both the training and the service model. Horder's theory appears particularly useful in planning the 'first and second order' of organizational and cultural change, before operational and educational structures are tackled. This seems parallel to the clinical practice of matching therapeutic theory with the child's needs and intervention goals, and of engaging clients before firing ahead with implementation. Cooper's complexity theory can help in weaving

128 Training in a service context

through overarching and often conflicting agency systems, and thus prevent mishaps by assuming that an inter-agency agreement will easily translate into, for example, inter-agency training, direct access to mental health services for children in care or health care access for homeless youth.

Learning objectives and format of delivery

Setting learning objectives from the outset is always important, even more so in the case of education provided in a service context. This can be particularly difficult for trainers, who may have experience in a particular topic, but are not automatically ready to relate to a certain audience, especially interprofessional groups. We are all relatively good at communicating knowledge and experience to those who are similar to us, usually in terms of profession. The more different the learner group though (in terms of discipline, experience, age, diversity, language, culture or working setting), the more the trainer's own skills and adaptability will be tested.

I have experienced training courses where trainers were approached by being asked 'What can you contribute?', instead of 'This is what the participants need, how can you best relate to it?' Next comes the question of 'how' to achieve this. Being knowledgeable about PTSD or depression will not be enough to equip practitioners with the necessary skills if they come from a different conceptual world. Discussions and patient planning between organizers and trainers can pay dividends. Even meticulous preparation though cannot fully equip one for the 'real thing' of meeting the learners, especially an interprofessional group with their own, new and evolving dynamics. Whilst attending an interesting family support workshop by an excellent Latin American NGO, one of the trainers asked me if I ever felt anxious when I was training. I laughed and said that I hoped that I was always anxious, because the moment I relaxed would lead to a complacent and ultimately poor delivery.

It is always a challenge, albeit an interesting one, to aspire to constructivist learning theory that enables trainer and trainees to build on previous knowledge and experience whilst remaining faithful to the learning objectives. There is no point in indulging in group dynamics and participants' stories if they divert from the pre-set goals. As in family therapy, working with the unknown, and processing interprofessional or other tensions in a boundaried and constructive way, can hopefully be mirrored by trainees in their practice. It may well be their first opportunity to work on a task with someone they previously perceived as being completely different and antagonistic.

All these real-life human interactions and learning tasks can best be achieved through interactive learning, discussion in pairs, small or larger groups, case material and role play. For those to be genuine and effective, one needs to build in time and facilitation. On the other hand, focusing on practical aspects without some understanding of the underpinning theory and evidence-base can leave participants confused about when and why to use an approach; furthermore, they may underestimate its limitations and have no Plan B if their preferred intervention does not work. Where more extensive courses allow for placements, observation and application within the learners' working environment between training sessions, these links between theory, evidence and practice become even clearer and clinical decisions can be made and justified with more confidence.

Trauma-related awareness and foundation knowledge

It is a good hypothesis that, when asked for their preference, the majority of practitioners will opt for training in therapeutic techniques such as cognitive behavioural therapy (CBT) or narrative therapy. This is fine, as long as it is based on key and broad knowledge, and is relevant to the client group and role. Realistically though this will be unlikely to be the case for most staff, at least to start with. The terms 'awareness' and 'foundation' training thus have different connotations for different groups.

The learning objectives of training programmes for frontline practitioners should be to provide: a broad understanding of the mechanisms through which different types of traumatic events affect children (not only through direct exposure but also through family and communities, which will inform further interventions); an understanding of how distress is expressed at different developmental stages; key knowledge on common mental health presentations; assistance in recognizing potential mental health problems, as appropriate to one's role; guidance on using information, observation and interviews to formulate a child's needs in a systematic way, before putting together a care plan; guidance based on available evidence that informs the selection of an intervention; and an interprofessional context in planning interventions to best meet children's needs. Admittedly, the last two objectives maybe a step too far for foundation training, nevertheless it is important to introduce these principles and rationale, and thus encourage a more critical and service-focused (contrasted with only one's own practice) thinking.

Course organizers should anticipate likely barriers and constraints from the beginning. Selecting the target staff group, ensuring time commitment and release from duties (especially those working with emergencies) and negotiating agreement from stakeholders across agencies is not easy, but, unless these issues are tackled early on, trainers will have to face low attendance, drop-outs and disengagement through lack of staff preparedness ('Why am I here?', 'Why am I training with other groups?', 'How will this help me in my work?', 'Is it really necessary for all our staff to attend?'). Such investment in gaining consensus in a common direction will pay off later, particularly if the overarching objective is to make an impact on children, and for this impact to be sustained.

Although it is possible to achieve most of the specific learning objectives, at least partially, in one day, this will not enable meaningful interactions, case-based discussion and processing new knowledge. A two-day course, with a few weeks between the training days to allow participants to implement new knowledge in their practice and to feed back their experiences, is possibly realistic for this purpose. Staff release for more than two days is likely to be regarded as coming under the next

130 Training in a service context

PHOTO 12.1 Not much time to plan, but an eventually intuitive co-facilitation with Gura Susanna, senior social worker, during care home staff training in Jakarta

section of more specialized training. If this training is an ongoing endeavour, achieving and maintaining consistency between the facilitators also requires planning and time investment (preferably two co-facilitators per training course, who complement each other in terms of agency roles and experience – Photo 12.1).

As already discussed, facilitators need to discover their own healthy balance between keeping to their goals during pre-planned sessions, and enabling participants to make their own mark, and thus influence the training. Interprofessional issues such as different agency cultures, priorities and approaches to children's needs, and establishing networks and joint-working are particularly challenging if they have not been experienced before. Consequently, these require built-in time and carefully designed activities. Participants' feedback, evaluation and ongoing monitoring should be integral to any training. These can be threatening at first (as shown in the Preface of this text), but is ultimately the only way to actively engage and bring together individual staff or agencies that have previously been operating in silo, whilst respecting and protecting their professional identity and service boundaries. A possible parallel is drawing a comparison between a collection of musicians and an orchestra or band – which one would you prefer to listen to?

Trainers and participants alike can have their own assumptions, fears and myths about each other. Whenever trainees asked if they contribute to a local inter-agency training programme, I would initially suggest that they first attended the training as

PHOTO 12.2 Closing the cycle: Following a training programme with child protection community volunteers in Uganda, including a career and life-turning human connection (see Preface)

students, mixed with the other participants and observed their learning style and interactions. Was it what they expected? Were they surprised? Then they could move on to the topic and delivery. This process would normally distinguish between adaptable future trainers who could function in an interprofessional context from those who were technically capable but rather uni-dimensional in their knowledge-transfer. For some trainers, 'newness' is tough. Relating to community leads and volunteers in African and Asian countries was the ultimate challenge but also the pinnacle of my training adventures (Photo 12.2). As during practice, reflecting on our style and accepting our limitations are wise training companions. Once these challenges are 'cracked' with fellow professionals, they can be extended to the public domain such as to parents or other caregivers, children and young people (usually through schools) and communities. To achieve this, we need to understand which key messages are important to them before delivering interventions through mental health awareness or promotion programmes.

Continuous professional development or lifelong learning

Moving up to the next level of training, but keeping to the same learning and interprofessional principles, what knowledge should all frontline workers in contact with vulnerable children and their families ideally have? And in what format, intensity and mode should it be delivered? The difference between this level and the previous foundation or introductory training is the need to delve into certain topics in more detail, use case material and learn and practise case-based skills during the training and between sessions. Unlike the next level of obtaining extensive skills in a particular therapeutic modality which involve the award of a postgraduate or therapy accreditation, and consequently require a year or more of input and the submission and marking of portfolios or other assignments, the continuous professional development (CPD) objective is to provide a broad overview of approaches and some core skills to facilitate the role as a minimum requirement. A usual format is a ten-day equivalent programme over two modules, which is delivered in intensive bursts or fortnightly, depending on the logistics of the target group. We will later consider how this can be complemented by e-learn methods. This requires the same careful matching of staff training needs in collaboration with the accrediting body, be it an academic, professional or other organization.

The focus and learning objectives could vary from child development to child protection or special educational needs. If mental health is the main remit of the CPD programme, it may again be tempting to start with mental health problems and strategies straightaway. The risk is that mental health concepts will not be linked to children's other needs or to interprofessional practice. Therefore, in similar situations, we have opted for one generic and one targeted mental health module. Generic topics include child legislation, implications of child development for practice, mental health awareness, school mental health (or literacy), cultural applications and a risk and resilience framework for mental health problems. Each topic is a challenge in its own right, but this logical flow builds up knowledge and meets expectations from a more solid basis rather than only from a mental health perspective.

Mental health problems can be addressed in the second module, again in relation to staff roles. These can include common child mental health presentations such as anxiety, depression and behavioural problems; PTSD and attachment difficulties; and neurodevelopmental conditions such as attention deficit hyperactivity disorders (ADHD), autism and learning difficulties. This is a tall order, but a balanced overview of key features, mechanisms and strategies can be more valuable for this purpose, whilst giving staff and their managers the choice of pursuing more in-depth training in some areas at the next stage, if this is available and is particularly relevant to their duties. Such a curriculum also sends a powerful message on the increasing availability and indications of different modalities, their evidence-base and, crucially, their limitations.

Sustainability clearly relies on supervision and obtaining further skills, but a booster component in CPD courses, often involving an e-learn or other online component, could be considered. The acquisition of specific therapeutic skills traditionally relies on lengthier, usually postgraduate courses. Increasingly though there are opportunities for brief training, either as an induction to the modality or as an adapted course for a non-specialist level. This is a major opportunity to enhance the skills base of the child workforce, particularly where specialist resources are sparse. There is, however, a responsibility on trainers, practitioners and their managers to focus and boundary the application of these skills in enriching staff roles rather than pretending that they are filling a therapy vacuum within their agency – this would not be in either the children's or the staff's interests. The different levels of postgraduate qualifications offer such options, with skills-based portfolios and often a research assignment or small project, either as a built-in or optional ingredient. Again, such choices and the resulting investment should ideally reflect both individual career choices and service needs.

Optimizing the deceptively scary use of new technologies

Embracing the unknown carries both opportunities and challenges. Remaining rigidly stuck in the past while the world is changing around us can, in our case, deprive access to many staff and volunteers, especially in remote and underprivileged regions of the world, and ultimately the benefit of their knowledge and competencies to millions of children. On the other hand, uncritically adopting approaches just because they are new and accessible can equally be naive and even unsafe. We clearly do not have fully developed training answers and models yet, certainly not enough supporting evidence, however there are interesting and constantly evolving examples that we need to take advantage of. These will hopefully not look frightfully outdated by the time you read this text!

The usual fear is 'Will technology take over and make my skills redundant?' This is rather unlikely. I recall the same fear (and sometimes naivety) in using questionnaires for service purposes such as referring children who scored above the cut-off to a mental health service without an assessment. 'Have you talked to the child and their carer before making the referral?' Or, 'Have you put the questionnaire scores in the context of other information and your specialist assessment?' Because, questionnaires are, well, just questionnaires . . .

These arguments are rather simplistic, as considerations on the use of technology are more complex, particularly when they involve children and young people. There are an increasing number of online apps, psychoeducational resources and self-help packages of variable quality and limited evaluation. Some are truly innovative and based on young people's preferences. For example, online screening and self-help materials through mobile phones have been shown to enhance the engagement of homeless youth, who found these alternatives to initial face-to-face less threatening to start with. These may or may not lead to them taking up a clinical offer, i.e. they have been designed as precursors of or complementary to other interventions. Similar dilemmas and options are presented for training purposes.

Where better to start with than one's own doubts? A face-to-face postgraduate mental health course with several levels had been successful for several years, as shown by the students' (all experienced practitioners) uptake and completion rates. But something was niggling me, and this was not an urge to embrace technology, as I was oblivious to it at the time. Instead it was the over-reliance on practitioners

134 Training in a service context

needing to commute long distances, the skewed nature of students from our region and the dangerous over-reliance on the same funding sources (e.g. health authorities and services seconding staff to the course). What really worried me though was missing the chance to relate to an international pool that would simply broaden and improve both quality and impact. Then came a period of self-doubt, experimentation and transition:

EXTERNAL TEACHING ADVISER: Have you considered changing it – or part of it – to distance learning?

AUTHOR: No, because I like meeting and seeing the students. On the first day of the course, we traditionally go for dinner, how can we drink online?

EXTERNAL TEACHING ADVISER: Maybe you need to look at some established distance-learning courses – they are actually not *that* new (a clear dig at being left behind training times . . .).

Indeed I looked at some of the more successful examples irrespective of the fields, (actually) talked to students and was convinced that technology was a communication tool to relate the same or similar skills, but in a different way. The message was loud and clear: 'You've got to change, don't just put Powerpoint presentations on the web; first, you have to understand the different psyche of technology, then adapt to it'. In that respect, the development period was intense, in terms of investment both in time and funding to set up new materials. The hardest task was facilitating a group of tutors to concurrently adapt within that period. We learnt a whole new language: podcasts (brief and succinct audio-recordings to accompany the text by highlighting key messages); vlogs (the visual equivalent); group discussions; journals (students' responses to a question or task individually, usually on more personal and reflective issues); and wikkies (students working as a team by adding layers of answers to a given task). 'Do you really expect me to use these?' 'Now?'

A few months later, this approach worked a treat. It broadened the geographical origin of the student group, its diversity in terms of roles and experience and, crucially, their international perspectives. My main observation, both in individual and particularly in group discussions and interactions, was that web-based participants replicated all human and training characteristics that we have been exhibiting since our schooldays. Some students contributed more than others, some were shy but came alive later in the course and some made minimal contributions and derived minimal benefit. There were encouragement, mutual learning and tensions. Tutors proved human too: proactive, responsive or passive, as indeed in any classroom around the world. My main reassurance was that, with all those parameters in place, practitioners from all over the world gelled together, despite language, cultural and service system differences.

This experience reminded me of Dylan's line 'don't criticize what you don't understand', which made me that little bit wiser when the considerably more important WACIT challenge came along, with the need to maximize social media

Training in a service context **135**

and web-based resources to enhance access, build global networks, bypass bureaucracy and hierarchies and establish partnerships. These included a blog, Facebook page, Twitter and YouTube. Conclusion: 'Just ask (very) young people and don't question their advice – just do it!'

Fortunately, there are more unexploited options, which can be linked and can feed off each other, in various combinations and order (i.e. stand-alone or, ideally, as prerequisites in a strategic way). E-learn courses also use interactive modes (activities, self-reflection, quizzes and different case materials based on participants' caseload, reading or watching a vignette). They are relatively short and not facilitated, i.e. the student takes responsibility for going through the course without external input, which is instead built in to the online training methods. There may or may not be a final pass rate and certification. The distinct feature here is that we must presume the participant's capacity to utilize this new or booster knowledge autonomously. For this reason, an e-learn course can serve as the next stage from foundation/awareness or, most commonly, as booster (mandatory or voluntary) training within a profession or organization (often child protection or cultural diversity refreshers). Such training is not confined to professionals, there are an increasing number of interesting examples of courses for caregivers like adoptive parents and foster carers, both prospective and approved.

In contrast, as already discussed, distance-learning training has active, live and ongoing external moderation. This may include an assignment or case portfolio, with a linked assessment. These training models are by no means mutually exclusive, with hybrid courses combining different elements for pragmatic or other reasons; for example, a face-to-face intensive induction can be followed by a distance-learning or e-learn component.

Organizational issues to be considered

These theory, practice or research-driven ideas will not suit all countries, services and circumstances. Crucially, unless a number of organizational safeguards are put in place, their benefits will not be sustainable. New knowledge increases awareness, expectations and uptake of more complex cases, hence risk. These will in turn increase demand. Supervision is essential for all staff, as well as volunteers. In places where this might not yet be available such as in conflict zones, external arrangements should initially be made for a parallel fast-track strategy to develop internal supervisory capacity across an agency.

If psychosocial support or mental health provision are relatively novel in an agency's mission, one needs to anticipate that it will take time before it is embedded across the organization, including the operational teams. Appointing a mental health lead or champion (I prefer the former, with some formalized commitment from their agency, rather than just relying on enthusiasm and initiative) can influence the direction of changes in service operational criteria, staff roles and skills and client characteristics over the initial period. These changes will need both direction and support, rather than being left to chance. Service user involvement at several

136 Training in a service context

training levels is relatively new in most countries, but is rapidly expanding. This should become central to service and training policy and ethos, rather than remain tokenistic, whilst still finding creative ways of protecting vulnerable groups, especially making use of children's expert advice. All these points mirror a genuine investment in the future. The same applies to developing a local and national pool of trainers through parallel – initially intensive – 'training the trainers' initiatives. Last but not least is the need to translate human potential into the next generation of leaders, across agencies, organizations, professional bodies and policy departments. Exciting and obvious as these ways forward might be, they will also require continuous monitoring and built-in evaluation that will enable adjustments and cost-effective prioritization. Both traditional and emerging methods such as participatory workshops (yes, even research can be fun!) provide options which are integral to educational activities, not dissimilar in style, cause minimum time burden and are perceived as being useful by staff and other stakeholders.

EPILOGUE

> We are, therefore, ready to build on what once seemed inconceivable, i.e. to systematically approach whole vulnerable groups rather than rely on chance for those who manage to get out and seek help on their own accord. We have access to theories, networks, narratives and sound evidence that we are on the right track. The next generation of inspired practitioners, researchers and policy-makers will move forward from the 'whether' to the 'how' in a more sophisticated way, and in parts of the world that we can still not imagine we can get remotely close to.
>
> *Vostanis, 2014a*

In the hope of not breaching copyright of my earlier text, it was interesting to compare notes with its conclusion. It sounded sensible enough, albeit rather remote, at the time. It then dawned on me that this was only three years ago! Could I possibly have imagined that, only three years and more than 100,000 air miles later, I would be plunging into the World Awareness for Children in Trauma (WACIT) programme in places and contexts that I had never even searched for on the internet? I would have certainly laughed off any suggestion, but the threads were there all along, I just needed a few catalysts to inter-connect them.

Innovation and evidence are emerging faster than previously anticipated. Technologies are enabling us to come closer to one another, share lessons and avoid repeating the mistakes of the past. More importantly though, both trauma and child mental health are becoming ingrained in global consciousness as requiring evidenced solutions rather than sympathy. Neither concept is any longer way down the priority lists of humanitarian and other international organizations, governments, services, public and the media.

So, having got the predictions horribly wrong last time, it would be wiser to refrain from any more guesses. Let us just build on the momentum, persevere in winning both hearts and minds and continue to integrate policy, research, service development, practice and training to the benefit of those who need it most.

BOOK REFERENCES BY CHAPTER

1 Ever-changing approaches to child trauma

Cicchetti, D. (1993). Developmental psychopathology: Reactions, reflections, projections. *Development Review*, 13, 471–502.

Coleman, J. & Hagell, A. (2007). *Adolescence, Risk and Resilience: Against the Odds*. Chichester: John Wiley.

Corsaro, W. (1997). *The Sociology of Childhood*. London: Sage.

Council of Europe (2006). *Rights of Children at Risk and in Care*. Strasbourg: Council of Europe.

Denov, M. & Akesson, B., Eds. (2017). *Children Affected by Armed Conflict*. New York: Columbia University Press.

Gabrielli, J., Gill, M., Koester, L.S. & Borntrager, S. (2014). Psychological perspectives on 'acute or chronic' trauma in children: Implications of the 2010 earthquake in Haiti. *Children and Society*, 6, 438–450.

Garmezy, N. (1985). Broadening research on developmental risk. In Emde, R., Frankerburg, W. & Sullivan, J., Eds., *Early Identification of Children at Risk: An International Perspective*. New York: Springer, pp. 45–58.

Green, H., McGinnity, A., Meltzer, H., Ford, T. & Goodman, R. (2005). *Mental Health of Children and Young People in Great Britain*. London: HMSO.

Helal, M., Ahmed, U. & Vostanis, P. (2011). The representation of low- and middle-income countries in the psychiatric research literature. *International Psychiatry*, 8, 92–94.

Kieling, C., Baker-Henningham, H., Belfer, M., Conti, G., Ertem, I., Omigbodun, O., Rohde, L.A., Srinath, S., Ulkuer, N. & Rahman, A. (2011). Child and adolescent mental health worldwide. *Lancet*, 378, 1515–1525.

Luthar, S., Cicchetti, D. & Becker, B. (2000). Research on resilience. *Child Development*, 71, 573–575.

Stuttaford, M., Hundt, G. & Vostanis, P. (2009). Sites for health rights: The experiences of homeless families in England. *Journal of Human Rights Practice*, 53, 257–278.

United Nations Children's Fund (UNICEF) (2011). *The State of the World's Children*. New York: UNICEF.

United Nations Children's Fund (UNICEF) (2012). *Measuring Child Poverty: Innocenti Report Card 10*. Florence: Innocenti Research Centre.

United Nations Conference of Plenipotentiaries on the Status of Refugees and Stateless Persons (1951). *Final Act and Convention Relating to the Status of Refugees*. Geneva: United Nations.

Vostanis, P. (2017). Global child mental health: Emerging challenges and opportunities. *Child and Adolescent Mental Health*, 22, 177–178.

World Health Organization (WHO) (2012). *Adolescent Mental Health*. Geneva: WHO.

2 Impact of trauma on child mental health

Attanayake, V., McKay, R., Joffres, M., Singh, S., Burkle, F. & Mills, E. (2009). Prevalence of mental disorders among children exposed to war. *Medicine, Conflict and Survival*, 25, 4–19.

Bean, T., Derluyn, I., Eurelings-Bontekoe, E., Broekaert, E. & Spinhoven, P. (2007). Comparing psychological distress, traumatic stress reactions, and experiences of unaccompanied refugee minors with experiences of adolescents accompanied by parents. *Journal of Nervous and Mental Disease*, 195, 288–297.

Bender, K., Ferguson, K., Thompson, S., Komlo, C. & Pollio, D. (2010). Factors associated with trauma and posttraumatic stress disorder among homeless youth in three US cities: The importance of transience. *Journal of Traumatic Stress*, 23, 161–168.

Betancourt, T., Borisova, I., Williams, T., Meyers-Ohki, S., Rubin-Smith, J., Annan, J. & Kohrt, B. (2013). Psychosocial adjustment and mental health in former child soldiers. *Journal of Child Psychology and Psychiatry*, 54, 17–36.

Bronfenbrenner, U. (1979). *The Ecology of Human Development: Experiments by Nature and Design*. Cambridge, MA: Harvard University Press.

Chitsabesan, P., Kroll, L., Bailey, S., Kenning, C., Sneider, S., MacDonald, W. & Theodosiou, L. (2006). Mental health needs of young offenders in custody and in the community. *British Journal of Psychiatry*, 188, 534–540.

Colins, O., Vermeiren, R., Vreugdenhil, C., Schuyten, G., Broekaert, E. & Krabbendam, A. (2009). Are psychotic experiences among detained juvenile offenders explained by trauma and substance use? *Drug and Alcohol Dependence*, 100, 39–46.

De Anstiss, H., Ziaian, T., Procter, N., Warland, J. & Baghurst, P. (2009). Help-seeking for mental health problems in young refugees. *Transcultural Psychiatry*, 46, 584–607.

Ellis, B.H., MacDonald, H., Lincoln, A. & Cabral, H. (2008). Mental health of Somali adolescent refugees: The role of trauma, stress, and perceived discrimination. *Journal of Consulting and Clinical Psychology*, 76, 184–193.

Fazel, M. & Steel, A. (2002). The mental health of refugee children. *Archives of Disease in Childhood*, 87, 366–370.

Fleitlich-Bilyk, B. & Goodman, R. (2004). Prevalence of child and adolescent psychiatric disorders in Southeast Brazil. *Journal of the American Academy of Child and Adolescent Psychiatry*, 43, 727–734.

Ford, T., Vostanis, P., Meltzer, H. & Goodman, R. (2007). Psychiatric disorder among British children looked after by local authorities: Comparison with children living in private households. *British Journal of Psychiatry*, 190, 319–325.

Goldin, S., Hägglöf, B., Levin, L., & Persson, L.Å. (2008). Mental health of Bosnian refugee children. *Nordic Journal of Psychiatry*, 62, 204–216.

Holt, S., Buckley, H. & Whelan, S. (2008). The impact of exposure to domestic violence on children and young people: A review of the literature. *Child Abuse and Neglect*, 32, 797–810.

140 Book references by chapter

Howell, K., Kaplow, J., Layne, C., Benson, M., Compas, B., Katalinski, R. & Pynoos, R. (2014). Predicting adolescent posttraumatic stress in the aftermath of war. *Anxiety, Stress and Coping*, 28, 88–104.

Huemer, J., Karnik, N., Voelkl-Kernstock, S., Granditch, E., Dervic, K., Friedrich, M. & Steiner, H. (2009). Mental health issues in unaccompanied refugee minors. *Child and Adolescent Psychiatry and Mental Health*, 3, DOI:10.1.1186/1753-2000-3-13

Hussey, D., Falletta, L. & Eng, A. (2012). Risk factors for mental health diagnoses among children adopted from the public welfare system. *Children and Youth Services Review*, 34, 2072–2080.

Jensen, T.K., Fjermestad, K.W., Granly, L., & Wilhelmsen, N.H. (2015). Stressful life experiences and mental health problems among unaccompanied asylum-seeking children. *Clinical Child Psychology and Psychiatry*, 20, 106–116.

Kim, J. & Cicchetti, D. (2010). Longitudinal pathways linking child maltreatment, emotion regulation, peer relations and psychopathology. *The Journal of Child Psychology and Psychiatry*, 51, 706–716.

Lazarus, R. & Folkman, S. (1984). *Stress, Appraisal and Coping*. New York: Springer.

Lustig, S.L., Kia-Keating, M., Knight, W.G., Geltman, P., Ellis, H., Kinzie, D., Keane, T. & Saxe, G. (2004). Review of child and adolescent refugee mental health. *Journal of the American Academy of Child and Adolescent Psychiatry*, 43, 24–36.

Mels, C., Derluyn, I., Broekaert, E. & Rosseel, Y. (2010). The psychological impact of forced displacement and related risk factors on Eastern Congolese adolescents affected by war. *Journal of Child Psychology and Psychiatry*, 51, 1096–1104.

Meltzer, H., Doos, L., Vostanis, P., Ford, T. & Goodman, R. (2009). The mental health of children who witness domestic violence. *Child and Family Social Work*, 14, 491–501.

Montgomery, E. & Foldspang, A. (2006). Validity of PTSD in a sample of refugee children: Can a separate diagnostic entity be justified? *International Journal of Methods in Psychiatric Research*, 15, 64–74.

Morgos, D., Worden, J.W. & Gupta, L. (2008). Psychosocial effects of war experiences among displaced children in Southern Darfur. *Journal of Death and Dying*, 56, 229–253.

Panter-Brick, C., Eggerman, M., Gonzalez, V. & Safdar, S. (2009). Violence, suffering, and mental health in Afghanistan. *The Lancet*, 374, 807–816.

Papageorgiou, V., Frangou-Garunovic, A., Iordanidou, R., Yule, W., Smith, P. & Vostanis, P. (2000). War trauma and psychopathology in Bosnian refugee children. *European Child and Adolescent Psychiatry*, 9, 84–90.

Porter, M. & Haslam, N. (2005). Pre-displacement and post-displacement factors associated with mental health of refugees and internally displaced persons. *JAMA*, 294, 602–612.

Sack, W., Clarke, G., Him, C., Dickason, D., Goff, B., Lanham, K. & Kinzie, J.D. (1993). A 6-year follow-up study of Cambodian refugee adolescents traumatised as children. *Journal of the American Academy of Child and Adolescent Psychiatry*, 32, 431–437.

Schmid, M., Goldbeck, L., Nuetzel, J. & Fegert, J. (2008). Prevalence of mental disorders among adolescents in German youth welfare institutions. *Child and Adolescent Psychiatry and Mental Health*, 2, DOI: 10.1186/1753-2000-2-2

Sempik, J., Ward, H. & Darker, I. (2008). Emotional and behavioural difficulties of children and young people at entry in care. *Clinical Child Psychology and Psychiatry*, 13, 221–233.

Shamia, A.N., Thabet, A.A. & Vostanis, P. (2015). Exposure to war traumatic experiences, PTSD and post traumatic growth among nurses in Gaza. *Journal of Psychiatric and Mental Health Nursing*, 22, 749–745.

Thabet, A.A., Abed, Y. & Vostanis, P. (2002). Emotional problems in Palestinian children living in a war zone. *The Lancet*, 359, 1801–1804.

Thabet, A.A., Tawahina, A.A., El Sarraj, E. & Vostanis, P. (2008). Exposure to war trauma and PTSD among parents and children in the Gaza strip. *European Child and Adolescent Psychiatry*, 17, 191–199.

Twardosz, S. & Lutzker, J. (2010). Child maltreatment and the developing brain: A review of neuroscience perspectives. *Aggression and Violent Behavior*, 15, 59–68.

Vostanis, P. (2015). Healthcare professionals in war zones are vulnerable too. *Journal of Psychiatric and Mental Health Nursing*, 22, 747–748.

Vostanis, P., Grattan, E. & Cumella, S. (1998). Mental health problems of homeless children and families: A longitudinal study. *British Medical Journal*, 316, 899–902.

Zinzow, H., Ruggiero, K., Resnick, H., Hanson, R., Smith, D., Saunders, B. & Kilpatrick, D. (2009). Prevalence and mental health correlates of witnessed parental and community violence in a national sample of adolescents. *Journal of Child Psychology and Psychiatry*, 50, 441–450.

3 Child vulnerability in a global context

Belfer, M. (2008). Child and adolescent mental disorders: The magnitude of the problem across the globe. *Journal of Child Psychology and Psychiatry*, 49, 226–236.

Department of Education (2013). *Statutory Guidance for Local Authorities and Adoption Agencies.* London: Department of Education.

Derluyn, I. & Broekaert, E. (2007). Different perspectives on emotional and behavioural problems in unaccompanied refugee children and adolescents. *Ethnicity and Health*, 12, 141–162.

Eruyar, S., Huemer, J. & Vostanis, P. (2017). How should child mental health services respond to the refugee crisis? *Child and Adolescent Mental Health*, DOI:10.1111/camh.12252

Griggs, D., Stafford-Smith, M., Gaffney, O., Rockström, J., Öhman, M., Shyamsundar, P., Steffen, W., Glaser, G., Kanie, N. & Noble, I. (2013). Sustainable development goals for people and planet. *Nature*, 495, 305–307.

He, A., Lim, C., Lecklinter, G., Olson, A., & Traube, D. (2015). Interagency collaboration and identifying mental health needs in child welfare: Findings from Los Angeles County. *Children and Youth Services Review*, 53, 39–43.

Howard, M. & Hodes, M. (2000). Psychopathology, adversity and service utilisation of young refugees. *Journal of the American Academy of Child and Adolescent Psychiatry*, 39, 368–377.

Lund, C., Tomlinson, M. & Patel, V. (2016). Integrating mental health into primary care in low- and middle-income countries. *British Journal of Psychiatry*, 208 (s56), s1-s3, DOI: 10.1192/bjp.bp.114.153668

Miranda, J. & Patel, V. (2005). Achieving the Millennium Development Goals: Does mental health play a role? *PloS Medicine*, 2, 962–965.

Montgomery, E. (2008). Long-term effects of organised violence on young Middle Eastern refugees' mental health. *Social Science and Medicine*, 67, 1596–1603.

Moses, T. (2010). Being treated differently: Stigma experiences with family, peers, and school staff among adolescents with mental health disorders. *Social Science and Medicine*, 70, 985–983.

Munro, E., Hollingworth, K., Meetoo, V. & Simon, A. (2013). *Adoption Reform: Messages from Local Authorities on Changes in Processes and Timescales: Findings from Wave 1.* Childhood Wellbeing Research Centre Working Paper No. 20, Childhood Wellbeing Research Centre.

142 Book references by chapter

Neil, E. (2012). Making sense of adoption: Integration and differentiation from the perspective of adopted children in middle childhood. *Children and Youth Services Review*, 34, 409–416.

Office of the United Nations High Commissioner for Refugees (2015). *World at War: UNHCR Global Trends*. www.unhcr.org/uk/statistics/country/556725e69/unhcr-global-trends-2014.html (last accessed August 2017).

O'Reilly, M., Taylor, H. & Vostanis, P. (2009). "Nuts, schiz, psycho": An exploration of young homeless people's perceptions and dilemmas of defining mental health. *Social Science and Medicine*, 68, 1737–1744.

Organisation for Economic Co-operation and Development (OECD) (2016). *Country Risk Classification*. www.oecd.org/tad/xcred/crc.htm (last accessed August 2017).

Patel, V. & Rahman, A. (2015). An agenda for child mental health. *Child and Adolescent Mental Health*, 20, 3–4.

Rutter, M., Kreppner, J. & Sonuga-Barke, E. (2009). Attachment insecurity, disinhibited attachment, and attachment disorders: Where do research findings leave the concepts? *Journal of Child Psychology and Psychiatry*, 50, 529–543.

Sayal, K., Tischler, V., Coope, C., Robotham, S., Ashworth, M., Day, C., Tylee, A. & Simonoff, E. (2010). Parental help-seeking in primary care for child and adolescent mental health concerns. *British Journal of Psychiatry*, 197, 476–481.

Schomerus, G. & Angermeyer, M. (2008). Stigma and its impact on help-seeking for mental disorders: What do we know? *Epidemiology and Psychiatric Sciences*, 17, 31–37.

Shatkin, J., Balloge, N. & Belfer, M. (2008). Child and adolescent mental health policy worldwide. *International Psychiatry*, 5, 81–84.

Taylor, H., Stuttaford, M., Broad, B. & Vostanis, P. (2006). Why a 'roof' is not enough: The characteristics of young homeless people referred to a designated mental health service. *Journal of Mental Health*, 15, 491–501.

United Nations Children's Fund (UNICEF) (2016). *A Post-2015 World Fit for Children*. New York: UNICEF.

Vostanis P., Meltzer H., Goodman R. & Ford T. (2003). Service utilisation by children with conduct disorders: Findings from the GB national study. *European Child and Adolescent Psychiatry*, 12, 231–238.

Wells, R., Steel, Z., Abo-Hilal, M., Hassan, A.H. & Lawsin, C. (2016). Psychosocial concerns reported by Syrian refugees living in Jordan: Systematic review of unpublished needs assessments. *British Journal of Psychiatry*, 1–8, OI: 10.1192/bjp.bp.115.1

4 Looking for answers: from Birmingham shelters to Mumbai slums

Anstiss, H. & Ziaian, T. (2010). Mental health help-seeking and refugee adolescents: Qualitative findings from a mixed-methods investigation. *Australian Psychologist*, 45, 29–37.

Baqui, A., Arifeen, S., Rosen, H., Mannan, I., Rahman, S., Al-Mahmud, A.B., Hossain, D., Das, M.K., Begum, N., Ahmed, S., Santosham, M., Black, R.E. & Darmstadt, G.L. (2009). Community-based validation of assessment of newborn illnesses by trained community health workers in Sylhet district of Bangladesh. *Tropical Medicine and International Health*, 14, 1448–1456.

Baqui, A., Arifeen, S., Williams, E., Ahmed, S., Mannan, I., Rahman, S., Begum, N., Seraji, H.R., Winch, P., Santosham, M., Black, R.E. & Darmstadt, G.L. (2009) Effectiveness of home-based management of newborn infections by community health workers in rural Bangladesh. *Pediatric Infectious Disease Journal*, 28, 304–310.

Bucher, C. (2008). Towards a needs-based typology of homeless youth. *Journal of Adolescent Health*, 2, 549–554.

Getanda, E.M., Vostanis, P. & O'Reilly, M. (2017). Exploring the challenges of meeting child mental health needs through community engagement in Kenya. *Child and Adolescent Mental Health*, 22, 201–208.

Groark, C., Sclare, I. & Raval, H. (2010). Understanding the experiences and emotional needs of unaccompanied asylum-seeking adolescents in the UK. *Clinical Child Psychology and Psychiatry*, 16, 421–442.

Hamoda, H. & Belfer, M. (2010). Challenges in international collaboration in child and adolescent psychiatry. *Journal of Child and Adolescent Mental Health*, 22, 83–89.

Jordans, M., Tol, W., Komproe, I. & De Jong, J. (2009). Psychosocial and mental health care for children in war. *Child and Adolescent Mental Health*, 14, 2–14.

Kalantari, M. & Vostanis, P. (2010). Behavioural and emotional problems in Iranian children four years after a parental death in an earthquake. *International Journal of Social Psychiatry*, 56, 158–167.

Karim, K., Tischler, V., Gregory, P. & Vostanis, P. (2006). Homeless children and parents: Short-term mental health outcome. *International Journal of Social Psychiatry*, 52, 447–458.

Rahman, A., Malik, A., Sikauder, S., Roberts, C. & Creed, F. (2008). Cognitive-behavioural therapy-based intervention by community health workers for mothers with depression and their infants in rural Pakistan: A cluster RCT. *The Lancet*, 372, 13–19.

Raikes, A., Yoshikawa, H., Britto, P.R. & Iruka, I. (2017). *Children, Youth and Developmental Science in the 2015–2030 Global Sustainable Development Goals*. Washington, DC: Society for Research in Child Development, Social Policy Report 30, 3.

Rutter, M. (2013). Resilience: Clinical implications. *Journal of Child Psychology and Psychiatry*, 54, 474–487.

Vostanis, P. (2014a). *Helping Children and Young People Who Experience Trauma: Children of Despair, Children of Hope*. London: Taylor & Francis.

Vostanis, P. (2014b). Meeting the mental health needs of refugees and asylum seekers. *British Journal of Psychiatry*, 204, 176–177.

5 An international perspective: the road to WACIT

Abera, M., Robbins, J. & Tesfaye, M. (2015). Parents' perception of child and adolescent mental health problems and their choice of treatment option in southwest Ethiopia. *Child and Adolescent Psychiatry and Mental Health*, 9, 40, DOI: 10.1186/s13034-015-0072-5

Amuyunzu-Nyamongo, M. (2013). The social and cultural aspects of mental health in African societies. *Commonwealth Health Partnerships*, 59–63.

Betancourt, T. & Khan, K. (2008). The mental health of children affected by armed conflict: Protective processes and pathways to resilience. *International Review of Psychiatry*, 20, 317–328.

Dornan, P. (2017). Children, poverty and sustainable development goals. *Children and Society*, 31, 157–165.

Fazel, M., Reed, R., Panter-Brick, C. & Stein, A. (2011). Mental health of displaced and refugee children resettled in high-income countries: Risk and protective factors. *The Lancet*, 379, 266–282.

Hodes, M., Jagdev, D., Chandra, N. & Cunniff, A. (2008). Risk and resilience for psychological distress amongst unaccompanied asylum seeking adolescents. *Journal of Child Psychology and Psychiatry*, 49, 723–732.

144 Book references by chapter

Hussein, S., Vostanis, P. & Bankart, J. (2012). Social and educational risk factors for child mental health problems in Karachi, Pakistan. *International Journal of Mental Health and Culture*, 5, 1–14.

Jordans, M., Tol, W., Komproe, I., Susanty, D., Vallipuram, A., Ntamatumba, P. & De Jong, J. (2010). Development of a multi-layered psychosocial care system for children in areas of political violence. *International Journal of Mental Health Systems*, 4, DOI: 10.1186/1752-4458-4-15

Maslow, A.H. (1943). A theory of human motivation. *Psychological Review*, 50, 370–396.

Miller, K.E. & Rasmussen, A. (2010). War exposure, daily stressors, and mental health in conflict and post-conflict settings: Bridging the divide between trauma-focused and psychosocial frameworks. *Social Science and Medicine*, 70, 7–16.

Pangallo, A., Zibarras, L. & Lewis, R. (2015). Resilience through the lens of interactionism: A systematic review. *Psychological Assessment*, 27, 1–20.

Reed, R., Fazel, M., Jones, L., Panter-Brick, C. & Stein, A. (2011). Mental health of displaced and refugee children resettled in low-income and middle-income countries: Risk and protective factors. *The Lancet*, 379, 250–265.

Tanner, T. (2010). Shifting the narratives: Child-led responses to climate change and disasters in El Salvador and the Philippines. *Children and Society*, 24, 339–351.

Tol, W., Komproe, I., Jordans, M., Gross, A., Susanty, D., Macy, R. & De Jong, J. (2010). Mediators and moderators of a psychosocial intervention for children affected by political violence. *Journal of Consulting and Clinical Psychology*, 78, 818–828.

Tol, W., Song, S. & Jordans, M. (2013). Resilience and mental health in children and adolescents living in areas of armed conflict. *Journal of Child Psychology and Psychiatry*, 54, 445–460.

Vostanis, P. (2016). New approaches to interventions for refugee children. *World Psychiatry*, 15, 75–77.

6 Children's safety should permeate policy, attitudes and environments

Barnes, J., Noll, J., Putnam, F. & Trickett, P. (2009). Sexual and physical revictimization among victims of severe childhood sexual abuse. *Child Abuse and Neglect*, 33, 412–420.

Barone, L. & Lionetti, F. (2011). Attachment and emotional understanding: A study on late-adopted pre-schoolers and their parents. *Child: Care Health and Development*, 38, 690–696.

Betancourt, T., Williams, T., Kellner, S., Genre-Mehdin, J., Hann, K. & Kayiteshonga, Y. (2012). Interrelatedness of child health, protection and well-being: An application of the SAFE model in Rwanda. *Social Science and Medicine*, 74, 1504–1511.

Carr, A., Fitzpatrick, M., Flanagan, E., Flanagan-Howard, R., Tierney, K., White, M., Daly, M. & Egan, J. (2010). Adult adjustment of survivors of institutional child abuse in Ireland. *Child Abuse and Neglect*, 34, 477–489.

Catani, C., Schauer, E. & Neuner, F. (2008). Beyond individual war trauma: Domestic violence against children in Afghanistan and Sri Lanka. *Journal of Marital Family Therapy*, 34, 165–176.

Cohen, J., Mannarino, A., Murray, L.K. & Igelman, R. (2006). Psychosocial interventions for maltreated and violence-exposed children. *Journal of Social Issues*, 62, 737–766.

Convention on the Rights of the Child (1989). *General Assembly Resolution 44/25, UN Document E.C. 12.1999.10*. New York: United Nations.

Department for Education (2010). *Haringey Local Safeguarding Children Board Serious Case Review 'Child a'*. London: Department for Education.

Gershoff, E., Lee, S. & Durrant, J. (2017). Promising intervention strategies to reduce parents' use of physical punishment. *Child Abuse and Neglect*, 71, 9–23.

Hamby, S., Finkelhor, D. & Turner, H. (2015). Intervention following family violence: Best practices and help-seeking obstacles in a nationally representative sample of families with children. *Psychology of Violence*, 5, 325–336.

Hodges, J., Steele, M., Hillman, S., Henderson, K. & Kaniuk, J. (2003). Changes in attachment representations over the first year of adoptive placement: Narratives of maltreated children. *Clinical Child Psychology and Psychiatry*, 8, 351–367.

Jalal, E. (2016). Professionals' perceptions of the implementation of the Multidisciplinary National Safety Programme in the Kingdom of Saudi Arabia, Unpublished PhD thesis, University of Leicester.

Jones, D., Lewis, T., Litrownik, A., Thompson, R., Proctor, L., Isbell, P., Dubowitz, H., English, D., Jones, B., Nagin, D. & Runyan, D. (2013). Linking childhood sexual abuse and early adolescent risk behaviour: The intervening role of internalizing and externalizing problems. *Journal of Abnormal Child Psychology*, 41, 139–150.

Jones, D., Runyan, D., Lewis, T., Litrownik, A., Black, M., Wiley, T., English, E., Proctor, L., Jones, B. & Nagin, D. (2010). Trajectories of childhood sexual abuse and early adolescent HIV/AIDS risk behaviors: The role of other maltreatment, witnessed violence, and child gender. *Journal of Clinical Child and Adolescent Psychology*, 53, 39, 667–680.

Jouriles, E., Vu, N., McDonald, R. & Rosenfield, D. (2014). Children's appraisals of conflict, beliefs about aggression, and externalizing problems in families characterized by severe intimate partner violence. *Journal of Family Psychology*, 28, 915–924.

Lampinen, J. & Sexton-Radek, K. (2010). *Protecting Children from Violence: Evidence-based Interventions*. New York: Psychology Press.

McDonald, R., Jouriles, E., Rosenfield, D. & Leahy, M. (2012). Children's questions about interparent conflict and violence: What's a mother to say? *Journal of Family Psychology*, 26, 95–104.

Mullender, A. (2004). *Tackling Domestic Violence: Providing Support for Children Who Have Witnessed Domestic Violence*. London: Home Office.

Neil, E., Beek, M. & Schofield, G. (2003). Thinking about managing contact in permanent placements: The differences and similarities between adoptive parents and foster carers. *Clinical Child Psychology and Psychiatry*, 8, 401–418.

O'Reilly, M. (2008). "I didn't violent punch him": Parental accounts of punishing children with mental health problems. *Journal of Family Therapy*, 30, 272–295.

Overbeek, M., de Schipper, C., Lamers-Winkelman, F. & Schuengel, C. (2014). American risk factors as moderators of recovery during and after interventions for children exposed to interparental violence. *American Journal of Orthopsychiatry*, 84, 295–306.

Ports, K., Ford, D. & Merrick, M. (2016). Adverse childhood experiences and sexual victimization in adulthood. *Child Abuse and Neglect*, 51, 313–322.

Rafferty, Y. (2013). Child trafficking and commercial sexual exploitation: A review of promising prevention policies and programs. *American Journal of Orthopsychiatry*, 83, 559–575.

Randall, J. (2009). Towards a better understanding of the needs of children currently adopted from care. *Adoption and Fostering*, 33, 44–55.

Richter, L., Komárek, A., Desmond, C., Celentano, D., Morin, S., Sweat, M. & Coates, T. (2014). Reported physical and sexual abuse in childhood and adult HIV risk behaviour in three African countries: Findings from project accept (HPTN-043). *AIDS and Behavior*, 18, 381–389.

Selwyn, J., Frazer, L. & Quinton, D. (2006). Paved with good intentions: The pathway to adoption and the costs of delay. *British Journal of Social Work*, 36, 561–576.

146 Book references by chapter

Sturgess, W. and Selwyn, J. (2007). Supporting the placements of children adopted out of care. *Clinical Child Psychology and Psychiatry*, 12, 13–28.

Thabet, A.A., Matar, S., Carpintero, A., Bankart, J. & Vostanis, P. (2010). Mental health problems among labour children in the Gaza Strip. *Child: Care, Health and Development*, 37, 89–95.

Tingvold, L., Hauff, E., Allen, J. & Middelthon, A. (2012). Seeking balance between the past and the present: Vietnamese refugee parenting practices and adolescent well-being. *International Journal of Intercultural Relations*, 36, 563–574.

Townsend, E., Wadman, R., Sayal, K., Armstrong, M., Harroe, C., Majumder, P., Vostanis, P. & Clarke, D. (2016). Uncovering key patterns in self-harm in adolescents: Sequence analysis using the Card Sort Task for Self-harm (CaTS). *Journal of Affective Disorders*, 206, 161–168.

Turner, H., Finkelhor, D., Ormrod, R., Hamby, S., Leeb, R.T., Mercy, J.A. & Holt, M. (2012). Family context, victimization, and child trauma symptoms: Variations in safe, stable, and nurturing relationships during early and middle childhood. *American Journal of Orthopsychiatry*, 82, 209–219.

Vu, N., Jouriles, E., McDonald, R. & Rosenfield, D. (2016). Children's exposure to intimate partner violence: A meta-analysis of longitudinal associations with child adjustment. *Clinical Psychology Review*, 46, 25–33.

Wadman, R., Clarke, D., Sayal, K., Armstrong, M., Harrow, C., Majumder, P., Vostanis, P. & Townsend, E. (2017). A sequence analysis of patterns in self-harm in young people with and without experience of being looked after in care. *British Journal of Clinical Psychology*, 56, 388–407.

Walsh, K., Latzman, N., & Latzman, R. (2014). Pathway from child sexual and physical abuse to risky sex among emerging adults: The role of trauma-related intrusions and alcohol problems. *The Journal of Adolescent Health*, 54, 442–448.

Zakar, M., Zakar, R., Aqil, N., Qureshi, S., Saleem, N. & Imran, S. (2015). 'Nobody likes a person whose body is covered with mud': Health hazards faced by child laborers in the brick kiln sector of the Okara district, Pakistan. *Canadian Journal of Behavioural Science*, 47, 21–28.

7 Nurturing attitudes and approaches

Altafim, E., Pedro, M. & Linhares, M. (2016). Effectiveness of ACT Raising Safe Kids parenting program in a developing country. *Children and Youth Services Review*, 70, 315–323.

Barth, R., Crea, T., John, K., Thoburn, D. & Quinton, D. (2005). Beyond attachment theory and therapy: Towards sensitive and evidence-based interventions with foster and adoptive families in distress. *Child and Family Social Work*, 10, 257–268.

Berrick, J. and Skivenes, M. (2012). Dimensions of high quality foster care: Parenting Plus. *Children and Youth Services Review*, 34, 1956–1965.

Betancourt, T., Ng, L., Kirk, C., Brennan, R., Beardslee, W., Stulac, S., Mushashi, C., Nduwimana, E., Mukunzi, S., Nyiranda, B., Kalisa, G., Rwabukwisi, C. & Sezibera, V. (2017). Family-based promotion of mental health in children affected by HIV: A pilot randomized controlled trial. *Journal of Child Psychology and Psychiatry*, 58, 922–930.

Betancourt, T., Yudron, M., Wheaton, W. & Smith-Fawzi, M. (2012). Caregiver and adolescent mental health in Ethiopian Kunama refugees participating in an emergency education programme. *Journal of Adolescent Health*, 51, 357–365.

Bowlby J. (1969). *Attachment and Loss. Vol. 1: Attachment*. London: Hogarth.

Book references by chapter **147**

Bowlby J. (1988). *A Secure Base: Clinical Attachment of Attachment Theory.* Abingdon: Routledge.

Bywater, T., Hutchings, J., Linck, P., Whitaker, C., Daley, D., Yeo, S. & Edwards. R. (2010). Incredible Years parent training support for foster carers in Wales: A multi-centre feasibility study. *Child: Care Health Development,* 37, 233–243.

Carnes-Holt, K. (2012). Child-parent relationship therapy for adoptive families. *The Family Journal: Counselling and Therapy for Couples and Families,* 20, 419–426.

Dybdahl, R. (2001). Children and mothers in war: An outcome study of a psychosocial intervention programme. *Child Development,* 72, 1214–1230.

Golding, K. (2003). Helping foster carers, helping children: Using attachment theory to guide practice. *Adoption and Fostering,* 27, 64–73.

Golding, K. (2007). Developing group-based parent training for foster and adoptive parents. *Adoption and Fostering,* 31, 39–48.

Holmes, B. & Silver, M. (2010). Managing behaviour with attachment in mind. *Adoption and Fostering,* 34, 65–76.

Howe, D. (2003). Attachment disorders: Disinhibited attachment behaviours and secure base distortions with special reference to adopted children. *Attachment and Human Development,* 5, 265–270.

Hughes, D. (1997). *Facilitating Developmental Attachment: The Road to Recovery and Behavioural Change in Foster and Adopted Children.* London: Aronson.

Jordans, M., Tol, W., Ndayisaba, A. & Komproe, I. (2013). A controlled evaluation of a brief parenting psychoeducation intervention in Burundi. *Social Psychiatry and Psychiatric Epidemiology,* 48, 1851–1859.

Kerr, L. & Cossar, J. (2014). Attachment interventions with foster and adoptive parents: A systematic review. *Child Abuse Review,* 23, 426–439.

Knerr, W., Gardner, F. & Cluver, L. (2013). Improving positive parenting skills and reducing harsh and abusive parenting in low- and middle-income countries: A systematic review. *Prevention Science,* 14, 352–363.

Knox, M., Burkhart, K. & Howe, T. (2011). Effects of the ACT Raising Safe Kids parenting program on children's externalizing problems. *Family Relations,* 60, 491–503.

Leathers, S., Spielfogel, J., Gleeson, J. & Rolock, N. (2012). Behavior problems, foster home integration, and evidence-based behavioral interventions: What predicts adoption of foster children? *Children and Youth Services Review,* 34, 891–899.

Leathers, S., Spielfogel, J., McMeel, L. & Atkins, M. (2011). Use of a parent management training intervention with urban foster parents: A pilot study. *Children and Youth Services Review,* 33, 1270–1279.

Leve, L., Harold, G., Chamberlain, P., Landsverk, J., Fisher, P. & Vostanis, P. (2012). Children in foster care: Vulnerabilities and evidence-based interventions that promote resilience processes. *Journal of Child Psychology and Psychiatry,* 53, 1197–1211.

McKay, K., Ross, L. & Goldberg, A. (2010). Adaptation to parenthood during the post-adoption period: A review of the literature. *Adoption Quarterly,* 13, 125–144.

Morris, J., Berrino, A., Okema, L., Jones, L., Jordans, M. & Crow, C. (2012). Does combining infant stimulation with emergency feeding improve psychosocial outcomes for displaced mothers and babies? *American Journal of Orthopsychiatry,* 82, 349–357.

Palacios, J. & Sánchez-Sandoval, Y. (2006). Stress in parents of adopted children. *International Journal of Behavioral Development,* 30, 481–487.

Pallett, C., Scott, S., Blackeby, K., Yule, W. & Weissman, R. (2002). Fostering changes: A cognitive behavioural approach to help foster carers manage children. *Adoption and Fostering,* 26, 39–48.

148 Book references by chapter

Panter-Brick, C., Grimon, M.P. & Eggerman, M. (2014). Caregiver-child mental health: A prospective study in conflict and refugee settings. *Journal of Child Psychology and Psychiatry*, 55, 313–327.

Puckering, C., Connolly, B., Werner, C., Toms-Whittle, L., Lennox, J. & Minnis, H. (2011). Rebuilding relationships: A pilot study of the effectiveness of the Mellow Parenting Programme for children with reactive attachment disorder. *Clinical Child Psychology and Psychiatry*, 16, 73–87.

Rushton, A., Mayes, D., Dance, C. & Quinton, D. (2003). Parenting late-placed children: The development of new relationships and the challenge of behavioural problems. *Clinical Child Psychology and Psychiatry*, 8, 389–400.

Rushton, A. & Monck, E. (2010). A "real-world" evaluation of an adoptive parenting programme: Reflections after conducting a randomized trial. *Clinical Child Psychology and Psychiatry*, 15, 543–554.

Rushton, A., Monck, E., Leese, M., McCrone, P. & Sharac, J. (2010). Enhancing adoptive parenting: A randomized controlled trial. *Clinical Child Psychology and Psychiatry*, 15, 529–542.

Selwyn, J., Del Tufo, S. & Frazer, L. (2009). It's a piece of cake? An evaluation of an adopter training programme. *Adoption and Fostering*, 33, 30–43.

Sourander, A., McGrath, P., Ristkari, T., Cunningham, C., Huttunen, J., Littley-Pottie, P., Hinkka-Yli-Salomaki, S., Kinnunen, M., Vuorio, J., Sinokki, A., Fossum, S. & Unruh, A. (2016). Internet-assisted parent training intervention for disruptive behavior in 4-year-old children: A randomized clinical trial. *JAMA*, 73, 378–387.

Spielfogel, J., Leathers, S., Christian, E. & McMeel, L. (2011). Parent management training, relationships with agency staff, and child mental health: Urban foster parents' perspectives. *Children and Youth Services Review*, 33, 2366–2374.

Thabet, A.A, Ibraheem, A., Shivram, R., Van Milligen, E. & Vostanis, P. (2009). Parenting support and PTSD in children of a war zone. *International Journal of Social Psychiatry*, 55, 226–237.

Tischler, V., Edwards, V. & Vostanis, P. (2009). Working therapeutically with mothers who experience the trauma of homelessness. *Counselling and Psychotherapy Research*, 9, 42–46.

Tischler, V. & Vostanis, P. (2007). Homeless mothers: Is there a relationship between coping strategies, mental health and goal achievement? *Journal of Community and Applied Social Psychology*, 17, 85–102.

Weine, S., Kulauzovic, Y., Klebic, A., Besic, S., Mujagic, A., Muzurovic, J. & Rolland, J. (2008). Evaluating a multiple-family group access intervention for refugees with PTSD. *Journal of Marital and Family Therapy*, 34, 149–164.

Weine, S.M., Raina, D., Zhubi, M., Delesi, M., Huseni, D., Feetham, S. & Pavkovic, I. (2003). The TAFES multi-family group intervention for Kosovar refugees. *Journal of Nervous and Mental Diseases*,191, 100–107.

Weymouth, L.A. & Howe, T. (2011). A multi-site evaluation of Parents Raising Safe Kids violence prevention program. *Children and Youth Services Review*, 33, 1960–1967.

8 Building resilience at school and in the community

Apfel, R.J. & Simon, B. (1996). Psychosocial interventions for children of war: The value of a model of resiliency. *Medicine and Global Survival*, 3, A2.

Betancourt, T., McBain, R., Newnham, E. & Brennan, R. (2014). Community character-istics and mental health among war-affected youth in Sierra Leone. *Journal of Child Psychology and Psychiatry*, 55, 217–226.

Bryan, J. & Henry, L. (2012). A model for building school–family–community partnerships: Principles and process. *Journal of Counselling and Development*, 90, 408–420.

Draper, A.K., Hewitt, G. & Rifkin, S. (2010). Chasing the dragon: Developing indicators for the assessment of community participation in health programmes. *Social Science and Medicine*, 71, 1102–1109.

Ellis, B.H., Lincoln, A., Charney, M., Ford-Paz, R., Benson, M. & Strunin, L. (2010). Mental health service utilisation of Somali adolescents: Religion, community, and school as gateways to healing. *Transcultural Psychiatry*, 47, 789–811.

Fazel, M., Patel, V., Thomas, S. & Tol, W. (2014). School mental health interventions in low-income and middle-income countries. *The Lancet Psychiatry*, 1, 388–398.

Finkelstein, N. & Rechberger, E. (2005). Building resilience in children of mothers who have co-occurring disorders and history of violence: Intervention model and implementation issues. *The Journal of Behavioural Health Services and Research*, 32, 141–154.

Folke, C. (2016). Resilience (Republished). *Ecology and Society*, 21, 4. DOI: https://doi.org/10.5751/ES-09088-210444

Graber, R., Turner, R. & Madill, A. (2016). Best friends and better coping: Facilitating psychological resilience through boys' and girls' closest friendships. *British Journal of Psychology*, 107, 338–358.

Holling, C. (2006). Engineering resilience versus ecological resilience. In Schulze, P., Ed., *Engineering within Ecological Constraints*. Washington, DC: The National Academies Press, pp. 31–44.

Howell, K., Kaplow, J., Layne, C., Benson, M., Compas, B., Katalinski, R. & Pynoos, R. (2014). Predicting adolescent posttraumatic stress in the aftermath of war. *Anxiety, Stress and Coping*, 28, 88–104.

Johnson, J., Wood, A.M., Gooding, P., Taylor, P.J. & Tarrier, N. (2011). Resilience to suicidality: The buffering hypothesis. *Clinical Psychology Review*, 31, 563–591.

Khamis, V. (2015). Coping with war trauma and psychological distress among school-age Palestinian children. *American Journal of Orthopsychiatry*, 85, 72–79.

Kia-Keating, M. & Ellis, B.H. (2007). Belonging and connection to school in resettlement: Young refugees, school belonging, and psychosocial adjustment. *Clinical Child Psychology and Psychiatry*, 12, 29–43.

Kovacev, L. & Shute, R. (2004). Acculturation and social support in relation to psychosocial adjustment of adolescent refugees resettled in Australia. *International Journal of Behavioral Development*, 28, 259–267.

Maltby, J., Day, L., Zemojtel-Piotrowska, M., Piotrowski, J., Hitokoto, H., Baran, T. & Flowe, H. (2016). An ecological systems model of trait resilience: Cross-cultural and clinical relevance. *Personality and Individual Differences*, 98, 96–101,

Marinus, H., Van Ijzendoorn, M. & Juffer, F. (2006). Adoption as intervention: Meta-analytic evidence for massive catch-up and plasticity in physical, socio-emotional, and cognitive development. *Journal of Child Psychology and Psychiatry*, 47, 1228–1245.

Meltzer, H., Dogra, N., Vostanis, P. & Ford, T. (2011). Religiosity and the mental health of adolescents in Great Britain. *Mental Health, Religion and Culture*, 14, 703–713.

Mohlen, H., Parzer, P., Resch, F. & Brunner, R. (2005). Psychosocial support for war traumatised child and adolescent refugees. *Australian and New Zealand Journal of Psychiatry*, 39, 81–87.

O'Reilly, M., Majumder, P., Karim, K. & Vostanis, P. (2015). "This doctor, I not trust him, I'm not safe": The perceptions of mental health and services by unaccompanied refugee adolescents. *International Journal of Social Psychiatry*, 61, 129–136.

Rousseau, C., Measham, T. & Nadeau, L. (2012). Addressing trauma in collaborative mental health care for refugee children. *Clinical Child Psychology and Psychiatry*, 18, 121–136.

150 Book references by chapter

South, R., Jones, F., Creith, E. & Simonds, L. (2015). Understanding the concept of resilience in relation to looked after children. *Clinical Child Psychology and Psychiatry*, 21, 178–192.

Sullivan, A. & Simonsen, G. (2016). A systematic review of school-based social-emotional interventions for refugee and war traumatized youth. *Review of Educational Research*, 86, 503–530.

Taylor, S. & Distelberg, B. (2016). Predicting behavioral health outcomes among low-income families: Testing a socioecological model of family resilience determinants. *Journal of Child and Family Studies*, 25, 2797–2807.

Tyrer, R. & Fazel, M. (2014). School and community-based interventions for refugee and asylum seeking children. *PloS one*, 9, e89359.

Unterhitzenberger, J. & Rosner, R. (2014). Lessons from writing sessions: A school-based randomised trial with adolescent orphans in Rwanda. *European Journal of Psychotraumatology*, 5, DOI: 10.3402/ejpt.v5.24917

Vanhove, A., Herian, M., Perez, A., Harms, P. & Lester, P. (2016). Can resilience be developed at work? A meta-analytic review of resilience-building programme effectiveness. *Journal of Occupational and Organizational Psychology*, 89, 278–307.

Walker, B., Holling, C., Carpenter, S. & Kinzig, A. (2004). Resilience, adaptability and transformability in social-ecological systems. *Ecology and Society*, 9, 5, DOI: www.ecologyandsociety.org/vol9/iss2/art5/

9 Application of therapeutic approaches

Anderson, L., Stuttaford, M. & Vostanis, P. (2006). A family support service for homeless children and parents: User and staff perspectives. *Child and Family Social Work*, 11, 119–127.

Barron, I., Abdallah, G. & Smith, P. (2016). Randomized control trial of a CBT trauma recovery program in Palestinian schools. *Journal of Trauma and Loss*, 18, 306–321.

Ehntholt, K., Smith, P. & Yule, W. (2005). School-based cognitive-behavioural therapy group: Intervention for refugee children who have experienced war-related trauma. *Clinical Child Psychology and Psychiatry*, 10, 235–250.

Graham, R. & Cloitre, M. (2009). Review of creative interventions with traumatized children. *Journal of Child and Adolescent Psychopharmacology*, 19, 327–329.

Hollin, C. (2005). The meaning and implications of 'programme integrity'. In McGuire, J., Ed., *What Works: Reducing Re-offending*. Chichester: Wiley, pp. 195–208.

Kalantari, M., Yule, W., Dyregrov, A., Neshatdoost, H. & Ahmadi, S.J. (2012). Efficacy of writing for recovery on traumatic grief symptoms of Afghani refugee bereaved adolescents: A randomized control trial. *Journal of Death and Dying*, 65, 139–150.

Kohrt, B. (2013). Social ecology interventions for post-traumatic stress disorder: What can we learn from child soldiers? *British Journal of Psychiatry*, 203, 165–167.

Lange-Nielsen, I.I., Kolltveit, S., Thabet, A.A., Dyregrov, A., Pallesen, S., Johnsen, T.B. & Laberg, J.C. (2012). Short-term effects of a writing intervention among adolescents in Gaza. *Journal of Loss and Trauma*, 17, 403–422.

Lange, A., Rietdijk, D., Hudcovicova, M., van de Ven, J.P., Schrieken, B. & Emmelkamp, P.M. (2003). Interapy: A controlled randomized trial of the standardized treatment of posttraumatic stress through the internet. *Journal of Consulting and Clinical Psychology*, 71, 901–909.

Midgley, N., Hayes, N. & Cooper. M., Eds. (2017). *Essential Research Findings in Child and Adolescent Counselling and Psychotherapy*. London: Sage.

Book references by chapter **151**

Peltonen, K. & Punamaki, R.L. (2010). Preventive interventions among children exposed to trauma of armed conflict. *Aggressive Behaviour*, 36, 95–116.

Tol, W., Komproe, I., Jordans, M., Gross, A., Susanty, D., Macy, R. & De Jong, J. (2010). Mediators and moderators of a psychosocial intervention for children affected by political violence. *Journal of Consulting and Clinical Psychology*, 78, 818–828.

10 Therapeutic interventions

Adler-Tapia, R. & Settle, C. (2009). Evidence of the efficacy of EMDR with children and adolescents in individual psychotherapy: A review of the research published in peer-reviewed journals. *Journal of EMDR Practice and Research*, 3, 232–247.

Becker-Wiedman, A. (2006). Treatment for children with reactive attachment disorder: Dyadic developmental psychotherapy. *Child and Adolescent Mental Health*, 13, DOI: 10.1111/j.1475-3588.2006.00428.x

Bjorn, G.J., Boder, C., Sydsjo, G. & Gustafsson, P. (2013). Brief family therapy for refugee children. *The Family Journal*, 21, 272–278.

Bolton, P., Bass, J., Betancourt, T., Speelman, L., Onyango, G., Clougherty, K., Neugebauer, R., Murray, L. & Verdeli, H. (2007). Interventions for depression symptoms among adolescent survivors of war and displacement in Northern Uganda: A randomized controlled trial. *JAMA*, 298, 519–527.

Booth, P. & Jergberg, A. (2009). *Helping Parents and Children Build Better Relationships through Attachment-based Play*. San Francisco: Jossey Bass.

Borduin, C. & Dopp, A. (2015). Economic impact of multisystemic therapy with juvenile sexual offenders. *Journal of Family Psychology*, 29, 687–696.

Carrion, V. & Hull, K. (2010). Treatment manual for trauma-exposed youth. *Clinical Child Psychology and Psychiatry*, 15, 27–38.

Cohen, J., Mannarino, A. & Iyengar, S. (2011). Community treatment of posttraumatic stress disorder for children exposed to intimate partner violence: A randomized controlled trial. *Archives of Paediatrics and Adolescent Medicine*, 165, 16–21.

Cooper, M., Rowland, N., McArthur, K., Pattison, S., Cromarty, K. & Richards, K. (2010). Randomized controlled trial of school-based humanistic counselling for emotional distress in young people: Feasibility study and preliminary indications of efficacy. *Child and Adolescent Psychiatry and Mental Health*, 4, DOI: 10.1186/1753-2000-4-12

Coulter, S. (2011). Systemic family therapy for families who have experienced trauma: A randomized controlled trial. *Journal of Social Work*, 41, 502–519.

Dallos, R. (2006). *Attachment Narrative Therapy: Integrating Narrative, Systemic and Attachment Approaches*. Maidenhead: Open University Press.

Davey, T. (2004). A multiple-family group intervention for homeless families: The weekend retreat. *Health and Social Work*, 29, 326–329.

Deblinger, E., Mannarinno, A., Cohen, J., Runyon, M. & Steer, R. (2011). Trauma-focused cognitive behavioral therapy for children: Impact of the trauma narrative and treatment length. *Depression and Anxiety*, 28, 67–75.

De Roos, C., Greenwald, R., Den Hollander-Gijsman, M., Noorthoorn, E., Van Buuren, S. & De Jongh, A. (2011). A randomized comparison of cognitive behavioural therapy (CBT) and eye movement desensitization and reprocessing (EMDR) in disaster-exposed children. *European Journal of Psychotraumatology*, 2, DOI: http://dx.doi.org/10.3402/ejpt.v2i0.5694

Ehntholt, K. & Yule, W. (2006). Assessment and treatment of refugee children and adolescents who have experienced war-related trauma. *Journal of Child Psychology and Psychiatry*, 47, 1197–1210.

152 Book references by chapter

Figley, C. & Figley, K. (2009). Stemming the tide of trauma systemically: The role of family therapy. *Australian and New Zealand Journal of Family Therapy*, 30, 173–183.

Geldard, K., Geldard, D. & Yin Foo, R. (2013). *Counselling Children: A Practical Introduction*. London: Sage.

Goldenberg, H. & Goldenberg, I. (2013). *Family Therapy: An Overview*. Belmont, CA: Brooks/Cole.

Grover, S. & Kate, N. (2013). Child psychopharmacology: How much have we progressed? *World Psychiatry*, 12, 133–134.

Harvey, S. & Taylor, J. (2010). A meta-analysis of the effects of psychotherapy with sexually abused children and adolescents. *Clinical Psychology Review*, 30, 517–535.

Henggeler, S., Schoenwald, S., Borduin, C., Rowland, M. & Cunningham, P. (2009). *Multisystemic Therapy for Antisocial Behaviour in Children and Adolescents*. New York: Guilford Press.

Howe, D. (2006). Developmental attachment psychotherapy with fostered and adopted children. *Child and Adolescent Mental Health*, 11, 128–134.

Hughes, D. (2007). *Attachment-Focused Family Therapy*. New York: W. Newton and Company.

Hughes, D. (2017). *Building the Bonds of Attachment: Awaiting Love in Deeply Traumatized Children*. Lanham, MD: Rowman & Littlefield.

Ingley-Cook, G. & Dobel-Ober, D. (2013). Group work with children who are in care or who are adopted: Lessons learnt. *Child and Adolescent Mental Health*, 18, 251–254.

Johnides, B., Borduin, C., Wagner, D. & Dopp, A. (2017). Effects of multisystemic therapy on caregivers of serious juvenile offenders: A 20-year follow-up to a randomized controlled trial. *Journal of Consulting and Clinical Psychology*, 85, 323–334.

Kangaslampi, S., Garoff, F. & Peltonen, K. (2015). Narrative exposure therapy for immigrant children traumatized by war: Study protocol for a randomized controlled trial of effectiveness and mechanisms of change. *BMC Psychiatry*, 15, DOI: 10.1186/s12888-015-0520-z

Klasen, H. & Crombag, A. (2013). What works where? A systematic review of child and adolescent mental health interventions for low and middle income countries. *Social Psychiatry and Psychiatric Epidemiology*, 48, 595–611.

Kuester, A., Niemeyer, H. & Knaevelsrud, C. (2016). Internet-based interventions for post-traumatic stress: A meta-analysis of randomized controlled trials. *Clinical Psychology Review*, 43, 1–16.

Lieberman, A., van Horn, P. & Ippen, C.G. (2005). Towards evidence-based treatment: Child-parent psychotherapy with preschoolers exposed to marital violence. *Journal of the American Academy of Child and Adolescent Psychiatry*, 44, 1241–1248.

Lustig, S., Weine, S., Saxe, G. & Beardslee, W. (2014). Testimonial psychotherapy for adolescent refugees: A case series. *Transcultural Psychiatry*, 41, 31–45.

May, J. (2005). Family attachment narrative therapy: Healing the experience of early childhood maltreatment. *Journal of Marital and Family Therapy*, 31, 221–237.

McGrea, K. (2014). 'How does that itsy bitsy spider do it?' Severely traumatized children's development of resilience in psychotherapy. *Journal of Infant, Child and Adolescent Psychotherapy*, 13, 89–109.

McMullen, J., O'Callaghan, P., Shannon, C., Black, A. & Eakin, J. (2013). Group trauma-focused CBT with former child soldiers and other war-affected boys in the DR Congo. *Journal of Child Psychology and Psychiatry*, 54, 1231–1241.

Morina, N., Koerssen, R. & Pollet, T. (2016). Interventions for children and adolescents with posttraumatic stress: A meta-analysis of comparative outcome studies. *Clinical Psychology Review*, 47, 41–54.

Morina, N., Malek, M., Nickerson, A. & Bryant, R. (2017). Psychological interventions for PTSD and depression in young survivors of mass violence in low- and middle-income countries: Meta-analysis. *British Journal of Psychiatry*, 210, 247–254.

Murray, K., Davidson, G. & Schweitzer, R. (2010). Review of refugee mental health interventions following resettlement. *American Journal of Orthopsychiatry*, 80, 576–585.

Onuyt, L., Neuner, F., Schauer, E., Ertl, V., Odenwald, M., Schauer, M. & Elbert, T. (2005). Narrative exposure therapy as a treatment for child war survivors with posttraumatic stress disorder: Two case reports and a pilot study in an African refugee settlement. *BMC Psychiatry*, 5, DOI: 10.1186/1471-244X-5-7

Patel, V., Chowdhary, N., Rahman, A., & Vardeli, H., (2011). Improving access to psychological treatments: Lessons from developing countries. *Behaviour Research and Therapy*, 9, 523–528.

Porter, S., McConnell, T., McLaughlin, K., Lynn, F., Cladwell, C., Braiden, H.J., Boylan, J. & Holmes, V. (2017). Music therapy for children and adolescents with emotional and behavioural problems: A randomized controlled trial. *Journal of Child Psychology and Psychiatry*, 58, 586–594.

Robjant, K. & Fazel, M. (2010). The emerging evidence for narrative exposure therapy: A review. *Clinical Psychology Review*, 30, 1030–1039.

Rodenberg, R., Benjamin, A., de Roos, C., Meijer, A.M., Stams, G.J. (2009). Efficacy of EMDR in children: A meta-analysis. *Clinical Psychology Review*, 29, 599–606.

Sanchez-Meca, J., Rosa-Alcazar, A. & Lopez-Soler, C. (2011). The psychological treatment of sexual abuse in children and adolescents: A meta-analysis. *International Journal of Clinical and Health Psychology*, 11, 67–93.

Schauer, M., Neuer, F. & Elbert, T. (2011). *Narrative Exposure Therapy: A Short-term Treatment for Traumatic Stress Disorders*. Cambridge, MA: Hogrefe.

Slobodin, O. & De Jong, J.T. (2015). Family interventions in traumatised immigrants and refugees. *Transcultural Psychiatry*, 52, 723–742.

Smith, P., Yule, W., Perrin, S., Tranah., T., Dalgleish, T. & Clark, D. (2007). Cognitive-behavioural therapy for PTSD in children and adolescents: A preliminary randomized controlled trial. *Journal of the American Academy of Child and Adolescent Psychiatry*, 46, 1051–1061.

Sveaass, N. & Reichelt, S. (2001). Refugee families in therapy: From referrals to therapeutic conversations. *Journal of Family Therapy*, 23, 119–135.

Vetere, A. & Dowling, E., Eds. (2016). *Narrative Therapies with Children and Their Families: A Practitioner's Guide to Concepts and Approaches*. London: Routledge.

Vigerland, S., Lennard, F., Bonnett, M., Lalouni, M., Hedman, E., Ahlen, J., Olen, D., Serlachius, E. & Ljotsson, B. (2016). Internet-delivered cognitive behaviour therapy for children and adolescents: A systematic review and meta-analysis. *Clinical Psychology Review*, 50, 1–10.

Weir, K., Canosa, P., Rodrigues, N., McWilliams, M. & Parker, L. (2013). Whole family theraplay: Integrating family systems theory and theraplay to treat adoptive families. *Adoption Quarterly*, 16, 175–200.

Westermark, P., Hansson, K. & Vinnerljung, B. (2007). Foster parent in multidimensional treatment foster care: How do they deal with implementing standardized treatment components? *Children and Youth Services Review*, 29, 442–459.

Wettig, H., Coleman, R. & Geider, F. (2011). Evaluating the effectiveness of theraplay in treating shy, socially withdrawn children. *International Journal of Play Therapy*, 20, 26–37.

11 Always a service model, whatever the constraints

Anstiss, H., Ziaian, T., Procter, N., Warner, J. & Baghurst, P. (2009). Help-seeking for mental health problems in young refugees: A review of the literature with implications for policy, practice, and research. *Transcultural Psychiatry*, 46, 584–607.

Barratt, S. & Lobatto, W., Eds. (2016). *Surviving and Thriving in Care and Beyond*. London: Karnac.

Bethancourt, T., Newnham, E., Birman, D., Lee, R., Ellis, H. & Layne, C. (2017). Comparing trauma exposure, mental health needs and service utilization across clinical samples of refugee, immigrant, and US-origin children. *Journal of Traumatic Stress*, 30, 209–218.

Biehal, N., Ellison, S. and Sinclair, I. (2012). Intensive fostering: An independent evaluation of MTFC in an English setting. *Adoption and Fostering*, 36, 13–26.

Birman, D., Beehler, S., Harris, E.M., Everson, M.L., Batia, K., Liautaud, J. & Fogg, L. (2008). International Family, Adult, and Child Enhancement Services (FACES): A community-based comprehensive services model for refugee children in resettlement. *American Journal of Orthopsychiatry*, 78, 121–132.

Bone, C., O'Reilly, M., Karim, K. & Vostanis, P. (2015). "They're not witches . . .": Young children and their parents' perceptions and experiences of child and adolescent mental health services. *Child: Care, Health and Development*, 15, 450–458.

Butterworth, S., Singh, S., Birchwood, M., Islam, Z., Munro, E., Vostanis, P., Paul, M., Khan, A. & Simkiss, D. (2017). Transitioning care-leavers with mental health needs: "They set you up to fail". *Child and Adolescent Mental Health*, 22, 138–147.

Chamberlain, P. (2003). The Oregon multidimensional treatment foster care model: Features, outcomes and progress in dissemination. *Cognitive and Behavioral Practice*, 10, 303–312.

Cooper, M., Evans, Y. and Pubis, J. (2016). Interagency collaboration in children and young people's mental health: A systematic review of outcomes, facilitating factors and inhibiting factors. *Child: Care, Health and Development*, 42, 325–342.

Dang, M., Whitney, K., Virata, M.C., Binger, M. & Miller, E. (2012). A web-based personal health information system for homeless youth and young. *Public Health Nursing*, 29, 313–319.

Davies, J. & Wright, J. (2008). Children's voices: A review of the literature pertinent to looked-after children's views of mental health services. *Child and Adolescent Mental Health*, 13, 26–31.

Davies, J., Wright, J., Drake, S. & Bunting, J. (2009). 'By listening hard': Developing a service user feedback system for adopted and fostered children in receipt of mental health services. *Adoption and Fostering*, 33, 19–33.

Ellis, H., Miller, A., Abdi, S., Barrett, C., Blood, E. & Betancourt, T. (2013). Multi-tier mental health program for refugee youth. *Journal of Consulting and Clinical Psychology*, 81, 129–140.

Grossman, S.F., Lundy, M., George, C. & Crabtree-Nelson, S. (2010). Shelter and service receipt for victims of domestic violence in Illinois. *Journal of Interpersonal Violence*, 25, 2077–2093.

Hall, P., Weaver, L. & Grassau, P.A. (2013). Theories, relationships and interprofessionalism: Learning to weave. *Journal of Interprofessional Care*, 27, 73–80.

Leathers, S., Atkins, M., Spielfogel, J., McMeel, L., Welsey, J. & Davis, R. (2009). Context-specific mental health services for children in foster care. *Children and Youth Services Review*, 31, 1289–1297.

Long, T., Dann, S., Wolff, M. & Brienzabc, R. (2014). Moving from silos to teamwork: Integration of interprofessional trainees into a medical home model. *Journal of Interprofessional Care*, 28, 473–474.

Book references by chapter **155**

Michelson, D. & Sclare, I. (2009). Psychological needs, service utilisation and provision of care in a specialist mental health clinic for young refugees. *Clinical Child Psychology and Psychiatry*, 14, 273–296.

Monck, E. & Rushton, A. (2009). Access to post-adoption services when the child has substantial problems. *Journal of Children's Services*, 4, 21–33.

National Institute of Clinical Excellence (NICE) (2010). *Promoting the Quality of Life of Looked After Children and Young People*, NICE Public Health Guidance 28. London: NICE.

NHS England (2014). *Model Specification for Child and Adolescent Mental Health Services: Targeted and Specialist Levels (Tiers 2/3)*. London: Department of Health.

NHS England (2015). *Future in Mind: Promoting, Protecting and Improving Our Children's and Young People's Mental Health and Wellbeing*. London: Department of Health.

Losa, N. & Effat, R. (2017). Service users and carers in low- and middle-income countries. *British Journal of Psychiatry International*, 14, 4–6.

Martin, P., Davies, R., MacDougall, A., Ritchie, B., Vostanis, P., Whale, A. & Wolpert, M. (2017). Developing a case mix classification for child and adolescent mental health services: The influence of presenting problems, complexity factors, and services on number of appointments. *Journal of Mental Health*, Early Online 1–8, DOI: 10.1080/09638237.2017.1370631

O'Carroll, V., McSwiggan, L. & Campbell, M. (2016). Health and social care professionals' attitudes to interprofessional working and interprofessional education: A literature review. *Journal of Interprofessional Care*, 30, 42–49.

O'Reilly, M., Vostanis, P., Taylor, H., Day, C., Street, C. & Wolpert, M. (2013). Service user perspectives of multi-agency working: A qualitative study with parents and children with educational and mental health difficulties. *Child and Adolescent Mental Health*, 18, 202–209.

Patel, V., Flisher, A., Nikapota, A. & Malhotra, S. (2008). Promoting child and adolescent mental health in low and middle income countries. *Journal of Child Psychology and Psychiatry*, 49, 313–334.

Rao, P., Ali, A. & Vostanis, P. (2010). Looked after and adopted children: How should specialist CAMHS be involved? *Adoption and Fostering*, 34, 58–72.

Ratnayake, A., Bowlay-Williams, J. & Vostanis, P. (2014). When are attachment difficulties an indication for specialist mental health input? *Adoption and Fostering*, 38, 159–170.

Rousseau, C., Measham, T. & Moro, M.R. (2011). Working with interpreters in child mental health. *Child and Adolescent Mental Health*, 16, 55–59.

Ryan, S. & Nalavany, B. (2003). Adopted children: Who do they turn to for help and why? *Adoption Quarterly*, 7, 29–52.

Skokauskas, N. & Belfer, M. (2011). Global child mental health: What can we learn from these countries with limited financial resources? *International Psychiatry*, 8, 45–47.

Slesnick, N., Prestoopnik, J., Meyers, R. & Glassman, M. (2007). Treatment outcome for street living homeless youth. *Addictive Behaviors*, 32, 1237–1251.

Street, E., Hill, J. and Welham, J. (2009). Delivering a therapeutic wraparound service for troubled adolescents in care. *Adoption and Fostering*, 33, 26–33.

Taylor, H., Stuttaford, M., Broad, B. & Vostanis, P. (2007). Listening to service users: Young homeless people's experiences of new mental health service. *Journal of Child Health Care*, 11, 221–230.

Tischler, V., Karim, K., Rustall, S., Gregory, P. & Vostanis, P. (2004). A family support service for homeless children and parents: Users' perspectives and characteristics. *Health and Social Care in the Community*, 12, 327–335.

Tischler, V., Vostanis, P., Bellerby, T. & Cumella, S. (2002). Evaluation of a mental health outreach service for homeless families. *Archives of Disease in Childhood*, 86, 158–163.

156 Book references by chapter

Vostanis, P. (2010). Mental health services for children in public care and other vulnerable groups: Implications for international collaboration. *Clinical Child Psychology and Psychiatry*, 15, 555–571.

Vostanis, P., Ed. (2007). *Mental Health Interventions and Services for Vulnerable Children and Young People*. London: J. Kingsley.

Wolpert, M., Harris, R., Jones, M., Hodges, S., Fuggle, P., James, R., Wiener, A., McKenna, C., Law, D. & Fonagy, P. (2017). *Thrive: The AFC-Tavistock Model for CAMHS*. London: CAMHS Press.

Wolpert, M., Vostanis, P., Martin, K., Munk, S., Norman, R., Fonagy, P. & Feltham, A. (2017). High integrity child mental health: Focusing on the person, not the problem. *British Medical Journal*, 357, DOI: https://doi.org/10.1136/bmj.j1500

World Health Organization (WHO) (2005a). *Child Mental Health Services: Global Concerns – Implications for the Future*. Geneva: WHO.

World Health Organization (WHO) (2005b). *Mental Health: Facing the Challenges, Building Solutions*. Report from the WHO European Ministerial Conference. Copenhagen: WHO Regional Office for Europe.

World Health Organization (WHO) (2005c). *Atlas: Mental Health Resources in the World*. Geneva: WHO.

12 Training in a service context

Alderson, P. & Morrow, V. (2004). *Ethics, Social Research and Consulting with Children and Young People*. Ilford: Barnardos.

Allen, J. & Vostanis, P. (2005). The impact of abuse and trauma on the developing child: An evaluation of a training programme for foster carers and supervising social workers. *Adoption and Fostering*, 29, 68–81.

Barr, H. (2013). Toward a theoretical framework for interprofessional education. *Journal of Interprofessional Care*, 27, 4–9.

Baum, N., Cardozo, B.L., Pat-Horenczyk, R., Ziv, Y., Blanton, C., Reza, A., Weltman, A. & Brom, D. (2013). Training teachers to build resilience in children in the aftermath of war: A cluster randomized trial. *Child and Youth Care Forum*, 42, 339–350.

Beauchamp, T. & Childress, J. (2008). *Principles of Biomedical Ethics. Sixth edition*. Oxford: Oxford University Press.

Betancourt, T. & Williams, T. (2008). Building an evidence-base on mental health interventions for children affected by armed conflict. *Intervention*, 6, 39–56.

Boet, S., Bould, M.D., Burn, C.L. & Reeves, S. (2014). Twelve tips for a successful interprofessional team-based high-fidelity simulation education session. *Medical Teacher*, 36, 853–857.

Cooley, M. & Petren, R. (2011). Foster parent perceptions of competency: Implications for foster parent training. *Children and Youth Services Review*, 33, 1968–1974.

Dorsey, S., Farmer, E., Barth, R. & Greene, K. (2008). Current status and evidence base of training for foster and treatment foster parents. *Children and Youth Services Review*, 30, 1403–1416.

Ensign, J. (2003). Ethical issues in qualitative health research with homeless youths. *Journal of Advanced Nursing*, 43, 43–50.

Evans, S., Knight, T., Sonderlund, A. & Tooley, G. (2014). Facilitators' experience of delivering asynchronous and synchronous online professional education. *Medical Teacher*, 36, 1051–1056.

Festinger, T. & Baker, A. (2013). The quality of evaluations of foster parent training: An empirical review. *Children and Youth Services Review*, 35, 2147–2153.

Ford, K., Sankey, J. & Crisp, J. (2007). Development of children's assent documents using a child-centred approach. *Journal of Child Health Care*, 11, 19–28.

Furness, P., Armitage, H. & Pitt, R. (2011). An evaluation of practice-based interprofessional education initiatives involving service users. *Journal of Interprofessional Care*, 25, 46–52.

Hanna, E., Soren, B., Telner, D., MacNeill, H., Lowe, M. & Reeves, S. (2013). Flying blind: The experience of online interprofessional facilitation. *Journal of Interprofessional Care*, 27, 298–304.

Hussein, S. & Vostanis, P. (2013). Teacher training intervention for early identification of common child mental health problems in Pakistan. *Emotional and Behavioural Difficulties*, 18, 284–296.

Madge, N., Foreman, D. & Baksh, F. (2008). Starving in the midst of plenty: A study of training needs for child and adolescent mental health service care delivery in primary care. *Clinical Child Psychology and Psychiatry*, 13, 473–478.

Maltby, J., Day, L. & Hall, S. (2015). Refining trait resilience: Identifying engineering, ecological and adaptive facets from extant measures of resilience. *PloS One*, 10, e0131826, DOI: https://doi.org/10.1371/journal.pone.0131826

Mann, K.V., McFertridge, D., Martin-Misener, R., Clovis, J., Rowe, Beanlands, H. & Sarria, M. (2009). Interprofessional education for students of the health professions: The 'Seamless Care Model'. *Journal of Interprofessional Care*, 23, 224–233.

Matheson, C., Robertson, H., Elliott, A.M., Iversen, L. & Murchie, P. (2016). Resilience of primary healthcare professionals working in challenging environments: A focus group study. *British Journal of General Practice*, 66, e507–515.

Minnis, H., Pelosi, A., Knapp, M. & Dunn, J. (2001). Mental health and foster carer training. *Archives of Disease in Childhood*, 84, 302–306.

O'Reilly, M. & Parker, N. (2014). *Doing Mental Health Research with Children and Adolescents: A Guide to Qualitative Methods*. London: Sage.

O'Reilly, M., Ronzoni, P. & Dogra, N. (2013). *Research with Children: Theory and Practice*. London: Sage.

Oriana Linares, L., Min Min, L. & Shrout, P. (2012). Child training for physical aggression? Lessons from foster care. *Children and Youth Services Review*, 34, 2416–2422.

Pacifici, C., Delaney, R., White, L., Nelson, C. & Cummings, K. (2006). Web-based training for foster, adoptive and kinship parents. *Children and Youth Services Review*, 28, 1329–1343.

Rahman, A., Nizamim, A., Minhas, A., Niazi, R., Slatch, M. & Minhas, F. (2006). E-mental health in Pakistan: A pilot study of training and supervision in child psychiatry using the internet. *Psychiatric Bulletin*, 30, 149–152.

Rice, E. & Barman-Adhikari, A. (2014). Internet and social media use as a resource among homeless youth. *Journal of Computer-Mediated Communication*, 19, 232–247.

Robson, S. & Briant, N. (2009). What did they think? An evaluation of the satisfaction and perceived helpfulness of the training programme developed as an indirect intervention for foster carers. *Adoption and Fostering*, 33, 34–44.

Sebuliba, D. & Vostanis, P. (2001). Child and adolescent mental health training for primary care staff. *Clinical Child Psychology and Psychiatry*, 6, 191–204.

Thistlethwaite, J. & Moran, M. (2010). Learning outcomes for interprofessional education (IPE): Literature review and synthesis. *Journal of Interprofessional Care*, 24, 503–513.

Vostanis, P. (2014). *Helping Children and Young People Who Experience Trauma: Children of Despair, Children of Hope*. London: Taylor & Francis.

Vostanis, P. (2016). *A Practical Guide to Helping Children and Young People who Experience Trauma*. London: Speechmark.

World Health Organization (WHO) (2010). *Framework for Action on Interprofessional Education and Collaborative Practice* (WHO/HRH/HPN/10.3). Geneva: WHO.

Young, S. & Rice, E. (2011). Online social networking technologies, HIV knowledge, and sexual risk and testing behaviors among homeless youth. *AIDS and Behavior*, 15, 253–260.

INDEX

abuse 59–61
adoption 25, 69–70, 93–4
age 15
aggression 11
anxiety 11, 107
art therapy 49, 105
asylum-seekers 25, 51–2, 99–101
attachment theory 66–7, 92–5, 107
Australia 24
autonomy 62
awareness training 129–31

Bangladesh 80
behaviour 11, 89–92, 96–7, 107
belonging 82–4
biochemical factors *see* biological factors
biological factors 16–17
Brazil 17, 26
Bronfenbrenner, U. 14

case scenarios: applications 97–9;
    interventions 110–13; safety 64–5;
    service modelling 124–5
charities *see* NGOs
child and adolescent mental health services
    (CAMHS) 6–8
child rights 2, 28, 31, 56–8, 60–2 *see also*
    safety; welfare
child-centredness 4, 34, 61–2
child-parent psychotherapy 105
cognitive behavioural therapy (CBT) 33,
    97, 104–5
community 19, 72–3, 79–86

conflict 22, 77
consultation 38, 119
continuous professional development
    (CPD) 131–3
Cooper, M. 127–8
coping strategies 16
creative therapy *see* art therapy
criminal responsibility 4
culture 19–20, 31–3, 59–60

delivery formats 128–9
depression 11
developing countries *see* low-income
    countries; middle-income countries
dialectical behavioural therapy (DBT) 106
discrimination 77
distance-learning 134–5
domestic violence 32, 59, 61

ecological theories *see* resilience systems;
    socioecological theory
economic development 32–3 *see also*
    high-income countries; low-income
    countries; middle-income countries
education: attainment 16–19, 77; further
    education 84–5; high-income countries
    23–5; low-income countries 29–30;
    psychoeducation 88–9 *see also* school;
    service modelling
emotional literacy 16, 18–19, 76–7,
    84–5
emotional regulation 96–7, 107
employment 84–5

160 Index

environmental factors *see* resilience systems; setting
evaluation *see* service evaluation
evidence 5–6
experience reprocessing 103–6
eye movement desensitization and reprocessing (EMDR) 104

family 17, 61; adoption 25, 69–70, 93–4; kinship care 68–9, 93–4; parents 66–8, 107; therapy 92–5, 105–7
family support 67–8
Folke, C. 76
Folkman, S. 16
fostering 25, 93–4
foundation training 129–31
Freud, S. 103
further education 84–5

Gaza Strip 17, 77
gender 56
genetic factors *see* biological factors
globalization 32, 39
goal setting 91, 93–4, 97, 102–3
Greece 26, 51–2

hard-to-reach groups 35
health: high-income countries 23–5; low-income countries 29; middle-income countries 26–7 *see also* service modelling
hierarchy of needs 40, 48
high-income countries 23–5, 36–8, 122–3
hormonal factors *see* biological factors
human rights *see* child rights

implementation 58–9
income inequality 7, 22, 24, 32, 61 *see also* high-income countries; low-income countries; middle-income countries
India 26, 42, 80
indirect activities 119
individual vulnerability factors 15–17
inequality *see* income inequality
integration: service 36–8, 116–18; social 82–4
inter-agency partnerships 36–8, 116–17, 119, 122, 127–8 *see also* service modelling
intermediate approaches 106
interprofessional training 63–4, 127–8, 130–1

interventions 75; community-based 79–81; emotional literacy 76–7; mentors 81–2; school-based 78–9; social integration 82–4 *see also* therapeutic approaches; therapeutic interventions
Islam 19–20
Italy 26

joint working 36–8, 117–18

Kenya 42–6
kinship care 68–9, 93–4

Lazarus, R. 16
learning difficulties 16, 91
learning objectives 128–9
legislation 57–9, 94
life events 13
lifelong learning 131–3
low-income countries 28–30, 38–9, 123–4 *see also* WACIT model

Maslow, A. H. 40, 48
medication 108–9
meditation 97, 107
memories 103–6
mental health 3–4, 10–12, 60; service modelling 6–8; social acceptance 32, 78, 80; training 132; vulnerability 9–10, 12–13, 115–16 *see also* resilience systems; service modelling
mentors 81–2
methodologies 5–6
middle-income countries 25–7, 38–9, 123–4 *see also* WACIT model
mindfulness 107
modelling *see* service modelling; WACIT model
motivational therapy 106–7
multi-level framework *see* resilience systems; socioecological theory
multimodal programmes 109
multisystem therapy (MST) 109
Mumbai 42
music therapy *see* art therapy

narrative therapy 104–6
nature/nurture 12–13 *see also* resilience systems
negative reinforcement 91–2
Netherlands 24
network-building events 49
neurodevelopmental conditions 11–12

NGOs 8, 26–30, 42, 53
Nordic countries 23–5
nurturing: adoption 69–70; community practitioners 72–3; kinship care 68–9; parents and extended family 66–8; residential care 70–2

organizational change 62–3
organizational training 135–6
outreach 37–8

Pakistan 77
parents 66–8, 107 *see also* family
participation *see* user participation
peer mentors 81–2
pharmacological treatment *see* medication
physical environment *see* setting
physical punishment 32, 57, 91–2
policy 57–9, 116–17 *see also* service modelling
Portugal 26
post-traumatic stress disorder (PTSD) 11, 104
poverty *see* income inequality; low-income countries
practice *see* service modelling
privacy 62
privileges 91–2
psychiatric emergency 37
psychoanalysis 105
psychoeducation 88–9
psychosis 12
psychosocial model *see* WACIT model
psychotherapy *see* therapeutic approaches; therapeutic interventions
public attitudes 59–60

re-processing interventions 103–6
reflective exercises 21, 99–101
refugees *see* asylum-seekers
reinforcement 91
relaxation techniques 107
religion 19–20, 42, 86
research 5–6, 35
residential care 28, 70–2
resilience 12–13, 76
resilience systems 14–15, 20; community 19, 72–3, 79–86; family 17, 25, 61, 66–70, 93–5, 105–7; individual 15–17; school 17–19, 49, 76–9; societal 19–20, 22–3
resources 7, 63
responsibility 57–8
rewards 91

risk factors *see* resilience systems; vulnerability
Rwanda 42–3, 45–6

safety 56–7, 60–2, 94; implementation 58–9; interprofessional training 63–4; policy and legislation 57–8; public attitudes 59–60; setting 62–3
school 17–19, 49; emotional literacy 76–7; interventions 78–9 *see also* education
self-control *see* emotional regulation
service evaluation 121–2
service modelling 6–8, 33–5, 53; absence of 114–16; case scenarios 124–5; evaluation 121–2; high-income countries 36–8, 122–3; indirect activities 119; inter-agency partnerships 116–17, 119, 122; joint working 117–18; low-income countries 38–9, 123–4; middle-income countries 38–9, 123–4; specialist competencies 118–19; training 126–8; user participation 119–21; vulnerability 116 *see also* nurturing; safety; WACIT model
setting 62–3
sexual exploitation 58
skills *see* training
social changes 31–3, 59–60
social integration 82–4
social media 39, 134–5
social workers 58
societal vulnerability factors 19–20, 22–3
socioecological theory 14–20, 22–3, 108 *see also* resilience systems
Spain 26
specialist competencies 118–19
spirituality 86 *see also* religion
stigma 32, 78, 80
Sunshine Circles 72
systems *see* resilience systems; service modelling

target groups 42
technology 133–5
testimonial therapy 104
testing 95–6
therapeutic approaches 33, 75–6, 87–8; attachment theory 92–5; behavioural strategies 89–92; case scenario 97–9; cognitive behavioural therapy (CBT) 97; family approaches 92–5; psychoeducation 88–9; trauma-focused strategies 95–7

162 Index

therapeutic interventions 102–3; case scenarios 110–13; medication 108–9; multimodal programmes 109; re-processing memories 103–6; trauma related 106–8

theraplay 72, 105, 107

Third World countries *see* low-income countries

training 38, 46, 49–53, 118–19; continuous professional development (CPD) 131–3; interprofessional 63–4; learning objectives 128–9; new technologies 133–5; organizational 135–6; in service context 126–8; trauma-related awareness 129–31

trauma 1–3; strategies 95–7, 129–31; vulnerability 9–10, 12–13, 115–16 *see also* mental health; resilience systems; service modelling

Turkey 26

Uganda 80

UK 23–4, 36–7

UN Convention on the Rights of the Child 4

USA 23

user participation 119–21

violence *see* abuse; domestic violence

vulnerability 9–10, 12–13, 115–16 *see also* resilience systems; safety

WACIT model 40; building/second phase 49–52; Kenya 43–4; pragmatic challenges 42–3; preliminary 48; research question 41–2; Rwanda 45–6; target groups 42; testing 52–5

war *see* conflict

welfare 33; high-income countries 23–5; low-income countries 28–30; middle-income countries 26–7 *see also* residential care; service modelling

workshops 43–7

World Awareness for Children in Trauma *see* WACIT model